D1042086

THE MAN
WHO STOLE HIMSELF

THE MAN
WHO STOLE HIMSELF

THE SLAVE ODYSSEY OF
HANS JONATHAN

GISLI PALSSON

Translated from the Icelandic by Anna Yates

THE UNIVERSITY OF CHICAGO PRESS

CHICAGO AND LONDON

The University of Chicago Press, Chicago 60637
The University of Chicago Press, Ltd., London
© 2016 by The University of Chicago
All rights reserved. Published 2016.
Printed in the United States of America
Revised and updated from the original Icelandic edition *Hans Jónatan, maðurinn sem stal sjálfum sér*, published by Mál og menning, Reykjavík, © 2014 by Gisli Palsson.

25 24 23 22 21 20 19 18 17 16   1 2 3 4 5

ISBN-13: 978-0-226-31328-3 (cloth)
ISBN-13: 978-0-226-31331-3 (e-book)
DOI: 10.7208/chicago/9780226313313.001.0001

Icelandic
LITERATURE
CENTER
MIÐSTÖÐ ÍSLENSKRA BÓKMENNTA

This translation has been published with the financial support of The Icelandic Literature Center.

Library of Congress Cataloging-in-Publication Data

Names: Gísli Pálsson, 1949– author.
Title: The man who stole himself : the slave odyssey of Hans Jonathan / Gisli Palsson ; translated from the Icelandic by Anna Yates.
Other titles: Hans Jónatan. English
Description: Chicago ; London : The University of Chicago Press, 2016. | Includes bibliographical references and index.
Identifiers: LCCN 2016006354 | ISBN 9780226313283 (cloth : alk. paper) | ISBN 9780226313313 (e-book)
Subjects: LCSH: Hans Jónatan, 1784–1827. | Fugitive slaves—Iceland—Djúpivogur—Biography.
Classification: LCC DL373.H37 G5713 2016 | DDC 306.3/62092—dc23 LC record available at http://lccn.loc.gov/2016006354

For my grandchildren,
  Gisli Thor, Jon Bjarni, and Saga Ros

| Contents |

Choose yourself.

SØREN KIERKEGAARD, *Either/Or*, 1843

The views were immensely wide. Everything that you saw
made for greatness and freedom, and unequaled nobility.

KAREN BLIXEN, *Out of Africa*, 1937

All of our phrasing—race relations, racial chasm . . . , even
white supremacy—serves to obscure that racism is a visceral
experience, that it dislodges brains, blocks airways, rips muscle,
extracts organs, cracks bones, breaks teeth.

TA-NEHISI COATES, *Between the World and Me*, 2015

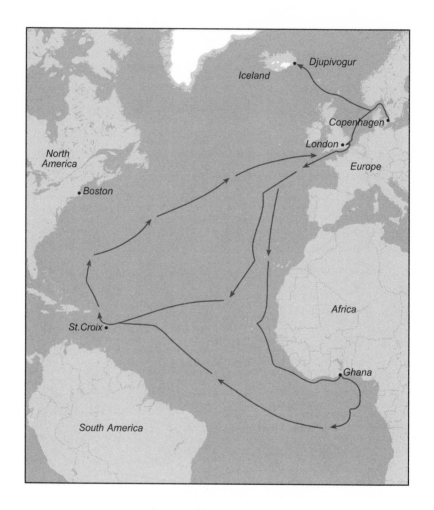

FIG. 1.1. The routes of the saga and the colonial world.

A MAN OF MANY WORLDS

THE FLOORBOARDS CREAK as I walk through the mansion at Amaliegade 23, just as they must have done more than two hundred years ago when sugar barons made their homes here in Copenhagen, in one of the most elegant districts of the colonial world. Many people lived under this roof: white and black, European counts and baronesses, slaves from Africa and the West Indies. The lives of masters and servants, free and unfree, were largely separate, connected only by the winding stair between upstairs and down. Mere traces of their vanished worlds remain, in the architecture of the house and in its lore. The concierge confides to me a legend of a young black slave who once had to live in that dark little space beneath the staircase: ultimately he had enough of his bondage and ran away. The concierge can tell me nothing of who that young man was or what happened to him.[1]

But I know. I know because an Icelandic woman, a neighbor of mine, in her old age had a dream. She dreamed that an ancestress, a black African woman, brought her roses and thanked her for thinking affectionately of her. She found she could not shake off this dream. Dagny Ingimundardottir was white; she lived in a little fishing village in the Westman Islands off the south coast of Iceland. She took pride in her great-great-grandfather, a dark-complected Danish shopkeeper and farmer named Hans Jonathan who was known to play the violin, and she was keenly interested in his origins. She told her grandson of her dream, and he began to investigate. From archives abroad he would occasionally bring Dagny a new piece of information. Other members of the family also contributed, and gradually Dagny's dream of her ancestress grew clear: the young black slave under the stairs at Amaliegade 23 and Hans Jonathan of Iceland were one and the same. And his story does not end there, in Iceland. Hans Jonathan's great-grandson Georg Bjorn, who was born in Denmark, emigrated to the United States in 1913. Only recently did his descendants in New England learn about their Icelandic relatives and their common African-Caribbean roots.

For some years a department of the Danish Ministry of Welfare concerned with immigration has been housed in this mansion at Amaliegade 23. Perhaps that is appropriate. When I first arrive, the staff assume I have come to make a complaint about some aspect of social services, and I am asked, "Do you have a number?"

I reply that I am looking into the case of a refugee named Hans Jonathan, a dark-skinned slave who lived in this house more than two hundred years ago and who was the defendant in an 1802 lawsuit (filed in Denmark) that raises fundamental questions about human rights: *The General's Widow Henrietta Schimmelmann versus the Mulatto Hans Jonathan.* No one here has heard of Hans Jonathan, or the lawsuit, beyond the concierge's story of the black boy under the stairs. Oral tradition in this case may not be reliable. It is not certain the boy in question is Hans Jonathan—but not many slave boys can have escaped from this grand house.

Hans Jonathan's story, this tall tale of a Caribbean slave who became an Icelandic peasant by way of one of the most notorious slavery trials in European history, spans two eras and three continents, from West Africa to the Virgin Islands, to Denmark, Iceland, and the United States. Hans Jonathan was born into slavery in 1784, but he would not submit to the shackles his black mother was forced to bear. His life was full of paradox and adventure: it recalls the heroic achievements of all those who campaign for freedom and human dignity. To tell it properly, one must recount not only his biography but *many* biographies—insofar as that is possible.

Biographers do not undertake their task lightly, but they may not be fully aware of their own motivations: the story simply will not leave them alone. My interest was piqued almost a decade ago when I saw a Danish TV documentary, *Descendants of Slaves*, in which one subject was an Icelander like me: Hans Jonathan. Much about his life sounded quite fantastical, and I felt it would repay my investigation. It seemed to me, an anthropologist, as though a long and important chapter in human history—the story of imperialism, colonialism, racism, human rights, and globalization—had been crammed into one brief life. Hans Jonathan casts light on questions of freedom and human rights that are as vital today as they ever were, all around the world. For he was a man who had the temerity, the courage, to steal himself.

| I |

THE ISLAND OF ST. CROIX

FIG. 2.1. Karolina Elisa Susanna Bjornsdottir (b. 1889), great-granddaughter of Hans Jonathan. (Photo: Hansina Regina Bjornsdottir. National Museum of Iceland, Reykjavik.)

"A HOUSE NEGRO"

HANS JONATHAN'S MOTHER, Emilia Regina, was a slave on the Caribbean island of St. Croix, at that time a Danish colony, now in the US Virgin Islands. In the eighteenth century the slaves of St. Croix were descended mainly from the Akan, Mandingo, Yoruba, Congo, and Ibo peoples of West Africa. They, or their ancestors, were first captured by fellow Africans, slave hunters who brought them to the Gold Coast (now Ghana), where Europeans had constructed trading posts with camps for slaves and slave traders, protected by fortresses.[1] The principal Danish stronghold was Christiansborg, built by Swedes in 1652 and later occupied by Dutch and Danish merchants. Now known as Osu Castle, it stands today in Accra as a tangible reminder of the slave trade.

Danes, and Icelanders, had engaged in long-distance trade during the so-called Viking Age, in the early Middle Ages. Sometimes these expeditions involved capturing European slaves. Later, from the seventeenth century onward, the growth in sugar production in the Danish West Indies demanded arrangements with more distant ports, in particular cheap and permanent labor provided by African slave traders through their brutal "hunting" of fellow Africans. These traders and their European partners formed lasting bonds and hybrid cultures, arranged and maintained partly through racial intermarriages.[2]

Some of the ships sailing from the Gold Coast to the Virgin Islands were Danish. Leaving Africa with their human cargo, they embarked upon the notorious Middle Passage, the journey across the wide Atlantic Ocean separating the enslaved Africans' homes from their destination in the New World. A number of factors influenced conditions on board: the number of slaves being transported, the size of the crew, and the preferences of the individual skipper. Some favored "loose packing," others "tight packing."[3] The atmosphere below deck was sometimes so airless that a candlewick would not light. On occasion the Africans were compelled to "dance" on deck in the sun, stretching themselves and shaking their limbs, while guards wielded guns and whips; this "exercise" was meant to ensure that the "goods" arrived at market in satisfactory condition.[4] Still, the business suffered considerable "wastage," as many a promising slave did not survive the long and difficult voyage. In the sixteenth century the Middle Passage might last three months; by the eighteenth century it was "only" one.[5]

After the hardships of the ocean passage, the Africans would be prepared for auction, perhaps by rubbing palm oil into their skin to make them look healthier. Planters, middlemen, and other speculators would feel the "goods," smell the Africans' skin, inspect them for wounds or sores, and estimate the physical stamina of men, women, and children, and their potential future value.[6]

Enslavement spelled a dramatic end to the captives' former lives. They disappeared into the anonymity of the plantations. Still, a remarkable amount of information can be gleaned from official records and reports, and not least from the slave registers. The colonial authorities, the various churches, and the employers all kept track of their citizens, subjects, and livestock. Standardized forms were used, divided into columns and filled out by scribes with widely varying handwriting and styles. From a twenty-first-century perspective, the slave registers give an almost surreal impression. They record detailed information on the slave owners; the name, age, and occupation of each enslaved person; whether he or she is a house slave or a field slave; and whether each is fit for work or not.

FIG. 2.2. The fort at Frederiksted. (Photo: Gisli Palsson.)

Enslaved Africans were classified as a type of livestock. The slave registers were often called "head tax lists": it was important to have an approximate head count in order to keep the plantation running efficiently, pay appropriate taxes, and so on, as in any other business. But beyond the neat columns of names and numbers was another reality, one that rarely made any appearance in the ledgers, although it is sometimes possible to read between the lines.

The occupation *bomba*, for example, appears on the lists from time to time. A *bomba* was a slave whose task it was to beat fellow slaves into submission. Its occurrence is an unsettling reminder of the divisions among enslaved persons and of the naked power entailed by the social contract of the plantation, if the terminology of contemporary philosopher Jean-Jacques Rousseau may be applied to the laws and rules of the colonial system—laws and rules imposed by the minority in order to keep the majority under control and thereby to safeguard their own interests.

"THE QUEEN"

Hans Jonathan's mother, Emilia Regina, was probably born in 1760 on the St. Croix sugar plantation La Reine (The Queen) under the ownership of a German baron, Christian Lebrecht von Prock (1718–80)—although it is possible that she was born in Africa. According to some of her descendants, she was the daughter of an African chief.

In 1755 Baron von Prock had been appointed governor of what was then the Danish West Indies, including St. Croix, St. Thomas, St. John, and many smaller islands. But he proved ineffectual in that role and was recalled about a decade later. Around the time Prock took over the governorship, King Frederik V of Denmark issued laws addressing the rights of slaves, including their housing, food, and medical care. This legislation was the first of its kind in the Danish realm; prior laws enacted in 1733 had made provision only for the rights of slave owners. Solicitous of the interests of his fellow sugar planters, Prock simply ignored the new legislation, which might have considerably improved the conditions of the slaves of St. Croix.[7] The baron performed no better in more northerly climes: two years after he left St. Croix he was appointed governor of Iceland, also a Danish dominion. Uninspired by his new post, he never actually went to Iceland and was replaced about a year later.

When he left St. Croix, Baron von Prock sold his sugar plantation to Thomas William Schäffer and his wife Henrietta Cathrina (1741–1816) née van Lexmond, later Schimmelmann. Little Emilia Regina, then about five years old, and the other Africans at La Reine passed to the plantation's new owners. Since she later is listed as a servant—a "house slave" or "house negro"—she was likely the daughter of one of the three adult slave women registered in the Schäffer home, Cato, Gertrude, or Mariana. Young children were generally allowed to stay with their mothers, at least partly in order to ensure the future value of the slave child.

Emilia Regina seems to have spent some of her childhood days in the nearby town of Christiansted instead of on the plantation. In 1772 eight house slaves were registered at the Schäffers' home at 12 Hospital Street. One of these was a girl named "Reina"—probably Emilia Regina, as she did not receive the name Emilia until she was baptized in 1787. On the 1773 slave register of the La Reine plantation the name Regina appears.

Interestingly, all three names—Reina, Regina, and La Reine— mean "queen." What does a slave's name imply? The names on the plantation lists are, as a rule, European: her brother was named Francis, her son Hans Jonathan, her daughter Anna Maria, the girl's father Andreas. Captains of slave ships allocated numbers to their "cargo" before it was put up for auction; afterward the owners gave their new slaves "Christian" names. These names are a clear indication of the subjection of the enslaved to their masters. We have no knowledge of the naming traditions of Emilia Regina's parents and their people, as we cannot say precisely where they came from in Africa. But slave names are subject to quite different rules from the names of free people. In slavery a woman does not own herself or even her name.

Slave names were similar in nature to nicknames: not chosen by a person or her parents, and often derogatory. Name-calling served to ensure that slaves felt marginalized. In Iceland, the island to which Emilia Regina's son Hans Jonathan would ultimately flee, people since the Middle Ages had been well aware of the power of name-calling—which, despite the old saying, can be as harmful as any sticks or stones—and special provisions were made to safeguard an individual's rights and honor. An example can be seen in Iceland's first written lawcode, from about 1118: "If a man calls a man by a name other than his own [. . .] the penalty is three years' exile, if he takes offence. The same applies if a man uses a nickname to mock him."[8]

Changes of name have occurred everywhere and in all periods for various reasons, but under slavery they were universally imposed. Slaves were often called by the names of heroes or great men, as if to underline their degradation. Cicero, a common slave name, served this ironic purpose. An enslaved man was not named after the Roman philosopher to acknowledge his intellect or eloquence; he was *branded* Cicero. The royal name Regina, "Queen" (or should we say Queenie?), may have had the same overtones. An enslaved African called by such a name was constantly reminded of his or her powerlessness.

When Thomas William Schäffer of La Reine died in 1775, his will valued his house slave Emilia Regina at "400 pieces of eight." The piece of eight, or *real de a ocho* (eight-real coin), was also known as the Spanish dollar. Nine house slaves were listed in Schäffer's will, valued from sixty pieces of eight up to six hundred. If Emilia Regina was valued at four hundred, what does that mean? The exchange rate of the Spanish dollar or piece of eight varied greatly from one colony to another, until it was eventually standardized in the late eighteenth century. In Emilia Regina's time, a complicated combination of currencies were in use in the Danish West Indies: in addition to the Spanish and the US dollar, the Danish rigsdaler and a special Danish West Indian rigsdaler were also legal tender.[9] When Emilia Regina was bought, sold, and valued in the slave registers of St. Croix, a Spanish dollar was worth approximately the equivalent of $260 today.[10] Hence the slave woman would have been worth about $100,000.

For comparison: Christian G. A. Oldendorp, a Moravian missionary who disembarked on St. Croix the year after Emilia Regina was valued at 400 pieces of eight, records that a good horse shipped from New York was worth 200 Spanish dollars.[11] Hence we may say that the slave woman Emilia Regina was worth two fine horses. In the same period, a pirate of the Caribbean might claim a hundred Spanish dollars for the loss of an eye, or for two-thirds of a leg. In other words, the slave woman was worth the equivalent of two horses, or four eyes, or a little less than three legs.

THE PLANTATION

The Virgin Islands owe their name to Christopher Columbus, who called there on his westward voyage of exploration in 1493, naming them after St. Ursula and the eleven thousand Virgins.[12] St. Croix, the largest island in the archipelago, came under French rule in 1650. Denmark acquired it in 1733, when it was purchased by the Danish West India-Guinea Company, along with other islands in what would then be called the Danish West Indies. In Emilia Regina's time, during the heyday of the sugar plantations, the slave population of St. Croix was about twenty thousand, while white residents numbered fifteen hundred to two thousand, counting landowners, government officials, and assorted clergy, physicians, police, and tradesmen. The principal centers of population were Frederiksted and Christiansted; sugar was the basis of the local economy.

On the plantations, houses and other buildings were often constructed on hilltops, where the breeze could cool the planters' homes and drive the windmills that processed the sugarcane. The elevated site also provided a good view of what was going on in the surrounding lowlands, for around their homes the planters had had the woods cleared and the soil prepared for growing sugarcane. Today, sugar production is a thing of the past on the La Reine plantation, but it has left its mark here and there on the landscape. A lane through densely wooded country leads to a fine eighteenth-century mansion. At the rear is a cabin where the house slaves slept. Here the young Emilia Regina spent her childhood and grew into womanhood.

The present owner of La Reine is William Fleming Cissel. The plantation has been in his family since 1841, and Cissel, who has a degree in history, has compiled a record of all its owners, of whom he is the thirteenth. The house is impressive, and largely in its original form. Paintings and Danish porcelain plaques embellish the lofty walls of its rooms. In the eighteenth century, these rooms must have echoed with conversations about sugarcane, hurricanes, ocean journeys, taxes, slaves, punishments, and revolts. In the basement is a hurricane shelter to which the household could retreat during severe storms: probably masters and house slaves could all be accommodated there, but hardly the army of Africans who labored in the fields.

Cissel and his family have also preserved old tableware and fur-

FIG. 2.3. Entrance to La Reine plantation. (Photo: Gisli Palsson.)

niture from plantation times, including a fine chair or chaise longue made of hardwood and leather. These "master's chairs" were not unlike a modern-day reclining La-Z-Boy; only a handful still exist on St. Croix. In the humid tropical heat, the masters of the plantations could lie back and imagine they were at home in the cool Danish climate, among the bustling street life and the dreaming spires of Copenhagen.

CHRISTIANSTED

In the latter half of the eighteenth century, Christiansted was a Danish town. Most of the inhabitants were white, numbering about a thousand, the vast majority of them male. It was by far the biggest community on St. Croix.[13] A number of streets had been neatly laid out in a grid around the fort and the harbor. The town was compact, with everything within easy reach. Houses were built close together—and everyone in Christiansted knew everyone else.

The La Reine sugar planter William Schäffer died in August 1775, and five months later his widow, Henrietta Cathrina, remarried. Her new husband was Judge Ludvig Heinrich Ernst von Schimmelmann (1743–93). He was thirty-three years old; she was thirty-five. Henrietta Cathrina sold her plantation but kept several of her slaves, including Emilia Regina, and the couple settled in Christiansted, where Schimmelmann was a rising star: in 1771 he had been appointed to the government of the Danish West Indies; a decade later he was nominated vice governor by the king of Denmark; and in 1784 he rose to the position of governor general major, in the high-flown language of the Danish colonial administration. Henrietta Louise, the young daughter of Henrietta Cathrina and her late husband William Schäffer, lived with them. The Schimmelmanns' own first child, Heinrich Carl Jacob, was born in 1776. The next year came a daughter, Caroline Adelaide. A second son, Ernst Carl Heinrich, was born in 1780, and in 1785 a daughter, Sabina Johanna, who lived only for three weeks.

Records from 1777 tell us that Emilia Regina was "a negro" in the

FIG. 2.4. Behind 15 Queen's St. in Christiansted, where the house slaves of the Schimmelmann family may have lived, among them Emilia Regina. (Photo: Gisli Palsson.)

Schimmelmann household, but they provide little or no details about the slave girl's parentage or place of origin. She was seventeen years old by this time and capable of carrying out most of the tasks allotted to a housemaid, such as cooking, washing, cleaning, tidying, and childcare. The slaves Cato, Gertrude, and Mariana are not mentioned in the Schimmelmann records at this time.

The Schimmelmann household also included three male house slaves: Cicero, Hector, and Peter. One of these could have been Emilia Regina's father, though slaveholders did not regard the presence of a father as having any particular importance for a slave child and saw little reason to keep them in the same household. Male slaves fathered children, and the mothers nursed them at their breast, ensuring another generation of laborers, but in general family ties were irrelevant to the business of sugar production.

Yet slave masters had to be able to trust their house slaves. The white masters and their families lived in constant fear of being attacked without warning in the dead of night by a mob of revolting slaves. (Gun ownership, common among the white people of Christiansted, was seen almost as a civic duty.) House slaves, often intimate with the field slaves, could pass on important information if they chose, and if the master expressed an interest. Thus house slaves enjoyed certain privileges, perhaps even being able to keep their own families together. They established a closer bond with their masters and mistresses than the average enslaved person could expect.

SERVITUDE AND SALVATION

It is hard to tell what kind of life Emilia Regina lived. We must rely here on contemporary sources that throw light on the community and culture of St. Croix. An important document is the account of Oldendorp, who recorded the price of a good horse.[14] Sent to St. Croix in the spring of 1767 by the evangelical Moravian Brethren, Oldendorp spent eighteen months there and on nearby islands. His narrative expresses a sincere interest in local conditions. Having been commissioned to write a history of the Brethren's mission, in addition he made detailed observations on diverse aspects of nature and human society on the islands.

Oldendorp discussed the place of the person of mixed race, the mulatto, in Caribbean society. He wrote that relations between white and black generally reflected customs that had existed for a long time in the region. These customs forbade, for instance, white men from marrying black women, but white men sometimes lived with them— even with two or more. "The children born to such Negro women belong to the master to whom the mother belongs," he explained. "They are used as his slaves if they are not exchanged or bought out of servitude. However, many such mulattos are treated a little better than other slaves."[15]

Despite the "swift and firm beatings" (which he believed were necessary in order to keep the laborers at their work), Oldendorp concluded that the slaves of St. Croix were happy with their lot. "One would err . . . in imagining these Negroes as downcast and sad, spiritless in their work, and depressed by the hardship of their lot in life," he wrote. "Generally, they are cheerful at their work, chatting, joking, laughing, and singing Guinea songs. Although this behavior is in large part a result of their natural easy-going disposition, it is also possible, I believe, to arrive at the conclusion that they are not in fact as oppressed in their condition as is commonly supposed."[16] The Moravian missionary often seems to imply in his report that servitude and salvation are one and the same—and a universal blessing.

Oldendorp's interpretation must count as one of the early examples of what has come to be known as the "happy slave hypothesis," a persistent theme in colonial metropoles. Detailed historical studies and endless reports in newspapers portray an entirely different picture. Plantation slaves on St. Croix and elsewhere repeatedly risked their lives resisting bondage, pulling down fences, destroying equipment, setting fire to outbuildings, stealing cattle, food, and liquor, and running away.[17] Often such protests were highly symbolic attempts to denigrate the master's persona by attacking anything belonging to him, considered an extension of himself. Much evidence also testifies to slave suicide. While enslaved persons who ran away from it all in desperation did not leave suicide notes and newspaper accounts and other reports rarely elaborated on the slave's point of view, it seems clear that self-destruction was common and had manifold implications.[18]

House slaves had certain means of coping and resisting their masters.[19] They were in a position to poison their master discreetly, using easily available plants of which they had knowledge; they could neglect the children entrusted to their care; and they could keep discontented field slaves informed about what the masters were planning, and even about developments in the outside world. Natural conditions on the island of St. Croix were not favorable for anyone who wanted to go into hiding, but nonetheless enslaved Africans sometimes made a break for it.[20] While slave owners tended to describe runaways as ungrateful, slavery was anything but happiness.

FIG. 3.1. Mill tower at Constitution Hill with Schimmelmann's initials, 1778.
(Photo Mark Sellergren.)

"THE MULATTO HANS JONATHAN"

MOST OF THE ENSLAVED PEOPLE on St. Croix were called negroes. But since many white men on the island fathered children on black slave women, they saw the need for a more subtle system of classification. The term *mulatto* was used to refer to the child of a white man and a black woman (also, technically, to the child of a black man and a white woman, but such children were far rarer). *Mulatto* derives from the Spanish and Portuguese *mulato*, which in turn has its root in the Latin *mulus* (mule). The word *creole* originally referred to a European born in the New World and then later an African-descended slave born in the Americas. Other concepts of racial hybrids common in the colonial world were *mestizo*, *casta*, and *zambo*.[1] This system of racial classification evolved to a byzantine complexity—in stark contrast to the elegant simplicity of the system of taxonomy developed by Carl Linneaus (1707–78) to classify the nonhuman world. In some regions, over a hundred variants in racial mixing were minutely classified. And when resourceful officials came up with the idea of issuing documents proving that the holder was "white," the actual color of the person's skin became irrelevant.

Yet while a clear distinction was maintained between whites and people of color, between slave and free person, the barrier was occasionally, symbolically, lifted. Accounts from the nearby island of St. Thomas show that as early as 1740 planters would carouse with their slaves: copious quantities of drink were consumed, after which the revelers would march to a neighboring plantation beating drums, setting off fireworks, and firing guns.[2] Such festivities spread throughout the Caribbean, including St. Croix. Before long they developed into true carnivals, expanding from one plantation to the next and into the town of Christiansted. Oldendorp, who observed the fun on several occasions, appears to have found the experience quite affecting—although the pious evangelist says nothing of having joined in. "When I ascribe to them an aptitude for dancing," he wrote, "that is not to say that they are able to perform very artistic dances. Their dancing consists of jumping about, shaking their shoulders, and moving their arms, wherein the great suppleness and strength of their bodies are displayed to good advantage. Even more monotonous is the instrumental music to which they dance.... And when the dance has ended, the spectators show their appreciation with wild laughter and jubilation."[3]

The carnival atmosphere reached its high point over Christmas: planters provided treats for their slaves, and some even invited them into the big house to dance to the music of a violin or banjo. A visitor to St. Croix remarked that "the feelings of the slaves toward their master, throughout the year, depend very much on the treatment they receive at these times."[4] Like the ancient Roman Saturnalia, in a sense Carnival transcended the barriers of class, race, and gender, undermining the everyday rules by making everyone equal—more or less. "But their liberty expired with the day. They slept, and were again slaves."[5]

BREEDING STOCK

Children of slave women were a welcome addition, from the perspective of their lawful owners, regardless of whether the fathers were white or black. The productivity of a sugar plantation was largely dependent on the labor of slaves, so it was essential to ensure a constant supply. Field slaves died young due to their hard work and inadequate diet, and infant mortality was high. To make matters worse for the plantation owners, antislavery campaigners were gaining ever-increasing support in the latter half of the eighteenth century. Every indication was that the African slave trade would be banned before long.

The good health and fecundity of female Africans on the plantations thus became a political issue: the women were used as breeding stock. Black women, whether field slaves, house slaves, or concubines, were considered to be under a moral and legal obligation to give birth to strong and healthy children. Care of pregnant women and infants was of such vital importance to the sugar barons that they arranged for it to be provided by European physicians and older, experienced women.

Not surprisingly, slave women secretly rebelled. They resorted to various expedients to discreetly avoid conception or to abort a pregnancy, and when the need arose, they "exposed" the newborns, abandoning them outside to die. A French physician in the nearby colony of Santo Domingo on the island of Hispaniola (today's Dominican Republic) was horrified by the exposure of infants prior to the Haitian Revolution that began in August 1791. He wrote of one mother who sacrificed two of her children in order to "steal" them from slavery. She believed that after this earthly life the enslaved Africans would return to their ancestral homes in Africa, to resume their former lives with their family and friends. Women who exposed their children to die in this way, contrary to the "laws of nature," the physician wrote, were subjected to severe penalties.

In the case of a stillbirth, the mother was also deemed culpable, yet slave women persisted in using a number of herbal concoctions to bring on bleeding or to induce premature labor. The knowledge of these remedies, accrued by women in Africa and the Caribbean over centuries, was passed down from woman to woman. Maia Sibylla Merian, a German artist who visited the Dutch colony of Surinam in South America long before European women had started to travel there in any numbers, recorded her observations of women's herbal remedies; these were published in 1705. As an abortifacient, Merian wrote, the African slaves used the seeds of the peacock flower, or *Flos pavonis*.[6]

Another writer who remarked on such herbal remedies—and one who is more pertinent to Emilia Regina's situation—is Dr. Johan Christian Schmidt.[7] He and Emilia Regina were on the Schimmelmann estate at the same time. A physician, Schmidt surely knew about the Caribbean slave women's methods of avoiding pregnancy and inducing abortion, for he wrote, "I could describe various interesting cures of the Negroes, who, as is known, are knowledgeable about plants."[8]

Traditional herbal remedies—though not listed anywhere in European pharmacopeia—apparently could cure certain common complaints, and physicians like Schmidt saw no reason to object to their use.[9] On the contrary, they encouraged the healers and even tried on occasion to learn their medical skills. The doctors were less enthusiastic, however, about anything that smacked of sorcery or witchcraft. For example, after reporting that pregnant field slaves in St. Croix were normally granted two months off before the birth and another two once the child was born, Schmidt noted:

> The pregnant Negroes . . . are very hardy in giving birth. They bear children often, without anyone attending them. . . . In the fields it often happens that immediately after they have given birth, they can go and do what they need to do. In the first eight days after birth, they are given candles, some rice, and new French wine, when it is available. During the first eight days, the candles are lit by the midwives for the whole night. During the ninth night, a newborn child is watched carefully by more than twenty Negroes, so that it will not be stolen or eaten by witches.[10]

When, at the age of twenty-three, Emilia Regina became pregnant by a white man, many of these customs and ideas about pregnancy and birth and the classification of humans by color became relevant. Would the child be black or white? Or something in between? Emilia Regina must have known about traditional African remedies and potions, and perhaps she had personal experience of them. Should she end her pregnancy?

NEITHER BLACK NOR WHITE

Emilia Regina's mistress, Henrietta Cathrina Schimmelmann, owned or rented several houses in Christiansted, but from 1781 to 1784 she lived at 33 Strand Street—and that is probably where Hans Jonathan was conceived, one hot summer day in 1783 when the hurricane season was approaching and nature was in full bloom. Or perhaps the act of conception took place away from town, among the billowing fields of tall sugarcane on a plantation called Constitution Hill, which was the property of the Schimmelmanns. At that time the house slaves were formally registered as resident on this plantation, and not at the Schimmelmanns' Christiansted home, but it is unlikely that Emilia Regina would have been far from Henrietta Cathrina, who, like most plantation wives, lived principally in town and depended on her house slave for various daily tasks.

Was the sexual encounter a rape, a common plantation thing?[11] It is impossible to know whether Emilia Regina loved or despised her impregnator. From the slave woman's viewpoint, breeding was simply one more burden entailed by bondage. Emilia Regina probably did what she had to do, like other slaves, often against her will. In the end, this was the enslaved person's lot in life. Oldendorp wrote that the slave master "believes that he has unlimited rights over the bodies of his slaves of both sexes." Here as elsewhere, his colonial language is one-sided, evading abuse, failing to capture the inherent violence of slavery. An enslaved female who "might wish to resist" the master's sexual advances "is nonetheless subject to the power of her master, who can do with her as he pleases."[12] Sometimes the master, thinking himself generous, shared these privileges with other white men. We have no way of knowing what kind of master Schimmelmann was, but most masters were brutal to their slaves.

Emilia Regina gave birth to a baby boy on 12 April 1784, according to much later legal documents from Copenhagen.[13] Her friend Sabina Helena, her brother Francis's unofficial spouse, was present at the birth. No doubt the attention of everyone else present—the midwife and members of the household—was focused on the child's skin color, hair, and facial features.

But people were aware that the skin color of a newborn is not necessarily a reliable indicator of its parentage. Wrote Oldendorp, "They come into the world without their black color, though not without some trace of it. Within four days, however, Negro children, who initially were as white, or as red, as newborn European infants, become first brown, and then gradually their color darkens until in three or four weeks it becomes as black as that of their parents."[14] He gave thought to the significance of differences in skin color and to what characterized the skins of different nations and races. Noting that Europeans had many theories on this matter, he wrote, "Others consider the Negro's blackness as something quite intrinsic to him and look for its cause either in his blood or in a fine network under the outer skin. . . . This much is certain, namely that, in addition to the differences of color, the Negroes can be readily distinguished from all other brown and black nations by the thickness and particular softness of their skin, as well as by their woolly hair."[15] Philosopher Immanuel Kant, a contemporary of Oldendorp and Emilia Regina and a native of the Prussian town of Königsberg, not far from the Hamburg homes of the Schimmelmann family, observed that Europeans living in Africa produced white children and, similarly, Africans who settled in Europe had children with dark skin color, regardless of their respective environments.[16] Color, Kant concluded, was not acquired.

It became clear, after a few weeks had passed, that Emilia Regina's son was a mulatto, the offspring of a black mother and a white father.

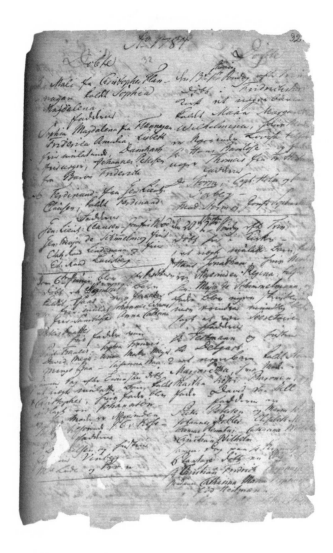

FIG. 3.2. Baptism of Hans Jonathan. Records of the Lutheran Church, St. Croix 1780–94, 1/770–4. (National Archives of Denmark.) Den evangeliske menighed, Skt. Croix. Enesteministerialbog for den evangeliske menighed på Skt. Croix (1740–1860) 1/770-4-4b.

FIG. 3.3.
The Lutheran Church in Christiansted
(rear entrance.). (Photo: Gisli Palsson.)

There must have been a lot of speculation about the father's identity. According to the church register of the Lutheran congregation in Christiansted, on 20 June 1784, the boy was christened Hans Jonathan.[17]

Accompanied by the witnesses and other family and friends, Emilia Regina must have walked, carrying her two-month-old son, the short distance from 33 Strand Street to the elegant Lutheran church at the harborside in Christiansted. Everyone would have worn white robes, in accordance with the custom of the congregation, as a sign that they were cleansed of their sins. From the viewpoint of planters and slaveholders, it was important to baptize slave children, whether they were categorized as negro, mulatto, mestizo, casta, zambo, or creole. It was not sufficient simply to make a head count of enslaved persons on the plantation and pay tax accordingly; it was also necessary to document the nationality, religious affiliation, and descent of each individual, so far as possible. This little multicultural community in the Caribbean had to be documented like every other dominion of the Danish king. Baby Hans Jonathan was officially a subject of the Danish crown.

THE GOVERNOR'S MANSION

Soon after the baptism of "the mulatto," as Hans Jonathan would later be called, the Schimmelmanns moved into the governor's mansion, the seat of government of St. Croix. Ludvig Heinrich Ernst von Schimmelmann now held the powerful position of governor general major, the highest office in the Danish islands of St. Croix, St. Thomas, and St. John. He was responsible for all official business and handled all military matters for the three islands. The family would live at the governor's mansion for about four years.

The residence of the governor and Lady Henrietta Cathrina was securely guarded. As the stronghold of power on which the plantation society was based, it was a target for disaffected slaves, and its present-day security measures recall the way the eighteenth-century slaveholders must have lived in constant fear of a sudden insurrection. Today all visitors wishing to enter the governor's residence must give an account of themselves, and those who enter by the main doors must empty their pockets and pass their possessions through a scanner as if entering airport security. Should the visitor have forgotten that this is now United States territory, the point is clearly underlined.

This mansion in Christiansted was the seat of the government of the Danish West Indies for nearly a century and a half. Attempts were made here to reconcile the attitudes of the government authorities in Copenhagen with those of the men who held power over the sugar plantations; these powerful men were often corrupted by the interests of the slaveowners—if they were not sugar barons and slaveowners themselves, as was Governor Schimmelmann. Work had commenced in 1742 on the oldest structure, the Schopen Wing of the mansion, which is the only part of the building Emilia Regina would have known. The building still contains marble statues of royalty and hundreds of black-and-white floor tiles of stone shipped from Oland in Sweden—the colonial masters wanted to bring with them some dazzling symbol of home.

CONSTITUTION HILL

Before he was a year old, Hans Jonathan was listed in a 1785 memorandum of slaves owned by the Schimmelmanns. He is included as one of three "mulattos" among the house slaves at Constitution Hill, a plantation the couple had acquired some years before. This slave register lists 163 men, women, and children—a considerable number. Constitution Hill was a large property, one of the major plantations on St. Croix. There the young Hans Jonathan most likely spent some time with the field slaves, who carried out the varied and arduous tasks involved in sugar production. He must surely have been a perceptive child, eager to learn. Perhaps it was his experience of the stark contrasts in plantation society—the privileged gentry in town, the oppressed slaves in the fields—along with his own ambiguous status as a mulatto, that led him to thirst for freedom and to realize that things need not necessarily be the way they were.

Perhaps the Schimmelmanns welcomed Hans Jonathan, the son of a white man (whoever that was), for they had lost their own eldest child, Heinrich Carl Jacob, in the same year that Hans Jonathan was born. The following year, 1785, their infant daughter lived for only three weeks. The presence of little Hans Jonathan may have assuaged their grief a bit. He may even have been permitted to play with the other Schimmelmann children: Ernst Carl Heinrich was only four years older than he, while Caroline Adelaide was seven years his senior.

Today Constitution Hill is but a shadow of its former self. The splendid drive and many of the buildings from the time of Emilia Regina and Hans Jonathan have been overrun by dense jungle, like the buildings on La Reine and most other eighteenth-century plantations in St. Croix. The land has been divided up among several owners. Constitution Hill itself, after which the plantation was named, and the surrounding area are now owned by the Sellergrens from

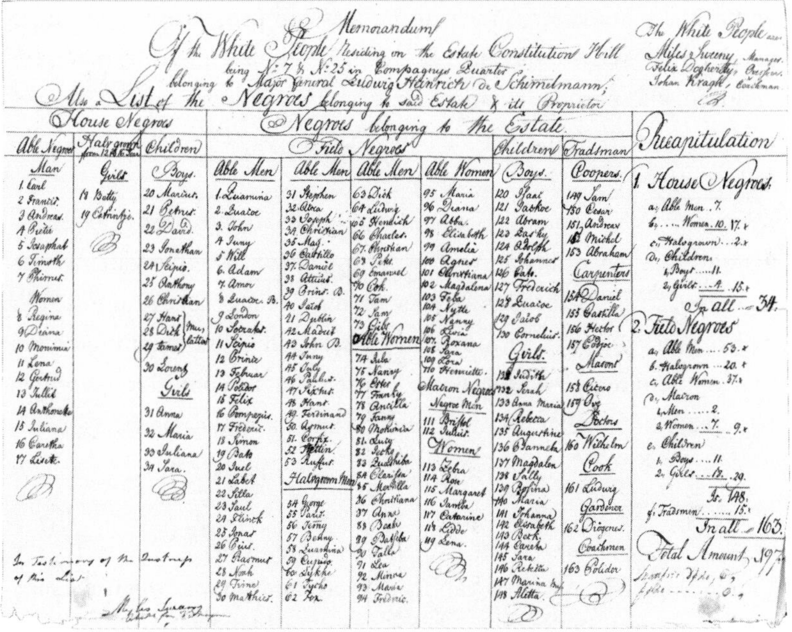
Memorandum
Of the White People residing on the Estate Constitution Hill being No. 7 & No. 25 in Compagnys Quarter belonging to Major General Ludwig Heinrich de Schimmelmann;
Also a List of the Negroes belonging to said Estate & its Proprietor

The White People are: Miles Sweeny, Manager. Felix Dogherty, Overseer. Johan Kragh, Coachman

House Negroes

Able Negroes — Man: 1 Carl, 2 Francis, 3 Andreas, 4 Pieter, 5 Josaphat, 6 Timoth, 7 Phirrus. Women: 8 Regina, 9 Diana, 10 Monimia, 11 Lena, 12 Gertrud, 13 Tullia, 14 Anthonette, 15 Juliana, 16 Caretha, 17 Lisette.

Half grown from 12 to … — Girls: 18 Betty, 19 Catrintje.

Children — Boys: 20 Marcus, 21 Petrus, 22 David, 23 Jonathan, 24 Scipio, 25 Anthony, 26 Christian, 27 Hans, 28 Dick, 29 James (Mulattos), 30 Lorenz. Girls: 31 Anna, 32 Maria, 33 Juliana, 34 Sara.

Negroes belonging to the Estate

Field Negroes

Able Men: 1 Quamina, 2 Quacoe, 3 John, 4 Juny, 5 Will, 6 Adam, 7 Amor, 8 Quacoe B., 9 London, 10 Sokrates, 11 Scipio, 12 Prince, 13 Februar, 14 Polidor, 15 Felix, 16 Pompejus, 17 Frederic, 18 Simon, 19 Bato, 20 Juel, 21 Labet, 22 Sitta, 23 Saul, 24 Klinck, 25 Jonas, 26 Prins, 27 Rasmus, 28 Noah, 29 Trine, 30 Matthies.

Able Men: 31 Stephen, 32 Alexa, 33 Joseph, 34 Christian, 35 Mag., 36 Castillo, 37 Daniel, 38 Atticus, 39 Prins B., 40 Jacob, 41 Dublin, 42 Madeit, 43 John B., 44 Juny, 45 July, 46 Paulus, 47 Sixtus, 48 Hans, 49 Ferdinand, 50 Asmus, 51 Corfix, 52 Hettin, 53 Rufus. Halfgrown Men: 54 George, 55 Paris, 56 Jemy, 57 Benny, 58 Quamina, 59 Cupido, 60 Sykke, 61 Tycho, 62 Fox.

Able Men: 63 Dick, 64 Ludwig, 65 Hendrich, 66 Charles, 67 Christian, 68 Peter, 69 Emanuel, 70 Coh., 71 Tam, 72 Sam, 73 Gibs. Able Women: 74 Bela, 75 Nanny, 76 Otter, 77 Franky, 78 Ancilla, 79 Fanny, 80 Mokinda, 81 Lucy, 82 Jecho, 83 Budsheba, 84 Clarissa, 85 Merilla, 86 Christiana, 87 Anna, 88 Beaky, 89 Batseba, 90 Talla, 91 Lea, 92 Minna, 93 Maria, 94 Frederic.

Able Women: 95 Maria, 96 Diana, 97 Abba, 98 Elisabeth, 99 Amelia, 100 Agnes, 101 Christiana, 102 Magdalena, 103 Feba, 104 Nytte, 105 Nanny, 106 Livia, 107 Roxana, 108 Sara, 109 Lora, 110 Henriette. Matron Negroes — Negroe Men: 111 Bristol, 112 Julius. Women: 113 Zebra, 114 Rose, 115 Margaret, 116 Jamba, 117 Catarine, 118 Lidde, 119 Lena.

Children — Boys: 120 Isaac, 121 Jackoe, 122 Abram, 123 Lasky, 124 Adolph, 125 Johannes, 126 Cato, 127 Frederich, 128 Quacoe, 129 Jacob, 130 Cornelius. Girls: 131 Juditha, 132 Sarah, 133 Anna Maria, 134 Rebecca, 135 Augustine, 136 Hanneka, 137 Magdalen, 138 Sally, 139 Rosina, 140 Maria, 141 Johanna, 142 Elisabeth, 143 Beck, 144 Caretha, 145 Sara, 146 Rebecca, 147 Marina, 148 Aletta.

Tradsman — Coopers: 149 Sam, 150 Cesar, 151 Andreas, 152 Michel, 153 Abraham. Carpenters: 154 Daniel, 155 Castilla, 156 Hector, 157 Codjoe. Masons: 158 Citero, 159 Ove. Doctors: 160 Wilhelm. Cook: 161 Ludwig. Gardener: 162 Diogenes. Coachmen: 163 Polidor.

Recapitulation
1. House Negroes
a, Able Men .. 7.
b, … Women .10. 17.
c, Halfgrown .. 2.
d, Children
1, Boys ….. 11.
2, Girls … 4. 15.
In all … 34.
2. Field Negroes
a, Able Men …. 53.
b. Halfgrown … 20.
c, Able Women . 37.
d, Matron
1, Men ….. 2.
2, Women .. 7. 9.
e, Children
1, Boys …. 11.
2, Girls .. 18. 29.
148.
f. Tradsmen ….. 15.
In all 163.
Total Amount 197

In Testimony of the Exactness of this List
Miles Sweeny

FIG. 3.4. Head tax list from Constitution Hill, 1785. (National Archives of Denmark.) Den vestindiske regering. Gruppeordnede sager. Matrikeloplysningskemaer (1772–1821) 3.81.493 for plantagerne 1785.

Iowa. They run a business selling hardwood furniture made in Bali and elsewhere in Indonesia, and they spend part of each year on St. Croix. Their home is fragrant with scents of teak and mahogany. The Schimmelmanns' house next door is still standing, though considerably altered over the years. Not much remains to recall the heyday of sugarcane and slavery, but it was clearly the home of prosperous landowners.

The heart of a sugar plantation was the tower of the windmill where the sugarcane was processed. At Constitution Hill the tower remains standing. Though the windmill's sails are long gone and mosses and shrubs have taken root in the stone walls, it remains a proud and tenacious monument to the past, and to obsolete production methods. The cornerstone of the mill, dated 1778, bears Schimmelmann's initials, LHS. Other relics of the old plantation days include a tall stone wall built around a patch of land to catch rainwater and act as a reservoir. Traces of boilers and pans used in the sugar production process may also be seen. It was a dangerous place for children, and perhaps youngsters were kept indoors, or at least at a safe distance from the hot vats and machinery, when milling was in full swing.

Just as Hans Jonathan was old enough to start toddling about the plantation, the Caribbean was swept by one of the most violent hurricanes to strike in decades. The storm hit St. Croix on 24 August 1785 before passing over Puerto Rico, Jamaica, and Cuba, claiming nearly two hundred lives over five days. These were the conditions in which the young boy began his life: bondage and natural disaster.

A SISTER AND COUSINS

Emilia Regina herself was baptized on 4 January 1787, when she may already have been carrying her second child.[18] Known until then simply as Regina, she was given Emilia as her baptismal name. For slaveowners, baptism of adult slaves was a propitiatory gesture, a sign of their sincere desire to "civilize" the black "barbarians" from the Gold Coast of Africa. As for the slaves themselves, perhaps their baptism and participation in the Christian congregation provided them with a temporary respite from the shackles of their daily lives. Or perhaps not.

The Christiansted church register records that Emilia gave birth to a daughter three years after Hans Jonathan was born. On 6 January 1788 the baby girl was christened Anna Maria.[19] Ludvig Heinrich Ernst von Schimmelmann, Emilia Regina's master and owner, was the child's godfather—a role of considerable responsibility. Anna Maria was apparently not a mulatto. The church records name her father as Andreas, "a negro" owned by Schimmelmann. Andreas appears to have been about the same age as Emilia Regina and was likely raised on St. Croix. He is first seen in slave registers for the Constitution Hill plantation in 1784. Two years later he is listed among the Schimmelmanns' house slaves. Hence we know that Anna Maria's parents lived under the same roof for a time, and perhaps Andreas was Emilia Regina's unofficial spouse. Yet by 1787 Andreas is no longer registered as a house slave but as one of the field slaves on the plantation. Was the couple deliberately separated?

Emilia Regina was not the only slave woman in the Schimmelmann household to have children under the master's roof: in the same year that Hans Jonathan was born, Emilia Regina's brother Francis and his spouse Sabina Helena had a daughter, Juliane Sophie. In the year of Anna Maria's birth they had another daughter, Maria Christiana.

But Francis had two daughters who were both black. Emilia Regina, by contrast, was the mother of two children who differed greatly by the standards of a slave-owning culture: mulatto and negro, boy and girl. Given the racial thinking of the time, if the father was white the offspring was assumed to be mentally superior to children born to two "black" slaves. It is likely that the half-siblings' lives took very different directions right from the outset. Gender was an important factor in identity, role, and social status. But even the most subtle physical differences that indicated race or origin, not least skin color, tended to be given prominence.[20] It was one thing to be the child of an enslaved black man, quite another to have a free white man for a father.

What was the three-year-old Hans Jonathan's reaction to his little sister? Would he have been present at her christening? Was he jealous, restless? Did he run around the church? Did he and Anna Maria have the opportunity to play together as siblings or with their cousins? What objects from the sugar fields might have found their way into a child's hands on St. Croix? Perhaps they had pretty stones and shells from the seashore to play with, or just stalks and leaves of sugarcane. Nothing further is known of Anna Maria or her younger cousin, Maria Christiana. The two girls may have died in infancy. But it is also possible that they lived to grow up and to be traded away. Juliane Sophie, by contrast, would soon go to Copenhagen with Hans Jonathan.

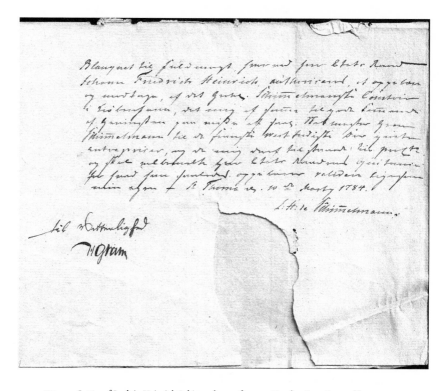

FIG. 4.1. Letter of Ludvig Heinrich Schimmelmann from 10 March 1784, witnessed by secretary
H. Gram. (National Archives of Denmark, Schimmelmann Private Archives, no 6285, box 31.)
Schimmelmann, Ernst. Breve fra generalguvenørerne i vestindien (1763–1808) 100. 1763–1833 m.m.

"SAID TO BE THE SECRETARY"

WHILE THE ST. CROIX church register clearly names the slave Andreas as the father of Emilia Regina's daughter, it is far from explicit
regarding the paternity of her son, "the mulatto Hans Jonathan."
The meaning of the Danish entry, "Fader blev ingen skriftlig udlagt
men erindrer mundtlig blev sagt at være Secretairen," is not clear, but
one must infer that the writer meant to state that "the father was said
to be the secretary." What should we make of this? Was it no more
than a local rumor? Or had Emilia Regina given some ambiguous
hint of who had fathered her son—perhaps because she could not be
sure who the father was, or she did not want to identify the man? All
theories are based on probability, but we must have in mind that clues
which may seem convincing today may not have carried as much
weight in the community where Hans Jonathan grew up.

No man came forward to claim the boy as his son, and he was the
lawful chattel of Governor Schimmelmann. Is it not enough to know
that his father was a white man of European origin, one of the colonial masters? One of Hans Jonathan's Icelandic descendants, Anna
Maria Sveinsdottir, declares that the most important thing to her is
to know who Hans Jonathan was—what kind of a man he was—
not who fathered him. On the other hand, knowledge of his true
paternity might enhance our understanding of the circumstances sur-

rounding the lives of Emilia Regina, Hans Jonathan, and the Schimmelmanns, as well as many more who play a part in this story.

It may appear obvious that Ludvig Heinrich Ernst von Schimmelmann himself could have fathered Emilia Regina's child. She had been a slave in his household from her teens, ever since he married Henrietta Cathrina. Many years later in Iceland, Hans Jonathan would name his own children Ludvik Stefan and Hansina Regina—possibly after both his parents, Ludvig Schimmelmann and Emilia Regina. Some documents even refer to Hans Jonathan by the surname Schimmelmann. While in the United States and some other contexts enslaved persons were commonly known by their masters' names, no matter who their fathers were, in the Virgin Islands the enslaved more often took their father's name.[1]

If we assume that Schimmelmann was the father, a new series of questions arise about the home life of mother and son. The presence of a black mother and a bastard child was not necessarily an embarrassment in the household of a planter; white fathers sometimes manumitted their enslaved children. The issue may, however, have been touchy in the residence of the governor of the Danish West Indies. It was not unknown, on the other hand, for freed slave women to become concubines of European officials: Peter von Scholten, who was governor from 1828 to 1848, separated from his Danish wife to live with a mulatto woman, Anna Heegaard (1790–1859).[2] By the time they made their home together in the governor's mansion, Anna had established a good life for herself: she owned a valuable house in Christiansted and a large number of slaves. Peter and Anna's relationship, though controversial, caused no major scandal. But Scholten was governor more than forty years after Schimmelmann's time, and in the intervening period some changes had taken place in race relations.

If Schimmelmann *was* Hans Jonathan's father, he may have had a hand in that ambiguous entry in the church register. The statement of the rumor about "the secretary" was entered into the register four days before Schimmelmann was appointed governor. The baptismal

FIG. 4.2.
Ludvig Heinrich Ernst von Schimmelmann.
(Kort- og Billedsamlingen, Royal Library,
Copenhagen.)

certificate states that the mother of the boy is property of "the governor," although he had not yet formally taken office. (Schimmelmann had served temporarily as governor ten years earlier, for half of 1773.) It is possible that he was keen to maintain his good reputation at this high point of his career.

We know that at the end of the eighteenth century, members of the Schimmelmann family in Copenhagen had concerns about "racial mixing" or interbreeding between black and white on St. Croix. Learning that interracial sex was taking place on their own plantations (just like everywhere else in the West Indies), the family decided to take action. In 1795 they dispatched Charles Bouden Vanderbourg and François Marquis de La Porte to St. Croix to uphold new and stricter moral standards, and to promote better living conditions for the slaves, in accordance with modern ideas. The plan was a dire failure. The family's overseer on the plantation was fired. The two new men, however, could not cope with the difficult tasks assigned to them, and before long they became as racist and colonialist in their views as their predecessors had been. One of them died within two years; the other found his way back to Europe the following year.

The news that both men had fathered mulatto children while on the island was received by the Schimmelmanns in Copenhagen with grave disappointment.[3]

Let us not forget the role of Henrietta Cathrina Schimmelmann. On St. Croix she was probably not in a position to keep her husband from taking a concubine, any more than other European wives in the colonies were. But Emilia Regina was her own property, inherited from her first marriage. This fact made Hans Jonathan officially her property as well. To Henrietta Cathrina, if he were her husband's son he would have been a constant reminder of infidelity—of Ludvig's intimacy with a negress from the Dark Continent, to use the terminology of the time. It was not a comfortable situation, although far from unique in the Danish realm or in the colonial world as a whole. Henrietta Cathrina was of an independent and determined character, even if her freedom as a woman was circumscribed by convention. Having inherited extensive assets from her first husband, Thomas William Schäffer, she was wealthy in her own right. When Hans Jonathan was later sent to Copenhagen, she must have been involved in the decision.[4] Henrietta Cathrina's consent to this arrangement is probably the strongest evidence that Schimmelmann was not in fact Hans Jonathan's father. If he had been, she would have been unlikely to agree to take the boy, this symbol of her husband's infidelity, to live with her in Denmark.

COUNT MOLTKE

Another theory about Hans Jonathan's paternity concerns a second renowned family, the Moltkes. Anna Maria Sveinsdottir recalls asking her father several times about his ancestors; he always described Hans Jonathan as the son of "Count Moltke." He told her that it was the count who arranged for Hans Jonathan to sail to Denmark, and who had him educated. Moltke had wanted to marry the mother of his child, the slave woman Emilia Regina, but that had proved impossible in light of his father's high position at the Danish royal court.

The family's reputation was at stake, and it had been regarded as wiser not to admit paternity. Another Icelandic descendant reports that her great-aunt Katrin Bjornsdottir (d. 1966) told a similar tale: Hans Jonathan's father had been of the Moltke family, his first name was probably Otto, and he was governor of St. Thomas. But no one of that name has ever been governor of St. Thomas.

Family tradition claims that before Hans Jonathan fled from Denmark in 1802, a friend of his father, or of his father's family, presented him with two or more objects, including a tobacco pouch or coin purse that still exists, property of Hans Jonathan's descendants in Norway. These were embellished with a motif of three birds, as on the Moltke crest. It is possible that the objects were entrusted to a person who had some other, unrelated business with Hans Jonathan. But we should not lightly dismiss what people say about their own descent, these traditions that have been passed down through generations.

Count Adam Gottlob Moltke (1710–92) was one of the most powerful men in Denmark in the eighteenth century.[5] His influence spanned the fields of politics and economics, culture and the arts. He was personally identified with the Danish absolute monarchy, especially during two crucial decades of the mid-eighteenth century when he was de facto ruler of the Danish-Norwegian realm, including Iceland.

At the age of nineteen he had become chamberlain to Crown Prince Frederik, then only seven. He gained the prince's confidence and came to be like a brother to him. When the prince came of age and ascended the throne, Frederik V proved himself not competent to rule: he was a drunkard and libertine with a violent temper. It fell to Moltke to do what the king could not.

The Swedish ambassador in Copenhagen, Baron Otto Flemming, described the count in 1751. Moltke, he wrote, "is tall of stature and has a quick and easy understanding, friendly and obliging, pleasant in conversation, observant, and untiring in all his undertakings—which sometimes overwhelm him, as he takes an interest in all matters, even where he has no specific role. He is a wise courtier, a stout character, solid and reliable with regard to what he promises. He takes care to acquaint himself well with all matters, being very jealous of his lord's honor."[6]

One of the king's—or Moltke's—first acts in office was to appoint Emilia Regina's initial owner, the German baron Christian Lebrecht von Prock of La Reine plantation, as governor of St. Croix. The name of Count Moltke has another tenuous connection with St. Croix: a map of the island made in 1766 was dedicated to him. The count, however, was not much of a traveler. He occasionally went to Germany, but he never ventured outside Europe. He certainly did not undertake, in his seventies, the long and arduous ocean passage to the Caribbean in order to father Hans Jonathan in the summer of 1783.

What of the other Moltkes? The count was the father of many sons: his first wife, Christiana Friderica, gave birth to thirteen children, of whom eleven lived. By his second wife, Sophia, he had another ten children, of whom five lived.[7] But there appears to be no record of the Moltke name among those who lived on St. Croix until the nineteenth century. One of the count's sons, nephews, or grandsons may have visited the Danish West Indies on his travels, without being recorded as resident. Could a Moltke have been Schimmelmann's secretary? The principal candidates are Christian (b. 1738), Caspar Herman (b. 1738), Christian Magnus (b. 1741), Adam Ludvig (b. 1743), Fridrich Ludwig (b. 1745), and finally Joachim Godske (b. 1746), whom the count designated his successor as head of the family.

Two powerful families such as the Moltkes and Schimmelmanns must surely have had some kind of interaction in the political, commercial, and social life of Copenhagen. Any Moltke who turned up on St. Croix would certainly have been offered hospitality by someone as influential as Ludvig Heinrich Ernst von Schimmelmann. And would it not have been the job of a slave woman or chambermaid to minister to such an honored guest? Perhaps Hans Jonathan's

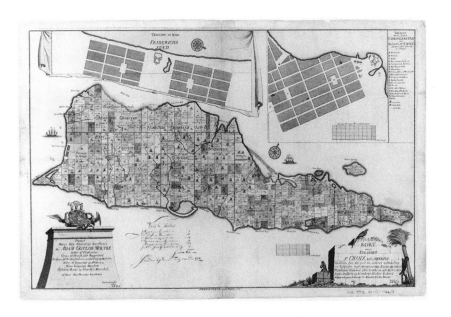

FIG. 4.3. St. Croix around 1766. The map was dedicated to Count Adam Gotlob Moltke. (Kort- og Billedsamlingen, Royal Library, Copenhagen.)

descendants simply put two and two together, knowing that his father, or someone close to him, had connections with the royal court and that Count Moltke was one of the most powerful men of his time in the Danish realm.

Perhaps Hans Jonathan knew the identity of his father and told his immediate family the truth. Or perhaps he was in the habit of talking about the Moltkes because one of them had been his benefactor. The name Ludvik, common among his descendants, might not derive from Ludvig Heinrich Ernst von Schimmelmann but from a Moltke: from Fridrich Ludwig, son of Count Adam Gottlob, or Adam Ludvig, the count's nephew.

THE MYSTERIOUS MR. GRAM

By that ambiguous reference to a rumor about an unnamed "secretary," the writer of the entry in the church register on St. Croix may have been concealing the fact that some eminent white man, such as Schimmelmann or Moltke, was Hans Jonathan's father. But the register contains dozens of baptismal records of infants who are called "illegitimate," whether white, black, or mulatto. One record for an illegitimate child states that "the pastor knows the identity of the father, but will not reveal it." If Hans Jonathan's father was a pillar of plantation society who wished to conceal his identity, it would have been simple to register the boy as "illegitimate," like so many other mixed-race babies. There was no cause for concern about such matters as inheritance and child support: the slave child was his master's property and the responsibility of his mother's owner or of whoever else purchased him.

While church registers may not always record the truth, and there may be many reasons for dissimulation, the simplest approach is to take the words at face value.[8] If Hans Jonathan's father was, in fact, the secretary, who might that be? Three secretaries are on record who are possible candidates: Gram, Hoffman, and Müller. The latter two, Hoffman and Müller, were public servants employed at the governor's residence before the Schimmelmanns' time there. Gram, on the other hand, was Schimmelmann's private secretary, who lived with the family at 33 Strand Street and on the Constitution Hill plantation from 1782 to 1784—perhaps under the same roof as Emilia Regina. The entry in the church register refers to *Secretairen*, *"the* secretary," as if the reader would know exactly who was being referred to. This indicates that there may indeed have been rumors about Emilia Regina and a specific secretary. The obvious conclusion is that "the secretary" must have been Gram.

Gram—he is given no first name in these records—seems to have made only a short sojourn on St. Croix. He is not listed in records from 1781 or earlier, and not in 1785 or later. He does not appear to have been a communicant in the Christiansted Lutheran church, even though his employer regularly took Communion there, sometimes accompanied by his house slaves. It seems that Gram spent only about three years on St. Croix before departing, never to return.

How can we trace his story? An obvious starting point is the Danish National Archives, adjacent to the Royal Library in Copenhagen. Nearby is the harbor where the sailing vessels of sugar barons used to dock, laden with goods from the Caribbean and Iceland—and sometimes with enslaved people too. The ships not only brought home the products of colonial territories but also carried letters between the city and the colonies. In the archives, the documents relating to the Danish West Indies amount to tens of tons. There newcomers communicate in whispers with the helpful staff. Other visitors head straight to the spacious and well-lit reading room, with its massive stone walls, to examine boxes of faded papers. Theirs is a silent encounter with the people and events of long ago; you could hear a pin drop.

The Schimmelmann documents fill a total of 117 boxes. Most are concerned with Heinrich Ernst von Schimmelmann, who, as Danish minister of finance from 1784 to 1813, was one of the leading lights of the Schimmelmann family. Superficially the archives appear to offer nothing relevant to Ludvig Schimmelmann, after whom so many Icelanders are supposed to have been named over the last two centuries. But a footnote in a recent book about the end of the Danish slave trade cites "Schimmelmannske privatpapirer (privatarkiv no 6285)."[9] It transpires that "private archive no. 6285" is a single box, number 31, containing two hundred documents referring specifically to Governor Ludvig Heinrich Ernst von Schimmelmann of St. Croix.

The oldest documents in the box date from the 1760s; the latest are from the year of Hans Jonathan's birth, 1784, when secretary Gram was working for the Schimmelmanns. Many are in the handwriting of Ludvig Schimmelmann, Hans Jonathan's master, and they were written where our story takes place, most of them on St. Croix. Some are in Danish, others in German, English, or French. The bulk of the documents are densely written pages, letters and memoranda, penned in Gothic script. One is addressed to the supreme authority in Denmark, the king himself. Another stands out for more subtle reasons. This letter Ludvig wrote from the island of St. Thomas, where he may have been attending to family business on the sugar plantations.[10] The note, only ten lines long, is addressed to his brother-in-law, Johan Friedrich Heinrich, who had sold him the Constitution Hill plantation some years earlier. In 1784 Heinrich was running the offices of the Schimmelmann family business in Copenhagen. The interesting point, however, is not the content of the note, nor its recipient, but the signature of the witness to the document: *H. Gram.* Now we know that the first name of the mysterious Mr. Gram begins with an *H.* The letter is dated 10 March 1784, about a month before Hans Jonathan was born. Gram must have sailed with Ludvig Schimmelmann to St. Thomas that spring, when Emilia Regina was about eight months pregnant.

So who was H. Gram? The name alone provides no real clue to his nationality: he may have been Danish, English, German, or from North America. A thorough search of Danish census records for the years after Gram disappears from the St. Croix population registers turns up nothing. A further search of Schimmelmann documents in Copenhagen is also unrewarding.

Hamburg, Germany, was the historic heartland of the Schimmelmann business empire, but repeated inquiries to archives in and around the city yield no result. Perhaps a search through the dozens, or even hundreds, of regional church registers would uncover an H. Gram. For now, a web search comes up with three promising men named Hans Gram. One of them, a professor at the University of Copenhagen, was a well-known linguist and medieval historian; another, also a professor at Copenhagen, was a pioneering bacteriologist noted for developing a technique (the Gram stain) for distinguishing classes of bacteria; and the third was a musician. Further exploration reveals that the last one is indeed the enigmatic secretary from St. Croix: "Mr. Gram, when a young man, was private secretary to the Governor of the Danish Island of Santa Cruz, [Spanish spelling of St. Croix]."[11] Following this line of inquiry, we learn that quite a bit is known, in fact, about the mysterious Mr. Gram. Now "the secretary" stands revealed. A new gateway into Hans Jonathan's story opens, and unclear elements come into focus.

AN ORGANIST IN BOSTON

Hans Gram was born in Copenhagen in 1754 into a family that made its wealth in shipping and commerce. His father, Niels Hansen Gram (1711–60), was a sea captain with the Asiatic Company, successor to the Danish East India Company, which held a monopoly of Danish trade east of the Cape of Good Hope. Hans Gram's mother, Maren née Brock (1734–1804), belonged to an influential family in Danish business life. Her brother Niels Brock had large business interests and left a substantial fortune at his death. He and his wife were childless, and their legacy went to found a commercial school in Copenhagen, which later developed into the prestigious Niels Brock Copenhagen Business College.

Hans Gram was the eldest of three children. His father died when he was three years old, and he and his siblings were raised by their mother's family. His uncle Niels Brock may have been like a father to him. The family was keen for Hans to go into business, but he chose another path, pursuing studies in music and literature. During his student years in Copenhagen he made friends who would later be renowned in the arts, such as the author Christen Henriksen Pram and the actor Joachim Daniel Preisler, both of whom made their mark in the 1770s. Gram himself translated a French play, *Le Tonnelier* (The cooper), by Nicolas-Médard Audinot, into Danish. It was staged in Denmark in 1780.

Hans Gram appears to have fled Copenhagen after some kind of a confrontation with the actor and literary scholar Knud Lyne Rahbek, later to be a professor and rector of the University of Copenhagen. The nature of the dispute between the two men is unclear.[12] Hans probably also fell out with his mother, who meant him to take over the family estates. In 1781 Gram sailed to St. Croix, where he became the governor's secretary. Perhaps his uncle or another relative had interceded on his behalf in order to help him toward a career in colonial administration. Or he may have been sent abroad to mend his ways, as was not uncommon when young gentlemen had misbehaved in some way.

At about the time of Hans Jonathan's birth, Hans Gram left St. Croix for Boston. Had Emilia Regina named her son Hans after his father, "the secretary"? That could have been an indication of real attachment between the couple—or it could have been an accusation of abuse or neglect. Was Gram's decision to leave motivated by his knowledge of the child he had fathered, or by talk about his encounter with a slave woman? Perhaps the rumors about the secretary were a contributory factor when the Schimmelmann family decided in 1795 to send two men to St. Croix in order to introduce higher moral standards on the island. Was Gram dismissed for his indiscretion?

It is possible that Gram went to Boston intending eventually to return to St. Croix. But while there he met Jane Burdick (1760–1806), daughter of the proprietor of the hotel where he was staying. The couple married on November 11, 1785, in Danvers, Massachusetts. Outraged, Gram's mother and her family disinherited him. Could a rumor about a bastard mulatto child on St. Croix have added to his offense in their eyes? Hans and Jane Gram went on to have five children: Hans Benjamin or Burch (b. 1787), Patrick Jeffry (b. 1790), the twins Neils and Nathaniel (b. 1793), and Joanna (b. 1801). The family lived at a series of places in Boston, their last home being on Common Street. A Boston directory lists Hans Gram as a "musician and composer."

Hans Gram was not a well man. He is said to have lived intemperately, and the family was impoverished. In 1795 he wrote a short letter to a newspaper in which he described the difficult conditions of his life in Charlestown, outside Boston. Having suffered two grave illnesses, he had earlier announced that he could no longer accept organ students, he wrote. But now he wished to inform his friends in Boston and the nearby area that he felt able to begin teaching music again.[13] In 1804 he learned that on her deathbed his mother had relented and bequeathed considerable assets to him. Invigorated by the news, Gram made plans to sail to Copenhagen to claim his inheritance. Foreseeing a great improvement in his fortunes, he planned celebrations for his fiftieth birthday, three weeks later. But on the eve of his departure from Boston he fell gravely ill, and within hours he was dead. Two years later his wife, Jane, died in Portland, Maine. She was said to have been virtuous and highly regarded.[14] In due course their children received their inheritance from Copenhagen, which amounted to twenty thousand rigsdalers.

Gram's death was widely reported by the press on the East Coast. An item in the *New Hampshire Centinel* was typical: "At Boston, Hans Gram, Esq. formerly of Copenhagen, a celebrated musician and organist."[15] He had taught music and played the organ at Brattle Street Church in Boston and was influential in establishing the custom of using seven syllables in the scale (*do, re, me, fa, sol, la, ti*) in place of the four syllables (*fa, sol, la, mi*) that had been customary. He is said to have reformed American music by lending it a European character. Among the best known of his compositions are *The Death Song of an Indian Chief* (1791) and *Sacred Lines, for Thanksgiving Day* (1793). The *Death Song* is the first orchestral work to appear in print in the

FIG. 4.4. "The Death Song of an Indian Chief" by Hans Gram. (Special Collections of the St. Louis Mercantile Library at the University of Missouri–St. Louis.)

United States. It became a standard work for choirs and orchestras—perhaps the first American "hit."[16] Some years after his death, a Hans Gram Musical Society was founded in Fryeburg, Maine, to uphold his musical legacy. In later years his works were honored in various ways, and his music has been discussed in detail in print.[17]

His *Death Song of an Indian Chief* was inspired by a series of poems by Sarah Wentworth Apthorp Morton. *Ouabi, or The Virtues of Nature: An Indian Tale in Four Cantos* ostensibly tells of love between European men and the women of a Native American tribe, but the author appears to have written it as a metaphorical representation of forbidden love in her own tangled private life.[18] In the poems, white men exploit their status in the colonial system, professing the romantic ideas of Jean-Jacques Rousseau about "free love" in a state of nature, while taking advantage of the women's vulnerability. The subject appears to have had no less relevance for Hans Gram than for the poet. Had Gram himself not disregarded, or rather taken advantage of, the social and racial divide on St. Croix—naively reaching out, perhaps full of ideas about innocent children of nature—impregnating a black woman, perhaps without her consent, and then departing as if nothing had happened? Slavery was an established institution in America at the time and likely contributed to the popularity of Gram's piece.

We might also glimpse his character in a verse he wrote to add to his translation of a German poem, "Hymns to Sleep." Gram, too, had had to come to terms with an alien environment when he settled in Boston, as New England society was very different from that of both Denmark and St. Croix. He wrote:

> *Come sweet sleep! The friendless stranger,*
> *Woos thee to relieve his woes—*
> *Shield his head from every danger,*
> *Guard the wand'ring youth's repose!*
> *Far from home and all the pleasures*
> *That his native country yields,*
> *What are his but fictious treasures,*
> *Dreams in sportive Fancy's fields—*
> *Ah! Prolong the ideal blessings,*
> *Which nor gems nor gold can buy—*
> *Rich is he while thee possessing,*
> *Poor, alas, when thou dost fly!*[19]

We have no detailed information on Hans Gram; his obituary describes him in platitudes that might apply to many men of his time—with the exception, perhaps, of this comment: "Though he possessed a peculiar eccentricity of character, yet he had virtues to imitate, and talents to admire, 'Misfortune's care-worn child,' his ambition, usefulness, and talents became observed—and, as monuments erected to human honor and glory decay by the violence of storms and the destructive touches of time, he gradually mouldered away. Alas how unstable is human knowledge and worth!"[20]

His eccentricity outlived him. More than forty years after his death, Hans Gram was still being written about in the Boston press. Under the headline "A Disgraceful Practice," the newspaper criticized the way the Boston police dragged prisoners in handcuffs down Leverett Street every morning to police headquarters, regardless of how serious or minor the offense of which they were accused:

> Some forty-five years since, we recollect an anecdote of a German musician, highly estimated in the way of his profession, a man of excellent heart, . . . might be said to be one of nature's noblemen;—but he would get tipsey, and was found lying in the gutter in one of the Boston streets, singing, in the most happy temper of mind, an old popular song of the day— *"Life let us cherish!"* A friend who happened to be passing, approached to see what was the matter; and on recognizing him and attempting to get him out of the gutter exclaimed, "Why Hans, is this you?—Is it possible this is Hans Gram?" "Yes," said Hans, with convulsive "hickup."[21]

The newspaper deemed it a scandal. The practice of chaining citizens and marching them through the streets before any warrant was issued against them "is, it seems, practiced in a puritan land which boasts of its abhorrence of slavery in all its forms and in every shape, and claims to be the pioneer in the cause of human liberty! Such indignity to men of sensitive feeling, and who may after all be innocent, is quite as degrading as the post." How ironic it would be if the secretary from Constitution Hill on St. Croix, the father of "the mulatto Hans Jonathan," had experienced for himself, however briefly, what it was like to be in chains.

FIG. 5.1.   The mill at Constitution Hill. (Photo: Gisli Palsson.)

AMONG THE SUGAR BARONS

HANS JONATHAN SPENT the first seven or eight years of his life on the plantations, among the sugar barons and their employees and servants in Christiansted. He would have wandered the fields and street barefoot and half-naked—in the tropical climate clothes were mostly a nuisance, especially for children. He was taught to read and write while also learning the principal languages of the West Indies: Danish, Creole, and English. In most respects, however, a clear distinction was made between white children and children of the enslaved. The Moravian missionary Christian G. A. Oldendorp was hardly thinking of white children when he commented that island children "find great pleasure in their instrumental music; quite early the children make a kind of fiddle for themselves, constructed by stretching several horse hairs over a shingle and then stroking them with a bow or plucking them with their fingers."[1]

There was much to catch a child's attention. The sugarcane grew high, and beyond it was dense jungle where it was easy to play and get lost. Down on the seashore, shoals of colorful fish could be seen swimming in the shallows, and an occasional giant turtle splashed around at the edge of the waves. In the treetops, birds of many species sang. The vivid plumage of flamingos, pelicans, parakeets, and hummingbirds caught the eye, while dainty half-tamed swallows glided through the air or swooped down to catch fleas and cockroaches.

Human society was no less colorful. Two street markets in Christansted offered a range of commodities, often attracting large crowds, especially on Sundays, when plantation slaves came to market to sell whatever they had been able to produce on the small plots of land allocated for their own use—mostly poultry, pigeons, eggs, cabbages, potatoes, and fruit. After darkness fell at around 7 p.m., the markets were lit by candles and lamps until they closed at about 8 p.m. Life on the plantations was busy and eventful, with shouting and exclamations, and sometimes mournful songs. This was a multicultural community with a babel of tongues spoken by people of all shapes and sizes. Some were "more equal than others," granted absolute authority, while others could only submit and obey or keep a low profile. Objections could be worded in only the most tentative way.

It was scary to be out at night. Best not to be alone, and wise to avoid passing bars, where shady characters gathered to down their mysterious rum drinks, made from sugarcanes—the canes that children sucked and gnawed for the sweet taste and the energy they provided. The revelers were noisy, and the din reverberated far out into the streets. The night was dark and menacing, providing plenty of scope for a vivid imagination. When the revelry died down there was a chance to dream, to forget the everyday world with its harsh heat and toil, to imagine a cool, enchanted world that featured in stories and books—a place where a person could be free.

The menace of slavery was not present only in the dark. Danger was an everyday reality both in the town and in the sugarcane fields. Screams and rhythmic blows from routine whippings of fifty to one hundred lashes were impossible to miss. Serious sickness (yaws, for instance) was rampant and painful to witness. The rhythms of production from early morning into the night were brutally enforced by the slaveholders and their staff. Death was often in view, sometimes sudden, sometimes in slow motion. Rebels and runaways were publicly displayed, humiliated, and physically abused.

Once he had put off childish things, where did a mulatto man belong?

THE FIRST ECONOMIC BUBBLE

Hans Jonathan had sugar in his blood; without sugar he would never have been born. Sugarcane originated in New Guinea in the Southwest Pacific. The term in fact applies to a number of species, but it is *Saccharum officinarum* that has played such an important role in history. Its stems are firm but juicy and up to two inches in diameter. The long and bittersweet story of sugarcane, as Sidney Mintz shows in his classic *Sweetness and Power*, tells us much about the relationship between production, consumption, and human society, about vicious and complex competition for power, and about potent symbolism.[2]

Honey had been the world's sweetener for millennia. In ancient Greece honey was ambrosia, the food of the gods. In the Koran it is called "healing for people." Sugarcane probably superseded honey as the sweetener of choice because it was easier to mass produce. In addition it was less likely to cause allergic reactions. Around 300 BC, sugar consumption became widespread in India, where it was classified into five types. One was *khanda*, from which the English *candy* is derived, along with its cognates in many other Indo-European languages. In 1374 sugar reached Copenhagen, which was to develop into one of the sugar capitals of the world.

After Columbus's first voyage to the New World in 1492, the Spanish introduced sugar cultivation on a large scale in the Caribbean islands, where the crop flourished in the rich soil. Before long a sugar revolution was under way in the Americas. Widely dispersed families of sugar barons in Brazil, North America, and Europe amassed gigantic fortunes—especially from the Caribbean—and forced millions of people into slavery. The vocabulary of the colonial world changed over time.[3] In the early days, the word *plantation* was used to designate European settlements in the New World, but it gradually came to be applied to the land inhabited or cultivated by the settlers. Eventually *plantation* took on the meaning of a very large farm: a sugar, cotton, or coffee plantation. But the plantation was not only the land itself. It was the whole colonial community—the people and social life of sugar cultivation.

In the Middle Ages sugar had been a rare and costly commodity. Royalty and the nobility had candlesticks and statues sculpted out of it. It was molded into likenesses of lions, elephants, and giraffes. At luxurious banquets, the elite sought to impress each other with sweet sugar concoctions, the forerunners of our modern desserts.

In the sixteenth and seventeenth centuries sugar became readily available to the general public. Consumption rose, and widely read cookbooks provided guidance about the nature of sugar and how to use it. Sugar was said to have many applications, for instance in hand lotion—and even for toothpaste. As Europe became industrialized and urban centers developed, sugar became an indispensable addition to a cup of tea, a cheap and tasty energy boost during the working day. Tea breaks became an established tradition for workers, which made for improved productivity. By 1800 sugar consumption in England was fifteen times what it had been a century earlier.

Sugarcane cultivation was probably the first global economic bubble. The sweet cane connected different continents and diverse peoples, compelling some into slavery while others spun sugar into gold and became barons and millionaires. The heyday of sugarcane came to end when new ways of producing sugar were developed, for instance from the sugar beet, a cheaper alternative.

THE SUGAR FACTORY

One of the best contemporary accounts of the Danish colony of St. Croix late in the eighteenth century was left by a Dane named Hans West.[4] He sailed to St. Croix in 1789 and remained there for some years. For about two years, he and Hans Jonathan were both on the island, though Hans Jonathan was only a child at the time.

In his early thirties Hans West applied for a teaching post in a new high school on St. Croix, established for pupils who would otherwise have had to go to Denmark to school. Apparently he did not put much effort into his teaching, as he was a worldly man whose interests lay elsewhere. But he was engrossed by his surroundings, writing descriptions of the community and of natural phenomena and talking to local people. He could not help observing that sugarcane was the focus of everything. Sugar, he wrote, is "the only product on whose cultivation—be it a success or a failure—the entire fortune or misfortune of the island depends. It determines the price of everything. To be sure, there is no product, with the exception of the spices of the East Indies, that is as rich and beneficial as sugar."[5]

West described in detail the working methods of a sugar plantation; the cultivation and processing were broadly similar throughout the New World.[6] The land had to be plowed before the crop was planted. Pieces of cane were then laid flat on the ground, so that they would grow shoots at both ends, and covered with earth. If all progressed normally, the cane crop could be harvested about a year later, using large, sharp machetes or billhooks. Enslaved persons worked in teams to chop the long canes, which were then tied into bundles and transported to the mill, which might be a windmill or one turned by animals. The juice was squeezed out of the canes via compression between three iron cylinders, and was channeled into a tank where it was filtered and boiled, then cooled until it thickened and crystallized. Up to twenty Africans worked in each sugar "factory," on the first production lines in industrial history.

Production using an unfree workforce required strict supervision. On each plantation was a guardhouse where one of the slaves, armed with a sword, stood watch over the fields and raised the alarm in case of fire. In the tropical heat of the sugar fields, fire sometimes broke out spontaneously; rebellious slaves also sometimes set crops alight. On some plantations the enslaved workers were summoned to their work by loud bells to ensure that everyone was quickly hard at work and functioned as an effective team. Although the enslaved Africans were kept at their work from morning until night under all but the most extreme weather conditions, it was important for them to pace themselves so that they would not succumb to heat exhaustion.

The heat and humidity of the Caribbean climate made their mark on the islanders' posture and gait. In some countries, a marked contrast can be observed between the compressed gait of people brought up in massive crowded cities and the swaggering stride of country folk. Even today the people of St. Croix seem to saunter about their business in a trancelike state—although these days few of them labor in the fields; many spend much of the day in air-conditioned spaces.

During West's time on St. Croix, no rain fell for months. When it finally began to rain, he noticed that the sugarcane grew at a phenomenal rate, by as much as two feet in two weeks. "The growth of the Negroes," West wrote, "seems to correspond to that of the plants. As infants they are carried on the back or hip of their mothers, or they are just placed naked on the ground while the mothers carry out their work. There they crawl and tumble, and through this natural freedom the body soon develops an unrestricted agility. A child of a year and a half therefore already looks after himself. . . . At the age of six, he is seen running errands, carrying burdens on his head and the like."[7]

Note that in West's account the Africans are "placed" in nature alongside the crops they cultivate—and set apart from white "civilization." West was well aware that the institution of slavery was already controversial by his time, and he sought to describe the conditions he saw as straightforwardly as possible. Yet a modern reader cannot avoid the impression that West was on the side of the planters. He was, admittedly, of the view that the slave trade was a bad thing and no longer defensible—that all forcible transport of Africans must be halted. But he reiterates common assertions that the conditions in which the slaves lived on the plantations were tolerable, and far superior to the living conditions they would have had in Africa.[8] No doubt Hans Jonathan and Emilia Regina should have been grateful for their good fortune!

THE SCHIMMELMANN EMPIRE

The Schimmelmann family originated in Germany and had business interests both there and in Denmark. An extensive history of the family and their influence in Europe and in the colonies reveals their far-reaching political and financial clout in the latter half of the eighteenth century.[9] The same Christian names (Ernst, Heinrich, and Carl) recur generation after generation in the Schimmelmann family tree, just like heritable DNA sequences—perhaps a sign of the family's solidarity and wealth.

The patriarch of the line, Heinrich Carl Schimmelmann (1724–82), began his career in Dresden as a subject of the king of Prussia. He rapidly made his fortune trading in commodities from the colonies, such as sugar, coffee, and tobacco. He moved in due course to Wandsbek—now part of Hamburg—and then to Copenhagen, where he became acquainted with the Danish royal family. He made his home in a splendid house on Bredgade at the heart of the Danish capital, adjacent to the royal palace of Amalienborg. Heinrich Carl had a reputation as an astute businessman, and he became the king's adviser on commercial matters. Heinrich Carl arranged for his nephew Ludvig Heinrich to receive training and experience in the business in Copenhagen and then sent him at the age of twenty-five to the Danish West Indies.

Ludvig Heinrich's parents lived in Stettin, which is now part of Poland but has been subject to Danish, Swedish, and German rule as the map of Europe has changed and changed again. His father Jacob (1712–78) apparently had no interest in sugar or slavery, unlike most of his kinsmen. Jacob was a theologian who made his mark in cultural history by translating into German the *Prose Edda* of Snorri Sturluson—one of the masterpieces of Old Icelandic literature[10]—at a time when the Germanic world was experiencing an awakening of interest in Norse culture.[11] In 1773, when he announced in the Stettin newspaper that his translation was about to be published, he declared that he saw the *Edda* as the oldest book in the world after the Bible and that it was especially important because it put forth the ancient religious mythology of the Norse and Germanic peoples.[12] Jacob Schimmelmann did not know Old Icelandic; his German version was based on existing translations into Latin (by Petrus Resenius in 1665)

FIG. 5.2.
Title page of Jacob Schimmelmann's
translation of the *Prose Edda*, 1777.

and French (David Mallet, 1756). In his translation he aimed to demonstrate the "harmony" between the *Edda* and the Bible, but his version and his approach have always been controversial. Jacob's translation of the *Edda* was published while the younger of his two sons, Ludvig, was on St. Croix, but Ludvig must have been well aware of his father's interest in Old Icelandic literature.

In 1763 Heinrich Carl Schimmelmann, Ludvig's grandfather, purchased four of the major plantations in the Danish West Indies, including La Grande Princesse and La Grange on St. Croix. These had originally been owned by the Danish West India-Guinea Company, which was dissolved in 1755. They had then passed into royal hands in the time of Frederik V, and Heinrich Carl bought them from the crown. This was probably a case of "insider trading," although that concept did not yet exist and probably was unthinkable under an absolute monarchy. Monarchs, after all, were regarded as receiving their power directly from God, and they could do with it as they pleased. Heinrich Carl also acquired a sugar refinery in Copenhagen and a whole fleet of slaving ships.

The Schimmelmann estates in the West Indies were among the most profitable properties in the Danish colonial empire. The soil was fertile, and Schimmelmann owned a huge number of enslaved Africans—peaking at over a thousand in 1784, the year of Hans Jonathan's birth. Heinrich Carl was a true sugar baron. He was vastly wealthy, with a global business network and a firm hand on every stage of the sugar industry, every aspect of the colonial triangular trade embracing Guinea on Africa's Gold Coast, the West Indies in the Caribbean, and Denmark. Sweetness brought power, and power was indeed sweet.[13]

Heinrich Carl's eldest son, Heinrich Ernst Schimmelmann, succeeded to his father's fortune in Denmark, where he rose to be minister of finance, but ironically enough he is best known for his role in abolishing the Danish slave trade and improving the country's colonial system. Heinrich Ernst Schimmelmann was known as an idealist, highly educated, kind, and generous. In spite of the fact that he had financial responsibilities, both public and personal, he was not much interested in money. From his youth his interests and passions were focused on the arts and sciences.[14] As a government minister he is said to have largely put aside all commercial attitudes and coldhearted calculations of profitability—although no doubt he was concerned with conditions in the global arena, growing opposition to slavery, shifting sugar prices, and new moves in the power games of the high seas.

Heinrich Ernst's wife, Charlotte, organized many social gatherings at Sølyst, the Schimmelmanns' country home, attended by artists and intellectuals of many different nationalities. She also corresponded with writers and thinkers all over Europe, including Charlotte and Friedrich Schiller. She was part of an extensive social network, as we would say today, whose members kept in touch by writing letters.[15] The intellectuals—beneficiaries of the profits of slavery and sugar cultivation—kept up with all political developments in Europe; they did many good deeds and lent support to a range of worthy causes, such as improving the lot of the poor and founding schools. But there is no indication that this privileged elite took any initiative to reform the conditions of those who toiled in slavery. Rarely did the sugar barons write about the Africans on their family plantations, except perhaps in abstract and general terms.

Two different stories are told of how the sugar baron and colonial administrator Ludvig Heinrich Ernst von Schimmelmann treated his slaves and other "colored" people in the West Indies. According to a Danish reference work of 1901, he was renowned for his human-itarian treatment of colored people on the islands.[16] Ludvig's own records, on the other hand, give the impression that he was a harsh master: on 20 April 1784, when Hans Jonathan was just a week old, Schimmelmann decreed that no slave should be sentenced to a milder penalty than a white man, and that a runaway slave should be subject to a penalty at least equivalent to that of a deserter from military ser-vice.[17] Black people were, in his view, particularly willful and impos-sible to control except by imposition of severe penalties—and severe penalties in those days were quite brutal.

THE PASSAGE TO COPENHAGEN

In 1788 Ludvig Heinrich Ernst von Schimmelmann resigned his post as governor, and the family left the West Indies for Copenhagen. Hans West's contemporary account states that Europeans on St. Croix and the other islands sometimes gave up on the intense heat of the place, which was physically and mentally debilitating. This ex-planation may be enough in itself for the Schimmelmanns' decision to return "home" to Denmark. Yet at that time opposition to slavery was growing in Denmark and elsewhere in Europe, and Ludvig must have known of this development before he returned to Copenhagen.

The Constitution Hill plantation remained in the hands of the Schimmelmann family for another decade or so. A plantation was like any other form of real estate: it could be sold at will. The house slaves, on the other hand, were in a category of their own. They were property, yet the Schimmelmanns must have known that they would have no market value back in Copenhagen, even though they might be useful as domestic servants. The family must have had to make a decision: who would they take with them to Copenhagen? They decided that Emilia Regina and Sabina Helena would accompany the family, but their children—along with their menfolk Andreas and Francis, who was also Emilia Regina's brother—would remain on St. Croix. Why did the Schimmelmanns make this arrangement?

When planter families from the West Indies journeyed to Copenhagen, they generally took some house slaves with them. The white masters and mistresses could not be expected to cope without servants on the long ocean passage to the north; they had to be provided with food and other services. Another probable factor was that the Schimmelmann children were attached to Emilia Regina and Sabina Helena, who had important roles in the household. Ernst Carl was now eight years old, Caroline Adelaide eleven. Emilia Regina and Sabina Helena had taken care of these two children all their lives, from their earliest infancy. Their own children, Hans Jonathan and Juliane Sophie, were only three years old—not yet old enough to be useful as servants—while the younger girls, Anna Maria and Maria Christiana, were still infants. The Schimmelmanns decided it would be best to leave the little ones behind. Their decision never to return to the West Indies may not have been made before they left.

We do not know where, or with whom, Hans Jonathan and his sister and cousins lived on St. Croix after the Schimmelmanns left. Hans was not at Constitution Hill, and he is not listed on slave registers after the household was dispersed. Presumably the children were farmed out to strangers. But three or four years after the Schimmelmanns departed, Hans Jonathan and his cousin Juliane Sophie set sail for Denmark. Had Emilia Regina begged the Schimmelmanns to bring her son to Copenhagen so she could have him with her? Or was there another reason? It seems obvious that Ludvig and Henrietta Cathrina must have known of the rumors regarding the boy's father, their former secretary, Hans Gram. It is not impossible that a connection with the Gram family in Copenhagen was the reason for sending for Hans Jonathan. Such a transfer to relatives in the Old World would not have been unique in the colonial world. One well-known case is that of Dido Elizabeth Belle (1761–1804), the daughter of an enslaved African, Maria Belle, in the West Indies and Sir John Lindsay, a British naval officer. Lindsay took Belle with him to England and entrusted her to his uncle William Murray, First Earl of Mansfield.

We do not know exactly when or with whom Hans Jonathan and Juliane Sophie sailed. Ludvig Heinrich Ernst von Schimmelmann may have returned to St. Croix on business and brought the two children back with him to Copenhagen. A Norwegian explorer who met Hans Jonathan more than twenty years after his journey from St. Croix to Copenhagen reported that Hans Jonathan said he had traveled "with Governor Schimmelmann."[18] So long afterward, Hans Jonathan may indeed have believed that he had gone "with" Schimmelmann even if that was not the case.

As he boarded the ship for Copenhagen, Hans Jonathan probably felt a strong connection to St. Croix, though he likely imagined he was leaving it forever. This was the only place he knew, and he was unsure what to expect. Perhaps he was preoccupied with the ocean voyage itself, excited by stories he had heard about adventures on the high seas, about battles and pirates. He may also have been apprehensive about his encounter with the Old World. Although slavery had been his life until then and he had no guarantee that would change at the end of the journey, he had enjoyed the privileges granted to house slaves. He may have been too young to give much thought to heavy issues of this kind, endlessly discussed by grown-ups, free people as well as slaves. But he was confident that he would reunite with his mother.

| II |

COPENHAGEN

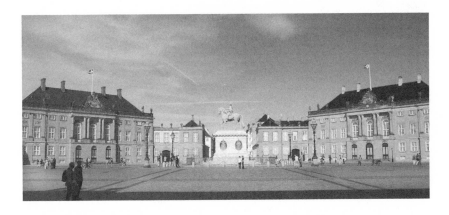

FIG. 6.1. The heart of Amalienborg, Copenhagen. (Photo: Gisli Palsson.)

A CHILD NEAR THE ROYAL PALACE

LITTLE HANS JONATHAN and his cousin Juliane Sophie, each only
seven or eight years old, were probably at sea for two to three months
on their journey to Copenhagen. Their ship would have sailed past
Puerto Rico, then set a course for St. Augustine in Florida, which was
the oldest continuous European settlement in North America. In the
shadow of the fort built there by the Spanish in the sixteenth century
for defense against Native Americans, pirates, and any other competition, the vessel was reprovisioned and goods were bought and
sold. From Florida the ship, now laden with passengers and a cargo
of mostly sugar, was carried on the Gulf Stream across the wide Atlantic, past the British Isles. It was steered into the North Sea, either
via the English Channel or past the Shetland Islands, and on through
the Skagerak and Kattegat, to dock in Copenhagen on the Øresund
Sound.

About thirty years before the children from St. Croix sailed to
Copenhagen, the Icelander Arni of Geitastekkur had taken this route
as he headed home after visiting China. His account of the ocean
journey is typically pithy: "On that journey . . . the liquor barrel was
up on deck during every watch, so we were half-drunk all the time,
lying on the deck like dogs in our jubilation. We dropped anchor
at Copenhagen . . . and went ashore, attired in garments of silk and
velvet."[1]

On their own journey, the children would have watched and learned. The sailors aboard their ship were rough men, probably in poor health, suffering from the various ailments and contagious diseases that accompanied a seafaring life. Yet they must also have been skillful sailors, for the ship would have carried only a minimal crew. On the westward passage from Africa to the Danish West Indies, sea captains needed many hands to keep slaves under control and to forestall the danger of insurrection; on the way back to Europe, on the other hand, a large crew was unnecessary—and unwelcome, for the whole point of the colonial economy was to transport sugar. Everything revolved around sugar, and extra sailors merely jacked up its cost. The captains dealt with this staffing problem in various ways. Some were cruel and harsh in their treatment of the crew, in the hope that men would jump ship and elect to remain in the colonies. The ships' owners even encouraged their captains to accuse crew members of imaginary offenses as an excuse to leave them behind.[2]

Seasickness was likely no problem for these old salts, but it may have affected our two young passengers. As the ship rolled in the waves and winds, the sense of balance and the digestive system joined forces in rebellion against the body. Every moment the ship plunged down into the flying spray seemed to last an eternity, and nausea was likely overwhelming. In due course the children would have grown accustomed to the rolling motion of the ship and gotten their sea legs, like most people on a long ocean journey. Perhaps they even enjoyed the rocking movement, as if they were back in the womb or the cradle. Hans Jonathan, at least, was apparently not put off by his first experience at sea. Years later he enlisted in the Danish navy, and still later in life, in the East Fjords of Iceland, he is said to have taught people the basics of navigation.

When their ship docked in Copenhagen harbor in 1792, Hans Jonathan and Juliane Sophie entered another strange and exotic world. The community on St. Croix was, of course, half-Danish, and some of what they saw in Denmark would have reminded them of Christiansted. But Copenhagen was a big city: even the grand residence of the governor and the sturdy fort in Christiansted were dwarfed by its magnificent mansions and palaces.

At that time nearly one hundred thousand people lived inside the walls of Copenhagen. As the city grew and expanded, some of those defensive walls would give way to new development, but for now the gates to the city were locked every night, keeping the inhabitants enclosed in an ever more crowded space. Copenhagen was a cosmopolitan city of many cultures and nationalities, each with its own customs and dress, manners and languages: Yiddish-speaking Jews, German-speaking soldiers, Francophone aristocrats, and students who showed off their knowledge of Latin. "Nowhere else in the world," said writer Ludvig Holberg, "do people take pride in not knowing their native language."[3]

Over the city lay a stinking miasma from open drains and canals, mingling with odors of malt and hops from the breweries in this beer-loving country. The contents of chamber pots were sometimes unceremoniously dumped into the street, so passersby had to be on the alert. And there were cases of small children drowning in the deep drainage channels.[4] Hans Jonathan and Juliane Sophie must have experienced culture shock, as we say today. But the children were likely quick to adjust to their new environment—as children are. They must have been delighted to be reunited with their mothers when they arrived at their new home at Amaliegade 23—though they may have felt a little uneasy after four years' separation. A lot had happened in the intervening period, and there had been no contact between mother and child.

As on St. Croix, Emilia Regina, her friend Sabina Helena, and the other enslaved Africans in the household were servants to the Schimmelmann family. The Schimmelmanns' Copenhagen home, with its servants' quarters in the back, had to be run in a manner that met the expectations of governors, counts, and other European aristocrats of that flamboyant rococo period. The servants—both slave and free—took care of the children and attended to the adults' needs, polished silver and furniture, washed and ironed laundry, and pre-

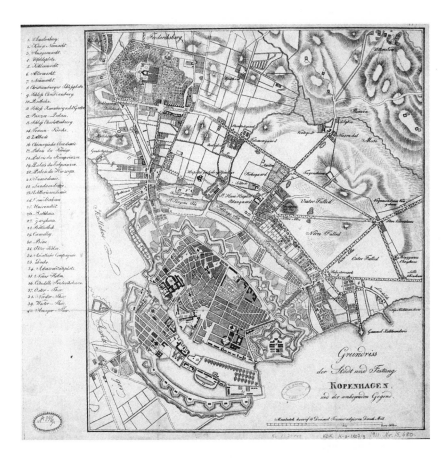

FIG. 6.2. Old Copenhagen. (Kort- og Billedsamlingen, Royal Library, Copenhagen.)

pared food. Their tasks may have been more diverse and complicated than before, but in another sense they were simpler—no longer subject to the thunderous bells that ruled the lives of plantation slaves.

Ludvig Heinrich Ernst von Schimmelmann probably called in from time to time at the nearby headquarters of the Schimmelmann family business, renewing his acquaintance with relatives with whom he had corresponded for so many years. He caught up on the latest developments in politics and the arts, passed on his experience of the plantations, and gave advice on business matters. Changing attitudes to slavery, in both Europe and North America, were a source of concern, even panic, in sugar circles. In the colonies, the world was being turned upside down. The Haitian Revolution (1791–1804) culminated in both the abolition of slavery and the founding of the Republic of Haiti.[5] Rebellions and revolts were also breaking out in several other colonial metropoles. Fierce debates took place about legal technicalities, economics and ethics, the profitability of the sugar industry, whether people could be chattel—about rights, obligations, and humanitarianism.[6] France, one of the most powerful states in Europe, was convulsed by revolution in 1789 and its king deposed. He was guillotined in 1793, and a new constitution was enacted establishing the rights of every citizen. The news of the execution of Louis XVI electrified Copenhagen: unrest broke out in the city, and student protests led the authorities to fear a revolution in Denmark as well. The common people took the side of the students against the police. The sugar bubble was about to burst—and sugar baron Ludvig Heinrich Ernst von Schimmelmann did not have long to live.

AMALIEGADE 23

The Schimmelmann mansion at Amaliegade 23 was right in the heart of Copenhagen in the Frederiksstaden district, which had been built in the mid-eighteenth century in honor of King Frederik V, to celebrate his absolute power. Count Moltke, who was responsible for the development, had made sure that the monarchy was indeed glorified through sophisticated urban planning and elegant architecture. When Frederiksstaden was completed, it was judged to be one of the most splendid urban districts in all of Europe, a tangible symbol of Denmark's colonial empire, its important position in global trade, and the glory and power of its king.

The focal point of Frederiksstaden was the octagonal plaza, Amalienborg, around which clustered the palaces of the royal family and the aristocracy. In the harbor nearby, merchant ships could often be seen lying at anchor, either unloading their cargo or on their way to the East or West Indies to sell European goods in exchange for commodities from the colonies. Parallel to Amaliegade Street was Bredgade, which was also lined with palatial homes. Sugar millionaires Ernst and Charlotte Schimmelmann lived at Bredgade 28, an elegant and sturdy mansion that was the Schimmelmann family seat; they had inherited it from the patriarch of the family, Heinrich Carl. It is not unlikely that Hans Jonathan was a visitor to this mansion, accompanying Henrietta Cathrina Schimmelmann and her children.

Amaliegade 23, the house where Henrietta Cathrina lived with her family, had been designed by the court architect Nicolai Eigtved, who also designed the royal palaces of Amalienborg.[7] The windows in the front wall of the mansion were glazed with clear "English glass," the rear ones with old greenish "French glass." At the rear of the building were other buildings, including the servants' quarters and a stable, which had originally been a bakery. Beyond them was a large fenced-in garden.

Amaliegade 23 was attached to number 25, and the two houses share an interesting history. At number 25 was the Mothers' Aid Society, a charity for unwed mothers founded by Queen Juliane Marie in 1783. One of the rooms, formerly an operating theater, is reputed to be haunted even today. A baby hatch is said to have been installed in the front of the building, an opening in which mothers could leave their illegitimate babies anonymously. Initially this led to a drop in the number of babies left outside to die. But in due course the hatch was closed, as the arrangement had been abused by parents

FIG. 6.3. Amaliegade 23 in Copenhagen, 1914. (Museum of Copenhagen.)

who "posted" a child through the hatch, then turned up at the charity to volunteer as foster parents, selected their own child, and were
paid for fostering him or her.

As Hans Jonathan grew older and more confident, his childhood
world expanded beyond the buildings at the back of Amaliegade 23
and into the garden. There he may have met and played with Adam
Wilhelm Moltke, who was about his age and whose home adjoined
the same garden. Eventually he explored Amaliegade and the surrounding area, at least during the day. The buildings there were orna-
mented with motifs reflecting contemporary ideas about the colonial
world—colorful images of wild beasts, birds, and butterflies which
would have caught the boy's eye. Facing Hans Jonathan's home was
a fine row of buildings, once the houses of sea captains on the East
Asian routes. Could his great-grandfather Niels Gram have lived
there?

Hans Jonathan had a more comfortable life than most enslaved
children. He enjoyed many privileges that the Danish social elite re-

garded as indispensable. He seems to have had music lessons, for example, as we know from his lifelong love of the violin. He was also taught to read, write, and calculate. In the 1780s many private schools were established in Copenhagen, but they are unlikely to have been open to slave children. It is far more probable that Hans Jonathan was homeschooled by tutors at Amaliegade 23. The upper classes who had enslaved workers in their homes often employed educated men, generally theology graduates, to teach their own children and those of the house slaves. The Schimmelmanns, renowned for their interest in education and enlightenment, would have done likewise.[8] Eager to learn, Hans Jonathan reveled in all the latest developments in Copenhagen society. Yet he was not free, any more than a field slave back on the plantation.

PEOPLE OF COLOR

In his excursions outside the garden fence, Hans Jonathan may have met others like himself, for in the late eighteenth century increasing numbers of people of color were to be seen on the streets of Copenhagen. By 1800 about fifty house slaves are estimated to have been living in the city, but there may have been twice that number.[9] On occasion slave traders sought to profit by transporting some of their human cargo from West Africa not to the colonies but to Copenhagen. These individuals entered a true "black market," as they were not officially registered anywhere. Danes referred to *vilde karle* (wild men) in the city and debated whether it was lawful to sell such people in Denmark, whether auctioning off human beings was befitting for Danes, and whether granting residence permits was advisable.[10] With the escalation of the slave trade and increasing profits in the production of sugar, Copenhageners and other Europeans had collapsed all the dark-skinned people they encountered in the streets under the category "negroes." Bondage, it was assumed, was in the nature of blackness. The notion of "free" blacks was odd, demanding special explanation.[11]

Occasionally large groups of enslaved Africans had an impact on city life. For instance, in 1802 about four hundred slaves escaped from vessels in the harbor. August Henning, an official from outside the city, was then visiting a friend in Copenhagen, a member of the Schimmelmann family. He wrote about the slave escape in his diary, commenting that Danes were no longer safe in the streets. It was difficult to induce the escapees to return to the ships, he said: they roamed around in a drunken state and were a constant problem. Some of the fugitives even broke into the Schimmelmann family's grand country home at Sølyst.[12]

In the latter half of the eighteenth century, the Danish aristocracy kept a close eye on developments in the capitals of other colonial powers. There intellectual discourse increasingly focused on concepts of beauty and taste—in spite of the brutality of slavery, or perhaps precisely because of it. The word *aesthetic* itself was coined by German philosophers during the heyday of the sugar trade to describe a "science of sensual recognition" to complement "rationalist" perspectives.[13] In the aesthetics of these slaveholding societies, the marginalized—women, the poor, enslaved blacks—often served as a foil to the white males who held power, whose superiority was highlighted by this contrast with "the other." Black boys featured prominently in this aesthetic, both in North America and in Europe. In the spring of 1771, for example, the citizens of Copenhagen were treated to the spectacle of King Christian VII, then in his early twenties, at play with two black boys on the balcony of the royal palace. The three lads threw books, porcelain, and other valuables off the balcony, until palace guards intervened to shoo them indoors. The boys were treated as the king's pets.[14] It is entirely possible that Hans Jonathan served this ornamental purpose in his master's home, an exotic proof of the aesthetic and moral standards of the sugar trade.

Yet Hans Jonathan's skin was not as dark as that of many Africans: he was a mulatto. We have little evidence of mulattos' position in Danish society or of how they felt about their life in the city, but some clues can be provided by Hans Christian Andersen, a writer best known today for fairy tales like "The Little Mermaid." Andersen's play "*Mulatten* (The mulatto), a romantic drama in five acts, premiered at the Royal Danish Theatre in Copenhagen in 1840. The leading character is the mulatto Horatio, who is a free man and thus has little in common with rebellious black slaves. Yet he does not belong in the world of the white slave owners either. He seeks to work his way up the social ladder, hoping to establish himself as an intellectual. The plot is propelled by emotional and sexual tensions as Eleonore, wife of the master of the La Rebelliere plantation, falls in love with Horatio. In act 5 the master sneers at his wife, "I suppose you want to see my bison—the mulatto!" Eleonore replies, "Indeed I do. I have never seen a more beautiful man! The radiance in his eyes is evidence of the soul of a king!"[15] Skin color signified a social barrier, marking something exciting and forbidden, and the power of Andersen's play arose from its challenge to these boundaries. The work marked a turning point in the writer's career, and it was performed repeatedly in both Denmark and Sweden during his lifetime. Interestingly, Andersen sets the action on a plantation on the Caribbean island of Martinique; perhaps it might have offended the sensibilities of Copenhagen society if it had been set in their own backyard.

THE ICELANDERS

Exploring the streets farther and farther from the mansion at Amaliegade 23, young Hans Jonathan may also have met Icelanders—though he probably did not recognize them as such. Around the time that Hans Jonathan arrived in Copenhagen in 1792, there was a sizable Icelandic community in the city, mainly made up of young men who were students at the university. Iceland, under Danish rule since the Middle Ages, would not have its own university until 1911; over the centuries Icelanders seeking to pursue higher education went mostly to the colonial capital, Copenhagen, where they trained for the professions: medicine, the church, and the law.

These young men from a sparsely populated island with a sleepy, stagnant rural society found themselves among the multicultural crowds of Copenhagen. In 1801 the population of Iceland numbered about forty-seven thousand, on an island of about forty thousand square miles (the size of Virginia). The island's biggest town, Reykjavik, where urban development was in its infancy, had a population of three hundred—compared to Copenhagen's one hundred thousand. A student from south Iceland, Hogni Einarsson, wrote home in 1828 recounting his experience of the big city: "I arrived here on the tenth of this month, and it was like entering a different world—though no Paradise, for I can think of no smell fouler than what I noticed first. I could see neither sun nor sky, and I could hardly make my way for people and carts, whose din was driving me mad."[16] Hogni was eventually swallowed up by the city: in 1832 he "stumbled out into the darkness" after his twenty-seventh birthday party, never to be seen again.[17]

Icelandic students, as subjects of the Danish king, were not considered "foreigners" as such, but there is some evidence of their own interest in human diversity. In 1797, for instance, the Icelander Magnus Stephensen published "An Entertaining Compendium for Friends with Enlightening Discourses and Poems." A governor of Iceland and president of the Icelandic High Court, one of the most influential men of his age in Iceland, Magnus maintained that skin color was largely a matter of hygiene: "black people" simply did not wash enough. He seems to have been of the opinion that "white" was the essential color of the human race—the primal, unsullied appearance of the species. While the word *negro* was in general use for the people of Africa, said Magnus, the negroes were in fact "very diverse."[18]

Why did Magnus feel the need to discuss these issues with his fellow Icelanders in 1797? It is hard to imagine that human diversity was in any way an urgent issue in that period for Icelanders, most of whom had never seen a "person of color." It is almost as if Magnus had a premonition that one would soon be stepping onto Icelandic soil.

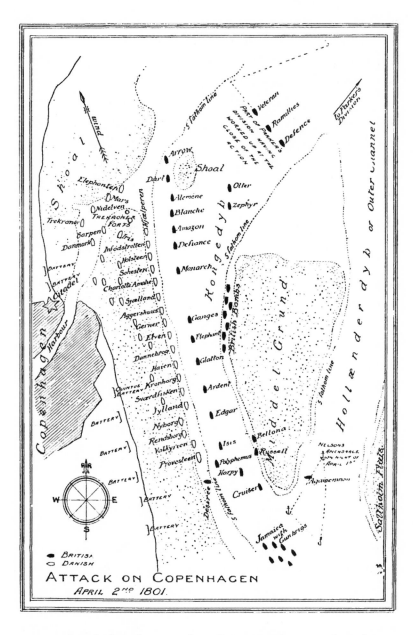

FIG. 7.1. The Battle of Copenhagen, 2 April 1801. (Source: W. L. Clowes 1899, *The Royal Navy: A History from the Earliest Times to the Present*, vol. 4 [London: Sampson Low, Marston, 1899].)

"HE WANTED TO GO TO WAR"

IN THE SPRING OF 1801 the atmosphere was tense in the mansion at Amaliegade 23. Henrietta Cathrina Schimmelmann maintained that she could do as she liked with "her" blacks—and many others in Copenhagen's aristocracy were of the same view. As a child Hans Jonathan may have submitted to her authority automatically, but as he grew up and learned more he began to resist. Those who are enslaved or otherwise coerced still have options.[1] They can resist, either covertly or through systematic protest. The late eighteenth century was an eventful time in Europe, and fresh breezes were blowing, carrying with them ideas about freedom and human rights. The French Revolution of 1789 heralded these new ideas, with spectacular consequences around the world. Everything, everywhere, was seen to be mutable. These ideas cannot have passed Hans Jonathan by: he was an intelligent young man with an inquiring mind; he had some education, and he spoke several languages. At age seventeen he could no longer meekly accept what his Danish masters said and did. He wanted to throw off the shackles of slavery and make his way in the world.

It is possible that his master, Ludvig Heinrich Ernst von Schimmelmann, had shielded Hans Jonathan because of his relationship with the family of the boy's father, Hans Gram. Or it may be that the master was impressed by the child's quick intelligence and ability to learn. But Hans Jonathan did not enjoy Schimmelmann's protection for long: Ludvig died at the age of forty-nine in December 1793, a year after Hans Jonathan arrived in Copenhagen. His will, which is extant, made no provision for Hans Jonathan.[2]

Henrietta Cathrina's father apparently had worked for the Cape Colony (now in South Africa), which had been established as a Dutch colony in the mid-seventeenth century. There the Boers (of Dutch origin) enslaved the native population and in due course, along with other white settlers, paved the way for the apartheid system, introduced in the mid-twentieth century by the white minority to brutally enforce separation of the races.

The twice-widowed Henrietta Cathrina at age fifty-two now became head of the Copenhagen household. She was financially comfortable, with her own family wealth and that of the Schimmelmann empire behind her. On the other hand, she had lost two children, which had cast a shadow over the Schimmelmanns' time on St. Croix, and after the death of her husband her relations with the enslaved household workers seem to have become increasingly strained.

Census records for Copenhagen show that in 1801 the widow was running quite a large home at Amaliegade 23: she had a household of eleven, including nine servants, of whom five were "negroes." The records list the following:

Henrietta Schimmelmann, 48; occupation: widow of Heinrich
    Ludvig; second marriage
Ernst Carl Schimmelmann, 20; son of Henrietta S.; unmarried
Michael William, 21; occupation: servant; unmarried
Hans Jonathan, 17; occupation: servant (negro); unmarried
Nicolai Hansen, 30; occupation: coachman; unmarried
Niels Bentsen, 26; occupation: laborer; unmarried
Sabina Helena (negro), 40; occupation: chambermaid;
    unmarried
Emilia Regina (negro), 36; occupation: chambermaid; unmarried

Christiane Jacobsen Schlengrich, 36; occupation: housekeeper;
unmarried

Inger Fredriksdatter, 30; occupation: kitchen maid; unmarried

Juliane Sophie (negro), 17; occupation: parlormaid[3]

The ages of Henrietta Cathrina Schimmelmann and Emilia Regina are incorrect here—the handsome widow has knocked twelve years off her true age—and the writer of the record has neglected to specify the skin color of Michael, who was a "negro" like four other servants in the household. Black and white, free servants and slaves, are listed without any distinction between "black" and "mulatto"—at least not in this census. The "negroes" are classified as servants and maids, not as slaves. The list probably reflects the hierarchy of the household, in which age and gender seem to have been more important than race. Sabina Helena is listed above her friend and unofficial sister-in-law Emilia Regina, presumably because she is older. Still, the status of the "servant" Hans Jonathan is interesting. He and his cousin Juliane Sophie are the youngest members of the household, but not only is he listed above his mother (although she is twice his age), but he is also placed above two white males, Nicolai and Niels, who are his elders. Did the mulatto boy have some special status in the Schimmelmann home?

Hans Jonathan had considerable freedom of movement within the city walls. He was able to associate with other young people and to go carousing in the evening. Sometimes he stayed out later than Henrietta Cathrina allowed; she waited up for his return, scolded him for the offense, and angrily locked the gate after him. Heated exchanges and the slamming of heavy doors disturbed the evening quiet and echoed around the garden.

Relations between Hans Jonathan and Henrietta Cathrina worsened steadily, reaching a low point when she discovered that the boy was trying to enlist in the Royal Danish Navy. Hans Jonathan said he wanted to do his part for Denmark in the forthcoming war with England. Outraged, Henrietta Cathrina forbade it, but Hans Jonathan refused to be cowed. When he insisted that he would not submit to her rules, his mistress grabbed a cane and struck the boy several times, according to testimony later given in court by her steward, Peder Hansen.

Hans Jonathan had had enough. He decided to run away. With a discreet farewell to his mother, he stealthily left the premises and went on his way. He must have felt a sense of relief, confident that the current discourse on human rights, which had had an impact all over Europe, would benefit him, and others like him—mulatto or black—in Copenhagen. And so he was lighthearted as he strode down the city streets, free as a bird.

THE LAWSUIT

When Henrietta Cathrina realised that Hans Jonathan had run away, she went straight to the police station to report him for dereliction of duty and for the theft of two hundred rigsdaler from her son, Ernst Carl—who had in fact already, visiting the police two days before, reported that sum missing from his chest at home at Amaliegade 23. Ernst Carl, however, appears not to have mentioned Hans Jonathan. Henrietta Cathrina felt it necessary to follow up her allegations with a formal letter. "Today," she wrote, "this mulatto ran away from me, and since he said yesterday evening that he wanted to go and fight against the English, etc., I presume that he wants to join the militia."[4] She requested that Hans Jonathan be arrested and that she be notified. This was not the first time that an enslaved person had been accused of theft: it was a classic response to rebellion.

The Schimmelmanns, not surprisingly, had apparently never had a portrait painted of their slave Hans Jonathan. Henrietta Cathrina's brief description is all we have—and perhaps, after all, there is some affection in her words: "He is sixteen years old, of small stature, and has a yellowish complexion and short curly hair. He left here wearing a blue cloak, long trousers, and short boots."[5] She goes on to say that even if the boy turned out to be guilty of theft, she would prefer to keep it a secret if possible. Her wish was not to punish him according to the strictest letter of the law, only to send him back to the Danish West Indies as soon as possible. But Henrietta Cathrina could not have it both ways: she could not initiate a lawsuit while also demanding confidentiality.

What was the "strictest letter of the law"? For theft it was death, according to a decree issued at the foundation of the Copenhagen City Court in 1771. At that time theft accounted for a large proportion of the cases brought before Danish courts, and many convicted thieves were beheaded in public. Amendments to criminal law in 1789 repealed the death penalty for minor offenses, but it remained in force for graver crimes.[6] Legal penalties were grounded in old Danish law and varied according to circumstances. A clear distinction was drawn, for instance, between a first offense and a repeated one; and it was one thing to steal a horse from a field, another, far worse, to go into a stable in order to steal it. Henrietta Cathrina may not have been aware of the amendments to the law, which were enacted the year after she arrived in Copenhagen. She was probably more familiar with the legal provisions in force on St. Croix, which were far more draconian.

In any case, Henrietta Cathrina's complaint appears not to have been taken seriously by the authorities. That is surprising in view of her high standing in society. Did the police judge her case absurd or suspicious in some way? Would the response have been different if the complaint had been made by her late husband? The police took no immediate action. Was it certain that Henrietta Cathrina had the rights she claimed over the boy? He lived under her roof, but that proved nothing. How were the police to know where people of color in the city had come from, and under what conditions?

Many nations look back to a time they see as their Golden Age. Denmark's Golden Age, when absolute monarchy came to an end and culture and the arts flourished, lasted a scant half-century, from about 1800 to 1850. Men such as physicist Hans Christian Ørsted, poet Adam Oehlenschläger, author Hans Christian Andersen, and finance minister Heinrich Ernst Schimmelmann made their mark on the era.[7] And so, in his own way, did Hans Jonathan.

THE BATTLE OF COPENHAGEN

In mid-March of 1801, Copenhagen's authorities called on all able-bodied men to come to the defense of the city against the English. Hans Jonathan was one of the many who volunteered to serve. Denmark had long been neutral in international affairs—for example, during the American Revolutionary War. In light of their economic interests in the West Indies and elsewhere, the Danes deemed it wise not to risk offending the superpowers of the time, England and France. In 1798, however, the Danes embarked on a more proactive foreign policy, largely on the initiative of Ernst Schimmelmann, who had by then risen to the position of minister of commerce and finance. Denmark soon became embroiled in the Napoleonic Wars. The sugar barons' vessels now had to sail the Middle Passage in convoy, escorted by Danish naval vessels. The following year English warships ambushed the frigate *Havfruen* and the twelve merchant ships it was escorting. Denmark's expanding colonial powers posed a threat to the English; hence confrontation between their navies was inevitable.

Ernst Carl Schimmelmann, the minister's twenty-year-old kinsman from Amaliegade 23, enlisted, intending to pursue a military career. Perhaps he and Hans Jonathan egged each other on. They were not only coming to the defense of Copenhagen but lending their support to old Schimmelmann, who was criticized by many in the city for having taken an unreasonable risk by abandoning the policy of neutrality that had served Denmark so well during the years of plenty. It is ironic that Hans Jonathan was so keen to join the military power that had enslaved him and other people of color to cash in on the sugar trade. But he may well have seen enlistment as the only way to escape his bondage—to stand on his own two feet and make his mark. And young men have often thought it glamorous to go to war.

In the court case initiated by Henrietta Cathrina, one witness testified about Hans Jonathan, saying simply, "He wanted to go to war." The youngster was keen to fight, and unafraid.

There had been no armed conflict between England and Denmark for three centuries—not since the Middle Ages, when the two countries clashed over control of Iceland from 1467 to 1490. But as the spring of 1801 progressed, it became clear that a conflict on the Øresund Sound was inevitable. Russia had arranged a league along with Denmark, Sweden, and Prussia, to facilitate free trade with France, which the British saw as a serious threat to their interests. In early 1801 the British government sought to break up the league, ordering Admiral Sir Hyde Parker to go to Copenhagen and detach Denmark from it by agreement or by force. On 30 March the British force passed through the narrows between Denmark and Sweden. Vice Admiral Lord Nelson, who was second in command, is famously reputed to have disobeyed Admiral Parker's order to withdraw by holding the telescope to his blind eye to look at the signals from Parker.

The Battle of Copenhagen took place on the anchorage just outside the city. The English were aware that the best time to attack the Danish fleet was in the spring, when most of the vessels would be in harbor. Danish men by the thousands responded to the authorities' call to arms, volunteering for the navy or joining army units to defend the anchorage. When news arrived that the English warships were sailing around the Skagen peninsula, everyone was in a state of high alert. But the odds were against the Danes. The English fleet was far larger, with experienced crews, while many of the Danish sailors were raw recruits. A letter written by Charlotte Schimmelmann, wife of the minister in charge, illustrates the fear and the nationalistic fervor engendered by the battle. "The land troops burned with the desire to measure themselves against the enemy," she wrote, "and every citizen of Copenhagen felt like a warrior. The enthusiasm, the bitterness was indescribable. These otherwise quiet people were completely inflamed and vengeful."[8]

On the Thursday before Easter, 2 April 1801, the English war-ships forced their way into the anchorage, one after the other, until it was crammed with vessels. Hans Jonathan was aboard the ship *Charlotte Amalie*. In ten days he would turn seventeen, if he lived. But the *Charlotte Amalie* faced two enemy vessels, the *Monarch* and the *Ganges*, both of them much larger. The Danish and English vessels were lined up less than three hundred meters apart, and they bombarded each other continuously throughout the four-hour battle—with even greater intensity toward the end.

Below decks a military surgeon treated the wounded, surrounded by mutilated corpses. It was a slaughterhouse, a demonic underworld—hell on earth. The English were astonished that the *Charlotte Amalie* held out for so long. Finally the *Ganges* compelled Captain Hans H. Kofoed to surrender. But while the English fleet had the advantage of size and numbers, it was difficult to maneuver in the crowded anchorage, and three English vessels ran aground. Admiral Horatio Nelson sent a man ashore to offer the Danes a truce, which Crown Prince Frederik accepted. At the battle's end, the deck of the *Charlotte Amalie* was awash in blood, and the ship was crippled. Of the 241-member crew, 39 had been killed or seriously wounded.[9] Hans Jonathan escaped unscathed.

Following the battle there was no attempt to care for the wounded sailors or to show solidarity. Some men—inadequately dressed, hungry, bloody—hurried away. Some were traumatized by their experience that day; others seized the opportunity to desert. Some had enlisted voluntarily, while others had been drafted or press-ganged. The Danes had had a narrow escape: Denmark retained its independence, but its navy had suffered severe damage.

Three days after the end of the Battle of Copenhagen, on the morning of Easter Sunday, crowds turned out to witness the funerals of the fallen. Church bells rang, and the somber assembly walked slowly through the streets after the hearses and coffins. The battle had taken a heavy toll: two thousand Danes died (English casualties were far fewer). Danish hearts swelled with patriotic fervor, and their fallen heroes were highly praised. Hans Jonathan's bravery had been noticed: Captain Kofoed spoke highly of him. Surely he must have a bright future in the navy?

Hans Jonathan was paid fifteen rigsdalers by the navy for his military service. It was probably the first time he had ever had any money of his own. As he was Henrietta Cathrina's "property," perhaps she had a claim to his pay. Can a man who does not own himself buy himself? Such transactions were not unknown, A slave from St. Thomas named Denmark Vesey (1767–1822)—originally called Telemaque—was lucky enough to win fifteen hundred dollars in a lottery when he was a house slave in Charleston, South Carolina. He used the money to buy his freedom. Vesey was later alleged to have been involved in a slave revolt in Charleston, for which he was executed.[10] Hans Jonathan's fifteen rigsdalers were just a fraction of the price of the average slave, so even if he might theoretically have had the right to buy himself, it would have been quite impractical. Nevertheless, his salary may have enabled him to leave home and purchase a violin.

A NAVAL CAREER

Hans Jonathan no doubt thought that when he came ashore following the Battle of Copenhagen, after his doughty service to king and country, the dispute about his alleged theft and dereliction of duty would disappear. In the context of life-and-death conflict, what did such trifles matter? He went home to Amaliegade 23, where he must have been warmly welcomed by his mother—but Henrietta Cathrina locked him up in the yard of the house. Her own son, Ernst Carl, had not distinguished himself by any heroic deeds in battle; was she offended by the contrast between the two boys? Two days later she appears to have had a change of heart. She handed Hans Jonathan over to the custody of the Danish navy.[11] He remained her property, but his market value was likely to rise rather than fall.

Perhaps Henrietta Cathrina felt it would be hard to keep Hans

Jonathan restrained in the garden after his fine military performance. Despite his traumatic experience in battle, he was keen for a naval career. Whatever Henrietta Cathrina's motivation, Hans Jonathan was promptly appointed to the crew of the warship *Denmark*, which had escaped damage in the battle. Was the house slave to embark on a career sailing the high seas, escorting slave vessels and defending the Danish capital from attacks by pirates and foreign sugar barons?

After a brief spell aboard the *Denmark*, Hans Jonathan was transferred to another ship, the *Elephant*, where he met another enslaved man, Peter Samuel, who would become his comrade in arms and who fought for his freedom as Hans Jonathan did. Peter Samuel, whose owner, the planter Isaak Brenner, had compelled him to enlist in the navy, had taken part in the Battle of Copenhagen aboard a ship that had survived with less damage than the *Charlotte Amalie*. He and Hans Jonathan got to know each other, compared stories, and agreed that both would demand their freedom. But ahead lay a complicated process that would ultimately lead to a historic lawsuit.

Among those who supported Hans Jonathan's efforts was the captain of the *Denmark*, Steen Andersen Bille. Hans Jonathan explained his situation frankly to the captain and told him about the legal dispute with Henrietta Cathrina. Bille had served the Danish Empire for many years and was familiar with the West Indies; he had a good reputation in the government and held the rank of privy councilor, with direct access to Crown Prince Frederik. Requesting a meeting, Captain Bille brought the plight of his two protégés to the attention of the prince.

This put Prince Frederik in a difficult position: the Copenhagen elite was a small society in which everyone knew everyone else. The prince was well acquainted with Henrietta Cathrina; they moved in the same social circles and met at parties and receptions. It was Prince Frederik himself who had appointed Henrietta Cathrina's late husband, Ludvig Heinrich Ernst von Schimmelmann, as governor of St. Croix. Yet the prince agreed to lend his assistance to Captain Bille, his privy councilor, by writing a letter. The prince indicated that to his knowledge no one in Denmark was denied freedom unless legally sentenced to bondage and, as a result "this person" could not "be considered a slave": "Nor do I believe that any lawyer would be able to grant Mrs. General Schimmelmann, so long as she stays in Denmark, other rights over this person than those which any lord may have over his servant. To that end he is considered free and enjoys rights when he dares to come ashore, not for evil reasons, with his comrades."[12]

Although the letter's phrasing is oblique, referring to "this person," possibly in order to avoid offending any of the judges or the sugar barons, neither Captain Bille nor anyone else who read it doubted that it referred to the case of Hans Jonathan. Henrietta Cathrina was not pursuing claims against anyone else. On 14 May 1801 Captain Bille granted Hans Jonathan his freedom. His shipmate Peter Samuel was also granted freedom on that day, presumably thanks to the position expressed in the prince's letter. Few people seem to have seen the letter, and Captain Bille may not have passed it on, but it has survived in Bille's private archive at the Danish Archives in Copenhagen.

Aged seventeen, Hans Jonathan was no longer a slave, or so it seemed—and that was cause for celebration. He rented a room at Kragh's tavern on Store Kongensgade 231, where he could relax, enjoy good food and drink, and amuse himself by playing the violin. He was confident that the letter written by Crown Prince Frederik, who was the de facto ruler of Denmark due to his father's mental illness, would outweigh anything that Henrietta Cathrina might claim.

Before long the widow learned that "her" mulatto was living at a tavern in the town, apparently believing that he owned himself and was free. The issue did not concern Hans Jonathan alone but all of her house slaves—and indeed dozens more like them in Copenhagen. The conflict at Amaliegade 23 must have been noticed by house slaves living in the vicinity. Henrietta Cathrina may have had the support of other slave owners in a similar situation; at any rate, she was not about to give up. She was a woman of powerful character, with long

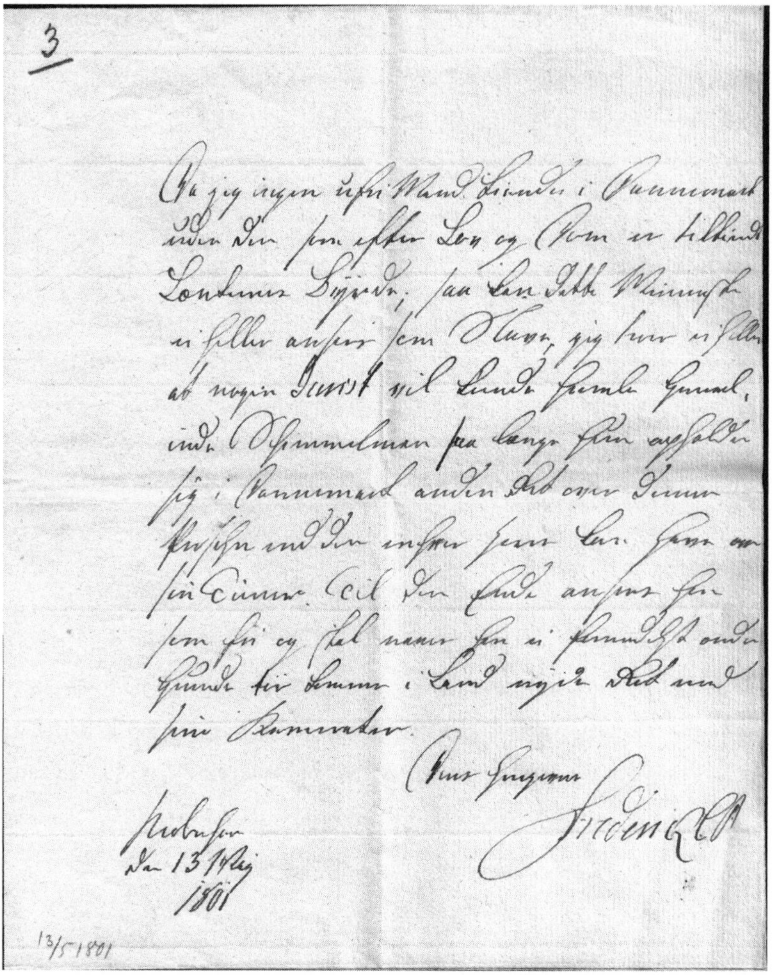

FIG. 7.2. Letter of Crown Prince Frederik in support of Hans Jonathan, dated 13 May 1801. (Privatarkiv Bille, Letters 1799–1816, Case 1; National Archives of Denmark.) Bille, Steen Andersen, søofficer, Breve, mm. Case 1.

experience in dealing with enslaved workers, both in the colonies and at home in Denmark. Just five days after the prince's letter declared Hans Jonathan a free man, she returned to the police station and submitted the following complaint in writing:

> Pro Memoria
>
> A mulatto boy, who belongs to me and is my born slave named Hans, left my house and service without my knowledge or consent. It is of great importance to me that this boy be apprehended for his crime in leaving my service (if not my right over him as my property), specifically in part as a means to prevent him from evading it altogether, and partly to have an investigation into several things that since his escape appear to be missing; thus I respectfully venture to request that Your Honor kindly vouchsafe me your assistance in having him arrested and interrogated. My steward can identify the place where I presume he is staying, and if Your Honor will send me a couple of officers, they can accompany my steward to the aforementioned location. I reserve the right to have the honor of presenting all that may be further necessary in this case when the boy is arrested. With esteem I remain Your Honour's most respectful servant.
>
> > Copenhagen, 19 May 1801
> > Henrietta, wife of General Schimmelmann,
> > resident at Amaliegade[13]

The deferential language of the memorandum is typical for the time: would it have the desired effect? Before long the police had tracked down Hans Jonathan in order to serve the complaint on him. A secretary recorded his response:

> He explained that it was true that he had been out on the defenses and in battle on 2 April last without the complainant's prior authorization, but that when this was over, he had arrived at the complainant's and she had then held him prisoner at her estate for two

days, after which he was sent aboard the *Denmark* and thereafter the *Elephant*, and presuming that he was then free under royal order, based on his application, was released and obtained permission to live wherever he wished. He was born on St. Croix on the plantation of the Governor General's wife, Henrietta Schimmelmann, the name of which he cannot recall, to the negress Emilia Regina; is eighteen years old; furthermore, in this city the complainant had him cared for, taught, and confirmed in the Lutheran faith, and he was in service to her thereafter. He held that he could not be considered to be the complainant's possession and wished not to return to her, whereas he desires to serve His Majesty the King by going to sea. He also insisted that he will provide proof that he was, as explained, set free.[14]

Hans Jonathan appears to have given misleading information about his age. Other documents indicate that he was born in April 1784, so he should have been seventeen years old. He may have wanted to appear older than his true age, or perhaps it was just a clerical error. On the other hand he may actually have been eighteen; some plantation recordkeepers recorded the birth of infants only after they had survived a year.[15] On this occasion Henrietta Cathrina accused Hans Jonathan of running away and of dereliction of duty, but not of theft, as before. The penalties, however, could be just as severe.[16]

Henrietta Cathrina was not present when the case came to court, but her steward Peder Hansen stated that she would submit documents within two days. She did not do so, and the steward returned to court empty-handed. Thus Henrietta Cathrina's demand that "the negro Hans" be imprisoned was dismissed. Once again freedom seemed to be within reach.

WAS HE FREE?

The next few months passed uneventfully, and Hans Jonathan walked the streets of Copenhagen like any free man. Meanwhile, another slave from St. Croix, David Tams, who had come to Denmark with his owner to live on a country estate, also determined to seize his freedom. But fortune was not on his side: as he made his way into Copenhagen via the North Gate on 20 July, guards arrested him. When his owner discovered that his slave had run away, he initiated a civil lawsuit against him in order to establish his rights of ownership. This inspired the widow Schimmelmann to follow his example. Dereliction of duty and theft would have been hard to prove in the criminal case, but a civil lawsuit to establish ownership would suffice.

Before the case of David Tams came up, Henrietta Cathrina had been negotiating with the navy to try to resolve the dispute. Hans Jonathan had indicated to the crown prince via Captain Bille that he wished to continue in military service. The matter was passed on to the navy, where it was agreed that his case should be considered in light of Hans Jonathan's heroism during the Battle of Copenhagen. Rear Admiral Otto Lütken, who had played a key role in the war with England, was of the view that Henrietta Cathrina should be consulted before any action was taken. After meeting with the widow, he proposed that the navy should purchase the slave and grant him his freedom so that he could be enlisted on the same terms as other naval personnel. But Henrietta Cathrina drove a hard bargain, demanding four hundred rigsdalers for Hans Jonathan—the price he would have fetched on St. Croix when she sold her plantation there. It was similar to the value placed on his mother Emilia Regina many years before—the equivalent of two fine horses. The navy would not agree to such a high price. Instead the royal lawyers were asked to consider the lawfulness of Henrietta Cathrina's claim on Hans Jonathan. Although a royal decree had banned the transport of enslaved persons from the West Indies to Denmark after 1795, the lawyers replied that there was no legal provision voiding ownership of slaves if they had been brought to Europe before then.

Henrietta Cathrina's claim this time was harder to dismiss. She appeared to own the man lawfully. She was entitled to sell her slave, and perhaps she intended to do so soon. Hans Jonathan's brief taste of freedom was over. He was arrested by four sturdy police officers at his lodgings. But he did not go quietly:

> Anno 1801, the 3rd of December at 5 o'clock in the afternoon, I, the undersigned Andreas Rohde, assistant by royal appointment to the royal bailiff's office here in the city, on behalf of the court and the king's steward, the Assessor Mr. Feddersen, attested by the court and the city's legal representatives Andreas Stenslev and Lars Jørgensen, proceeded with the Procurator Bierring, on behalf of the claimant, the wife of General Major Schimmelmann, to the mulatto Hans, lodging with tavern keeper Svend in Store Grønnegade in the baker's cellar, where I identified the aforementioned mulatto Hans (who said that his surname was Jonathan) bearing the requisition with the printed protocol supplied by the police office, after which I read out his explanation set out therein, which he now repeated, and further stated that the Crown Prince had given him his freedom, but proof of which he had none. Mr. Bierring held to the requisition and insisted that the mulatto Hans Jonathan's person be arrested, handcuffed, and brought to the capital's civil jail, where his assertion, devoid of all proof, is hereby denied as untrue. Thus it followed that, according to the requisition and the dismissed claim, the arrest and liability was legally declared of the mulatto Hans Jonathan's person, who was taken into custody in the capital's civil jail on the stroke of 6 o'clock in the evening.[17]

Conditions in jail were far from pleasant: the prisoners lived in crowded quarters and were fed miserly portions of poor food; the inmates were noisy and quarrelsome. Hans Jonathan felt that he had fallen among thieves and prostitutes.

The day after the arrest Henrietta Cathrina wrote another memorandum, which was later produced in court:

> When my mulatto boy Hans Jonathan, who is my born slave, had left my house and declared that he would not return to the same

(from where he should have been transported to the West Indies, since I am unable to keep him here because of his bad conduct), no trace of him could be found for several months, until a few days ago, when I was able to trace him; yesterday I was able to effect arrest of his person by the king's bailiff and have him held in the capital's civil jail. Therefore I venture to request that the afore-mentioned Hans Jonathan should be . . . [kept] under arrest until I can arrange passage aboard a ship to convey him to the West Indies.[18]

Now it was up to the court to decide Hans Jonathan's fate. Case number 345/1801, *The General's Widow Henrietta Schimmelmann versus the Mulatto Hans Jonathan*, came before the provincial court in Copenhagen, which had been established in 1771. Prior to that, the legal system had been an incomprehensible maze in which the juris-dictions of different courts overlapped and two courts might reach different verdicts in the same case. But if the restructured Danish legal system promised justice, the name of the lawsuit did not: The General's Widow v. the Mulatto was equivalent to Goliath v. David. And on this occasion there was no guarantee that David would be the victor.

FIG. 8.1. Henrietta Cathrina von Schimmelmann. (Kort- og Billedsamlingen, Royal Library, Copenhagen.)

THE GENERAL'S WIDOW V.
THE MULATTO

CHRISTMAS WAS COMING, and Copenhagen was chilly. Sooty smoke from coal-fired stoves hung over the city, blending with the stench of the open drains. Hans Jonathan had been in the city jail in the basement of city hall on the corner of Gammeltorv and Nytorv for eleven days, surrounded by thieves, prostitutes, and other criminals, when he was served with a summons by two court officials, Jensen and Andersen. They showed him a copy of Henrietta Cathrina's complaint and informed him that she was seeking confirmation of her ownership rights and intended to send him back to the West Indies. He was to attend court in one week, at nine o'clock in the morning on 21 December 1801, at which time further evidence would be presented.

On the day in question—the shortest day of the year—a nattily attired lawyer, N. C. Bierring, Henrietta Cathrina's advocate, arrived at the courthouse at Østergade 52 to submit the widow Schimmelmann's complaint against the mulatto:

> As Hans Jonathan's explanation has revealed, he is the de facto slave of the plaintiff and as a consequence thereof her property, because he was born on her plantation on St. Croix in America to her negress Emilia Regina. Therefore I do not need to expound

on her right, de jure, to dispose of him in compliance with the law, or to send him wherever she wishes. . . . Moreover, as far as the alleged release of His Royal Highness the Crown Prince is concerned, that alone shows the boy's temerity in uttering falsehood. . . . My assertion and reproof are thus . . . that the plaintiff be acknowledged as entitled to have Hans Jonathan as her slave and property, to transport him to the West Indies or anywhere else. And thus begins the case.[1]

When he was arrested, Hans Jonathan had stated that the crown prince had written a letter confirming that he had become a free man—that is, that he had once been a slave. That admission did not look good for his case. Hans Jonathan may have had some knowledge of the relevant legislation on slavery, which was rapidly being reformed, but for his court appearance he could not afford to engage a lawyer. The proceedings were adjourned until 4 January, and the court appointed an attorney to represent him. Court officers made preparations for the case and scheduled the examination of witnesses. The principal judge in the case, Anders Sandøe Ørsted (1778–1860), was only twenty-three years old at the time; he would go on to become influential as a jurist and a politician, being named prime minister in 1853. In accordance with custom, he, as the youngest of the five judges, took responsibility for the administration of the case and drafted the verdict.

The General's Widow v. the Mulatto would set a precedent for many other people in the same situation as Hans Jonathan. At that time dozens of Afrodescendent people from the Danish colonies were living in Copenhagen, most of them slaves from the West Indies or their descendants. Hans Jonathan's case would be a watershed.

CASE NO. 356/1801

Wine that is transported over long distances is sometimes said to travel well or badly. How well did property rights in a human being travel from St. Croix to Copenhagen? Were such rights compromised or reduced? Or did they cease to exist? Such questions were weighed by the judges in May 1802, under considerable pressure from wealthy individuals seeking to safeguard their own interests.

The court case had dragged on for four months—months of ritual and procedure and testimony. But some parties to the case were more equal than others. There is no record of Henrietta Cathrina Schimmelmann's attending the proceedings, nor of any request for her presence up to this point. She was represented by her lawyer, N. C. Bierring, whom she had commissioned to pursue all lawful means to ensure her right of ownership, as she had reason to believe that "her slave" might run away.

The documents in the case are in the Danish National Archives, sorted by size and stored in boxes dispersed around Copenhagen in order to make optimal use of the space available.[2] And those spaces are crammed—like the hold of a slave ship. These papers are, in a sense, the most vital evidence about the life of Hans Jonathan and about slavery in Denmark: dozens of pages in neat Gothic-style handwriting recording his origins and the matters in dispute in the case. Every document is stamped, dated, and signed with legal formality. In many cases the fee paid to the scribe is specified: half a rigsdaler, 25 skildings.

On 4 January 1802 the proceedings recommenced as planned. N. C. Bierring was present in court, representing the widow. Hans Jonathan's appointed defense attorney, Beyer (his full name is not provided in the court's documents), submitted a long written argument aimed at refuting Henrietta Cathrina's claims:

> Without providing any investigation of the extent to which the supposedly noble plaintiff's position in this case might be classified among noble or base deeds, . . . I will merely confine myself to examining the very nature of the case at hand. The plaintiff seeks to receive judgment that the defendant be regarded as her slave and property, so that she may do with him whatever she desires. It has

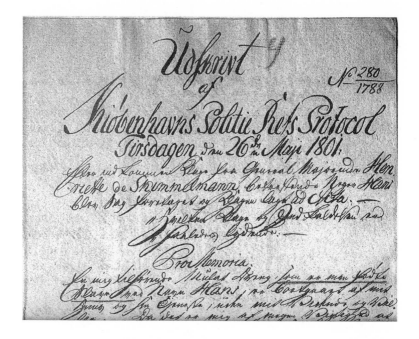

FIG. 8.2. One of the court documents regarding the case of Henrietta Cathrina von Schimmelmann and "negro" Hans Jonathan. Københavns Politi. Hovedjournal 1800 1-4211. Pådømte sager 1802 maj 24–juni 22. 1801, sag nr. 1448 (LAS). (National Archives of Denmark.)

not pleased her or her lawyer to demonstrate which part of Danish Law might support such a claim, but continued briefly and simply by saying that her rights need not be expounded. This was probably for the valid reason that they had not found anything to substantiate their case in the law of this kingdom. Perhaps the claim will find some basis in an applicable law of Morocco or Algeria?[3]

The sarcastic tone of Beyer's argument may not have helped his client's case. By the same token, he may have gone too far when he next claimed that Hans Jonathan might not necessarily be the son of Emilia Regina, as he was in no position to state with certainty who had given birth to him. Was it not a possibility, asked Beyer, that Hans Jonathan had been born before his mother became a slave of Henrietta Cathrina? The argument was not a strong one.

But the mainstay of Beyer's defense was that while West Indian law provided for the ownership of human beings as if they were chattel—"a dog or a horse or suchlike"—that point of view was not consistent with Danish law. And he added that Henrietta Cathrina had herself indicated that Hans Jonathan was not necessarily her property, when she lodged her complaint and demanded his arrest: she said that he had "left her house *and her service*," Beyer pointed out. He called for Hans Jonathan to be released and the case dismissed.

Some days later Beyer had Henrietta Cathrina served with a summons to court. Alleging that she had blackened Hans Jonathan's name and mocked, hurt, and inconvenienced him, the lawyer demanded that she pay the costs of the case and his own fee as defense attorney. The summons was delivered to the mansion at Amaliegade 23, but the widow was not at home. Her son, Ernst Carl, accepted it and undertook to pass it on to his mother and tell her what it contained. He and Hans Jonathan had grown up together, as we have seen, but now his "foster brother" was summoning his mother to court. While Ernst Carl is likely to have delivered the summons, he may have taken Hans Jonathan's side.

The following week Beyer submitted a complaint about the response to the summons: the case was making no progress, despite his best efforts. Henrietta Cathrina had not appeared in court, he said, and meanwhile his client was sitting in jail, unable to do anything, and in addition to that he was persona non grata—robbed of his honor, an undesirable, a foreigner, and an interloper. The consequences for Hans Jonathan were grave, he said, as his incarceration prevented him from pursuing his desired career in the Royal Danish Navy. And the situation worsened day by day. Fair compensation would be a thousand rigsdalers, plus another hundred for the damage to his reputation.

A ROBE OR A MAN?

Henrietta Cathrina still refused to be involved in the court proceedings and made no response to Beyer's arguments, but on 8 February her advocate Bierring launched his offensive, submitting a detailed rejoinder to the defense's arguments. First, he admonished Beyer for his sarcastic tone of voice, which he called an "attack" on Henrietta Cathrina; it was childish rather than clever and did not help his client's case, he said. Second, he claimed that innumerable laws and decrees made provision for the existence of slavery in the West Indies, and thus the enslaved must be the master's property. He would demonstrate, he proclaimed, that Hans Jonathan was truly the plaintiff's slave.

With regard to whether the property rights still existed if a slave was transported to Denmark, Bierring used an analogy that probably traveled better than most wines, and perhaps better than the slaveowner's right itself: "In the same way I could say to Mr. Beyer, if I met him in one of the provinces, 'Well, you have paid for the robe you have on, but you took possession of it first in Copenhagen, and since we are not in that city, your right of ownership over the robe ceases, and I might just as well take it for my own as leave it with you.'"[4] Bierring concluded by saying that Hans Jonathan had in fact undermined his own case by stating that the crown prince had "granted" him his freedom.

On 15 February, Beyer submitted another statement in Hans Jonathan's defense. The plaintiff, said Beyer, had still not produced one iota of evidence that she owned the defendant: the decrees and laws cited by Bierring established only that it was lawful to transport native blacks from Africa's Guinea coast to the Danish West Indies and that such property was subject to taxes. In the first place, Beyer proclaimed, Hans Jonathan was not black but a mulatto, the son of a black mother and a white father. Second, Hans Jonathan had not been transported from the Guinea Coast but was born on St. Croix, according to the plaintiff's own testimony, and thus was subject to different laws. Finally, Beyer suggested, it was "morally inconceivable" that Hans Jonathan could be a slave, as transport of slaves from the West Indies had been prohibited by a royal decree of 10 May 1792.

The decree cited by Beyer was the Forordning om Negerhandelen (Regulations on the Negro Trade) of 16 March 1792. It is undeniably odd that the defense counsel should misquote the date, as well as the contents, of the decree, which played such a key role in his argument. The regulations comprise six brief clauses.[5] The first clause provided that, effective 1 January 1803, slave *trading* outside the Danish West Indies would be prohibited. The final clause provided that, effective 1 January 1795, it was prohibited to *transport* slaves from the Danish West Indies. Hans Jonathan was probably still on St. Croix when the regulations were issued in 1792, but by the time the crucial clause took effect in 1795 he was already living in Copenhagen.

THE QUESTION THAT CANNOT BE ASKED

When the advocates had made their arguments, witnesses were called. Henrietta Cathrina's attorney questioned them in order to clarify key points of his case, especially with regard to Hans Jonathan's origins and conduct. The witnesses were all in Henrietta Cathrina's service: Emilia Regina; her friend Sabina, and Juliane, Sabina's daughter; the laborer Michael; Hansen the steward; and coachman Nicolai, "all resident at the home of the plaintiff on Amaliegade near the Public Hospital." The witnesses were summoned to appear in the first chamber of the city courthouse. The court had a number of chambers, each with its own supervising judge and court reporter and its own cases. The chambers were not large, with space only for the judges, the witness, and the court reporter. Cases were primarily conducted in writing, without oral arguments, and not in public.

On Monday 1 March 1802, court officers met with Hans Jonathan in the jail on the corner of Gammeltorv and Nytorv to inform him of the forthcoming examination of witnesses. He appears to have been present at some of the proceedings. How must he have felt as he entered the courthouse and went into the chamber, where he sat face to face with one witness after another? The two lawyers took turns, Bierring posing the first set of questions: he wanted to know when Hans Jonathan was born, how his mother related to the widow Schimmelmann. He asked whether Hans Jonathan had come to Copenhagen with his mother, where they stayed, whether Hans Jonathan had been confirmed, and if so, in what church. Finally he asked about Hans Jonathan's conduct in his mistress's home, especially in recent years, and why he ran away. Bierring's questions were first put to Emilia Regina.

Emilia Regina immediately stated that she understood Danish, that she had been confirmed, and that she was Hans Jonathan's mother. Her answers to Bierring's questions were recorded as follows by the court reporter:

> The witness came to Denmark from St. Croix in the West Indies with her master the late General Major Schimmelmann and the plaintiff, his wife. As to what year the witness came here, she cannot be more exact than to say that it was the year the Russian warships overwintered here. The court annotated that this was in 1788. Her son, the defendant, who was house negro to the late General Major Schimmelmann and his wife in the West Indies, came here two or three years after the witness. She cannot remember with complete certainty how old the defendant, her son, was when he came here, but she says he was four or five years old when the witness came here.[6]

Emilia Regina is suspiciously vague about the date of her arrival in Copenhagen and about when Hans Jonathan joined her. Perhaps she was being as uncooperative as she dared. But there is nothing imprecise about her response to the question about Hans Jonathan's confirmation:

> The defendant, the witness's son, was baptized in Christiansted in the West Indies but confirmed in the Garrison Church here in the city two years ago, as far as the witness recalls. The witness now showed a note on which was written that on the 12th of April, 1784, Regina's son was born and baptized in the Danish Church by

Mr. Øhm and named Hans Jonathan, whereupon the witness made known that she had not written this and cannot write, but that the plaintiff had written this at the witness's request, shortly after the defendant was born.[7]

How did Emilia Regina come to be carrying a note that her mistress had written when Hans Jonathan was born? It is interesting to note the emphasis on establishing beyond doubt that Hans Jonathan was baptized and confirmed. Why are six witnesses called to testify that these Christian rituals have taken place, while no other questions are asked about the conditions under which Hans Jonathan lived? The reason is that under Danish law, only an individual who had been baptized could be deemed a "person" and, if both confirmed and a free man, could act autonomously.

From the viewpoint of Henrietta Cathrina's advocate, however, the next question, about Hans Jonathan's conduct—especially in recent years—was perhaps the most important. Emilia Regina was careful in her answer. "The witness is not aware," the scribe wrote, "that the defendant, her son, has behaved other than well in his masters' service. What gave rise to the respondent going away from his mistress, the witness does not know, but other negroes in this country left their masters during the conflict between Denmark and England, and the respondent likewise left his mistress."

When it was Beyer's turn to ask questions, the case took an unexpected turn. "Who is the defendant's father?" Hans Jonathan's lawyer asked. "Was he a free white man or a slave?" It is hard to see what difference an answer to these questions could have made. As Bierring had already pointed out, and as Beyer surely knew, the owner of a female slave automatically owned her children, no matter who the father was. Could Beyer have hoped that the father, a respectable (white) man, or some member of his family, would come to Hans Jonathan's aid? Was this just one aspect of his attack on the alleged "ownership" of Hans Jonathan? Or did he intend to provoke Henrietta Cathrina by insinuating that the father may have been General Schimmelmann?

Before Emilia Regina could answer the question, Bierring objected to it as "irrelevant." Beyer persisted, demanding an answer, saying, "It has not been resolved whether the child of a slave woman was a slave, if the father was a free man." Bierring did not yield, and the court concluded that "it could not dismiss Mr. Bierring's objection and permit the witness to answer the question that was posed to her, as it was irrelevant to the case."

The moment passed, and Henrietta Cathrina's lawer went on to question the other witnesses. The steward, Hansen, gave an interesting answer to the question of why Hans Jonathan had run away:

> The witness has certainly noticed that the defendant, Hans Jonathan, has gone out carousing once or twice and has been away from home without permission, but the witness has not noticed any disloyalty or suchlike in him. The reason that the defendant ran away from the plaintiff was that the plaintiff confronted him, after he had been out of the house without permission, and rapped him a few times with a Spanish stick, whereupon the defendant went away and, like many others, "took the king's shilling" [15 rigsdalers] to serve on the Royal ships against the English fleet which lay in the Sound.[8]

As the testimony continued, Hans Jonathan's lawyer seemed to be losing the case. Some of his questions made no sense. Was Emilia Regina, Beyer asked, really Hans Jonathan's mother? Perhaps Beyer felt that the witnesses were not saying anything significant and that questioning was pointless. And, strangely, he somehow omitted to submit to the court—or was asked not to submit—the letter from Crown Prince Frederik supporting Hans Jonathan's claim to freedom. All Hans Jonathan's references to the letter thus appeared unreliable and even absurd. The court was astonished: was this mulatto boy, the Schimmelmanns' slave, claiming to have a letter from the prince himself? Prince Frederik, regent of Denmark, was a powerful man; one would expect his word to have at least as much influence as that of the sugar barons. Why was Captain Bille, to whom the letter was addressed, not called as a witness?

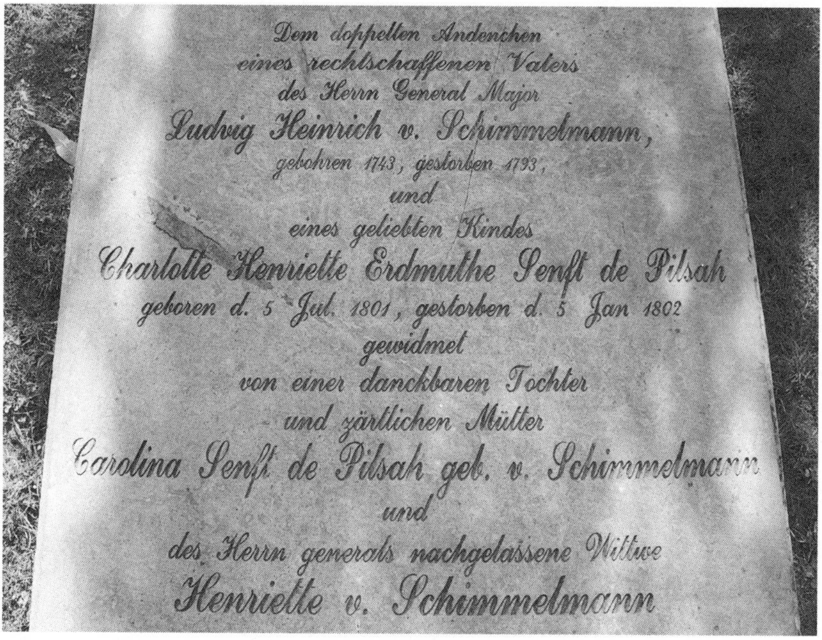

Dem doppelten Andenchen
eines rechtschaffenen Vaters
des Herrn General Major
Ludvig Heinrich v. Schimmelmann,
gebohren 1743, gestorben 1793,
und
eines geliebten Kindes
Charlotte Henriette Erdmuthe Senft de Pilsah
geboren d. 5 Jul. 1801, gestorben d. 5 Jan 1802
gewidmet
von einer danckbaren Tochter
und zärtlichen Mutter
Carolina Senft de Pilsah geb. v. Schimmelmann
und
des Herrn generals nachgelassene Wittwe
Henriette v. Schimmelmann

FIG. 9.1. Grave of L. H. Schimmelmann at Garnison Church, Copenhagen. (Photo: Gisli Palsson.)

THE VERDICT

THE WITNESSES' TESTIMONY was submitted to the court on 31 March 1802. Advocates Bierring and Beyer gave brief responses to it, although the testimony had yielded nothing unexpected. Judge Ørsted drafted a verdict, summarizing the arguments of his fellow judges, after which the five judges conferred. The case was concluded on 31 May, when the judges assembled in the courthouse on the corner of Østergade and Pilestræde, wearing their dark formal gowns, in order to hand down their verdict. Hans Jonathan was in court, dressed in a blue cloak, waiting to hear his fate. It was as follows:

> On those grounds the Court [rules]: the plaintiff, Henrietta, wife of General Major Schimmelmann, shall be entitled for fifteen days after this judgment's legal declaration, her behavior sanctioned by law, to transport the defendant, the mulatto Hans Jonathan, as her slave to the West Indies, and the arrest effected on the defendant's person (according to the requisition by the plaintiff of 3 December last year) on the same date, shall stand as lawful by the powers that be.[1]

The verdict was not surprising. Two days earlier a similar conclusion had been reached in the case of David Tams. The principal distinction between the two cases was that Tams's master had bought him, while Hans Jonathan had been born into slavery. Both men were deemed, however, to be chattel. Hence it was lawful to send them back to the West Indies. This was a formal legal judgment, not an arbitrary response by a police officer or the caprice of a count or a general's widow: the Danish legal system had spoken. A man who owned nothing—not even himself—was in no position to try to appeal the verdict, although that was possible in theory.

After the verdict was read, Hans Jonathan was released. He had not been convicted of any criminal offense and had no sentence to serve. The court had simply confirmed that he was a slave, property of Henrietta Cathrina Schimmelmann. He was to give himself up within fifteen days, unless he opted to appeal.

The verdict would give rise to vigorous debate among lawyers, but for Hans Jonathan the conclusion was stark. He must have found it hard to cope with his disappointment. He had been living in Copenhagen for ten years—more than half his life. He had served his country with honor in naval battle, and he had made many friends, some of them in high places. He thought he had gained his freedom, permitted to do so by the changing times in the city. But his connections had not helped his case. The judges were unanimous in their verdict, although they disagreed somewhat on the grounds: Hans Jonathan had been Henrietta Cathrina Schimmelmann's property from birth, in accordance with West Indian law; his arrest was lawful; and his owner was legally permitted to transport him back to the West Indies as a slave and to sell him there.

The judges' arguments and verdict are a function of the legal thinking of their time, and Hans Jonathan had certainly been permitted some rights in court. Yet aspects of the case are almost farcical—the choice of witnesses, in particular the absence of Captain Bille; the insinuations about the prince's letter; the distracting question about the identity of Hans Jonathan's mother—as if the verdict was a foregone conclusion. Overtly or covertly, Henrietta Cathrina must have enjoyed the backing of the Schimmelmann business empire, which had leverage throughout the administrative system—and even far beyond Denmark itself. Freedom and slavery were subject to their own rules: under the law, human rights within the Danish empire were contingent on geography and skin color.

Henrietta Cathrina may have seen the verdict as a moral victory—for the time being at least. But in the long run it gave rise to more problems than it resolved. She was not able to send "her" mulatto out of the country within the fifteen days provided in the verdict—or at least she did not do so. In accordance with the verdict, Henrietta Cathrina had two options: she could request official intervention and have Hans Jonathan arrested again for dereliction of duty, or she could do nothing. She apparently chose the latter option. Perhaps Henrietta Cathrina had been trying to teach Hans Jonathan a lesson by threatening him, a favored strategy among elite slave owners in North America and elsewhere.

The lawsuit may also, for her, have been a mistake. Hans Jonathan had grown up with her own children as their companion. Initially Henrietta Cathrina had tried to hush up the matter, but it had gradually gone beyond her control. Then, in the midst of her battle with Hans Jonathan, Henrietta Cathrina and her family suffered another shock. On 5 July 1801, her daughter Caroline had given birth to a baby girl, who was christened Henriette Charlotte, possibly after her grandmother and also Ernst Schimmelmann's wife. Six months later the child was dead.

Once the verdict was published in the official gazette, everyone in Copenhagen knew about the dispute between the general's widow and the mulatto. It offered a juicy scandal to be whispered about among the social elite who had frequented the Schimmelmann mansion at Amaliegade 23 and the grand country house at Sølyst—whether they felt for the widow's plight or sympathized with the persecuted slave and war hero. Perhaps it was to avoid the gossip that Henrietta Cathrina Schimmelmann and her family moved out of Copenhagen

FIG. 9.2.
The Schimmelmann mansion on Bredgade, Copenhagen. (Photo: Gisli Palsson.)

a year later; she died in Odense in 1816. The house at Amaliegade 23 was taken over by the Mothers' Aid Society next door, which expanded its services for unwed mothers.

As for Hans Jonathan, for some days after the verdict he remained at liberty in Copenhagen. He did not appeal, but neither did he give himself up within the required fifteen days. There is no indication that Henrietta Cathrina, or anyone else on her behalf, tried to track him down and arrest him. Once the verdict was given, he was apparently no longer of interest to the Copenhagen authorities—with one exception.

A month after the end of the case, the General Customs Office sent a letter to the governor of St. Croix, Ernst Frederik von Walterstorff, informing him of a rumor that a man named Hans Jonathan was to be sold on the island. The governor was requested to put the police on the alert: Hans Jonathan was regarded as likely to be a troublemaker.[2] The letter writer seems to have regarded Hans Jonathan as out of the ordinary—a rabble-rouser who might wreak havoc if he remained at liberty, perhaps even a threat to the Danish empire. This attitude toward individuals who challenged the system of slavery—whether in Europe or elsewhere—was fairly typical, but the customs officer need not have worried. For a long time nothing was known of the whereabouts of the slave, other than that he had not turned up on the plantation on St. Croix.

The General's Widow v. the Mulatto had several parallels in the colonial world. Britain, in particular, faced similar legal problems associated with slavery at home and in the colonies. In 1770 no fewer than fourteen to fifteen thousand slaves resided in the British Isles, in addition to an unknown number of free blacks—considerable numbers in comparison to the black population of Copenhagen at the time.[3] One of the interesting cases for comparison is *Somerset v. Stewart*. In 1772, three decades prior to the conclusion of the case of Hans Jonathan, Lord Mansfield, chief justice of the English Court of King's Bench, the highest common-law court in England, delivered an oral opinion in the case that would generate intense debates and legal scholarship throughout the Anglo-American world. The case involved a black man, James Somerset, who was born in Africa, taken to Virginia in 1749 by a slave owner, and later purchased by Charles Stewart. Somerset fled in 1771 while Stewart was away, but he was recaptured by his master, who arranged to sell him in Jamaica. Here, as in the case of Hans Jonathan, the key issue was the legality of ownership of humans in the metropole, on the one hand, and on the other hand in the colonies.

Lord Mansfield famously concluded that while the power of a master over his slave varied from one country to another, the "state of slavery is of such a nature, that it is incapable of being introduced on any reason, moral or political. . . . It's so odious that nothing can be suffered to support it."[4] Seeking to limit his judgment to the question of whether a person could be moved from one country to another against his or her will, Lord Mansfield concluded that "the black must be discharged."[5] This conclusion would inspire abolitionists, but slave owners mounted a counteroffensive. In England the issue was laid to rest by parliamentary emancipation in 1833. Issued on the eve of the American Civil War, however, Lord Mansfield's brief statement sparked intense controversies for American judges. Given his conclusion, it seems, the case of Hans Jonathan would have been readily dismissed.

THE AFTERMATH

All but one of the judges in Hans Jonathan's case saw it in very simple terms: the property rights over slaves were a fact. These rights included a general entitlement to dispose of the property freely— including the right to transport a slave from one country to another— although there were some restrictions and the owners had certain obligations when the property was human.

A dissenting opinion was put forward by the young judge Anders Sandøe Ørsted. While the laws of the Danish West Indies could not be challenged, he said, that did not mean they applied unconditionally in Denmark itself. His view was that when a slave arrived in Denmark his or her condition of slavery was altered to lifelong servitude—a concept firmly established in Danish law. The status of the individual as a slave was not abolished by his or her move to Denmark but remained *in suspenso* until the slave returned to the colony. Meanwhile, for as long as they remained in Denmark, slaves were indentured servants.[6]

Ørsted's theory shows that he was astute and inventive, but he overlooked—or perhaps deliberately ignored—an important and fairly obvious issue, which was later pointed out: under Danish law indentured servitude was a relationship based on an *agreement* between two parties, even though they were far from equal. The nature of slavery meant that it could have no such basis. While the distinction between slavery and servitude might often be subtle, an indentured servant legally owned him- or herself, while the enslaved person did not.

Ørsted's dissenting opinion soon attracted criticism. A young and daring jurist, Tage Algreen-Ussing, wrote a book in which he denounced Ørsted's views, as well as the verdict of the court. Algreen-Ussing argued that slavery in the West Indies entailed a use of force that was irreconcilable with justice. No legal provision explicitly permitted such a use of force, and hence it must be deemed unlawful.[7] He also addressed the fundamental differences between the rights of a slave and those of an indentured servant.

Algreen-Ussing and Ørsted continued their (sometimes heated) exchanges for a time, using Hans Jonathan's fate to hone their forensic skills. Readers have observed that while Ørsted cited certain foreign laws (for instance English and Prussian) to support his arguments, he never referred to a French decree of 1794, made during the French Revolution, which declared that any slave arriving on French soil was automatically free.[8] Nor does he seem to have discussed the *Somerset v. Stewart* case, which would have provided a serious challenge to his reasoning and conclusions.

The verdict in case number 356/1801 has interested Danish jurists ever since and is still discussed today, as it raises fundamental issues regarding human trafficking and the ownership of human beings.[9] Thus many Danish lawyers are surprisingly familiar with the story of Hans Jonathan—or at least the Danish chapter of the tale.[10]

WHERE'S HANS?

Hans Jonathan's story has also inspired historical fiction. *Druknehuset* (2008, The drowning house) by Maria Helleberg, for instance, is based on Henrietta Cathrina's lawsuit and the drama that took place at Amaliegade 23. The author allows herself poetic license in the book, imaginatively filling in the gaps. The novel is set in Copenhagen in 1807, by which time Hans Jonathan was long gone. It is told through the point of view of Victor, an enslaved man in the household of Henrietta Cathrina. Victor "knew [his mistress] inside out. It was said that she had pursued her husband's black lover, Emilia, and the son he had had with Emilia. The youth disappeared just after the Battle of Copenhagen and ran away from slavery. Wherever he may have landed thereafter, Victor wished him all the best."[11] That was the question. Where was Hans Jonathan? To the Danes, it seemed he had simply disappeared.

In 1964, more than a century and a half after the verdict was delivered in *The General's Widow v. the Mulatto*, Knud Waaben (1921–2008), a professor of criminal law at the University of Copenhagen, wrote a groundbreaking paper on the subject, skilfully outlining the key issues of the legal cases involving Hans Jonathan and David Tams, drawing attention to their continued significance for discussions of human rights. He addressed the circumstances and fate of both Hans Jonathan and David Tams, explaining the debates and the conclusions of the judges in terms of the conservative political culture of Denmark at the time and changing perspectives on race and slavery abroad. In his conclusion Waaben wonders what happened to Hans Jonathan and David Tams: "We do not know, therefore, whether the negroes were sent away. It may be that they had a chance to stay in Copenhagen. Even though they did not gain their freedom, they could have contented themselves with the conditions in the household of masters in a country whose legal system was not favorable to them, but where it was otherwise very good to be."[12] Waaben knew nothing of what had happened to Hans Jonathan, and neither did anyone else in Denmark until much later, around the turn of the twenty-first century, when one of Hans Jonathan's Icelandic descendants visited Waaben and explained who he was.

How did Hans Jonathan get to Iceland? He may have been able to join the crew of a merchant ship, perhaps thanks to his friends in the navy or to some Danish acquaintance with connections in the Iceland trade. Perhaps one of the Ludvigs in the Moltke family lent a helping hand. And when he set off for Iceland, he may not necessarily have intended to settle there.

Hans Jonathan must have heard about Iceland or read about the country. Perhaps when he was a child on St. Croix and his master's father, Jacob Schimmelman, published his translation into German of the Old Icelandic masterpiece the *Prose Edda* of Snorri Sturluson, with its tales of Norse mythology, the idea of Iceland lodged in his mind. Perhaps as a young man he met Icelanders in the Copenhagen bars, which were popular with students.

We do not know if Hans Jonathan had the chance to say good-bye to his mother and his friends in Copenhagen before he made his escape, but he managed to retrieve his violin and most likely some other belongings, including a clay pot his mother is reported to have brought to Copenhagen. It is unlikely that he remained in the city for long after the verdict was pronounced. It would have been hard for him to hide.

Beyer, Hans Jonathan's attorney, did not always display a gift for rhetoric, and sometimes he tripped himself up. Once, however, he hit the nail on the head. He and Henrietta Cathrina's lawyer had disagreed, among other things, on whether the Copenhagen police had denied Henrietta Cathrina's initial request and refused to arrest Hans Jonathan before the Battle of Copenhagen. The duty of the police was to resolve thefts and to safeguard people's property, said Beyer. "Had the chief constable considered the defendant the complainant's property, he would have been of assistance to her in apprehending and returning him to his owner, for then the respondent would have stolen himself from the complainant, and it is part of the police's duties to find and help an owner repossess things that have been stolen from them."[13]

Since March of 1801, Hans Jonathan had been beaten with a cane and had run away. He had been accused of stealing two hundred rigsdalers from his foster brother—half the price of a slave at West Indian values. He had answered Crown Prince Frederik's call to arms and fought aboard ship in the Battle of Copenhagen, earning fifteen rigsdalers. He had been locked up in his mistress's garden. He had served again in the navy, found a champion in Captain Bille, and been freed by a letter from the crown prince himself. He had lived as a free man in Copenhagen for more than six months, then spent another six months in jail. He had been through a grueling court case and heard his freedom denied. And now, in the summer of 1802, he had stolen himself.

Plantasien Constitution Hill paa St Croix   *August 1833*

PLATE I. The Constitution Hill plantation, 1833. (Frederik von Scholten, by permission of M/S Museet for Søfart, Helsingør, Denmark.)

PLATE 2. The harbor at Christiansted, St. Croix. (H. G. Beenfeldt [1767–1829], by permission of M/S Museet for Søfart, Helsingør, Denmark.)

PLATE 3. Heinrich Carl Schimmelmann and Caroline Tugendreich, around 1773–79. (Lorenz Lönberg; Museum of National History, Frederiksborg, Denmark.). (Photo: Hans Petersen.)

PLATE 4. The Battle of Copenhagen, 1801. (1901; C. Mølsted; Royal Danish Naval Museum, Copenhagen.)

PLATE 5. The ruins at Borgargardur, Djupivogur, Iceland. (Photo: Gisli Palsson.)

PLATE 6. "The races of men; from Southern Territories, dark people (Blamenn), also called Negroes." (From a manuscript written by Jon Bjarnason between 1845 and 1852; The National and University Library of Iceland.)

PLATE 7. Memorial service, Denmark, 2001. (Photo: Alex Frank Larsen.)

PLATE 8. Meeting of Icelandic and American descendants of Hans Jonathan in Djupivogur, Iceland, 1985. Left to right: Holger Eiriksson, Kristjan Jonsson, Roberta Eiriksson Dollase, Bjorn Jonsson, and Emil Bjornsson. (Courtesy of Roberta Dollase.)

| III |

ICELAND

FIG. 10.1. Djupivogur around 1820. (From Poul de Lovenorn, *Beskrivelse over den Iislandske Kyst og alle Havn* [Copenhagen, 1822].)

A FREE MAN

IN THE EARLY NINETEENTH CENTURY, travel to and from Iceland assumed a fairly regular pattern.[1] During the winter months drift ice made the sea journey too risky, but by May the ice had cleared, and Danish merchant ships would set sail for the colony in the North Atlantic. At the end of the short Icelandic growing season they returned to Copenhagen; around October the last of the Danish ships departed. The vessels usually had a capacity of 30–48 tons. The crew might number between three and seven, and the sea passage took about two weeks, unless disrupted by weather or the intervention of customs officers or coast guards.

The merchant ships usually carried a handful of passengers—perhaps Icelandic students or Danes employed in the Iceland trade. These were not slave-and-sugar vessels, like the ship Hans Jonathan had taken from the West Indies as a boy. Leaving the city, Hans Jonathan probably felt much as the Scottish missionary Ebenezer Henderson did when he traveled to Iceland some years later; the two men were of an age, and their paths would later cross in eastern Iceland. Wrote Henderson, "There was something peculiarly gratifying in the idea, that our vessel, instead of proceeding on any predatory or murderous expedition, was freighted with provisions for the inhabitants of a barren island; grain, and other articles for the support of temporal life."[2]

As his ship passed through the Øresund Sound between Helsingør and Helsingborg, Hans Jonathan would have marked the flags of many nations fluttering over the anchorage, where all vessels had to stop to pay a toll. Hans Jonathan was leaving behind the multicultural society of continental Europe as he set off across the North Sea and into the North Atlantic. In due time the ship sailed through the Fair Isle Gap between Orkney and Shetland, then on past the Faroes, taking the most direct route to Iceland, to call at Papey Island off the southeast coast before reaching port at Djupivogur. Hans Jonathan's knowledge of seamanship may have been useful, although he had never been in these northern seas before.

And then, *land ho!* On the horizon, an unfamiliar sight: high, craggy mountains and a towering white mass of glaciers. The island itself gradually rose into view above the horizon. As the ship sailed closer to shore, it was possible to see Papey Island; behind it, the striking pyramidal peak of Mount Bulandstindur; and farther east the legendary Godaborg (Gods' Fortress) cliffs. It is said that after the adoption of Christianity in Iceland around AD 1000, the new converts carried their heathen idols up onto Godaborg and flung them into the sea.

The days were long and bright during this summer journey in the north, where the midnight sun shines from May to August. With every nautical mile he put behind him, Hans Jonathan was getting closer to freedom. He must have felt it, as his dark days as a slave, prisoner, and fugitive gave way to hopes of a better life ahead. He must also have known that now there was no turning back; he would never see his mother again.

The ship slowly approached Papey Island, where the small landing place and the rough scrubland beyond must have struck him as wild and exotic. There were buildings on the flat land above the shoreline. The tiny island was home to an extended family of fifteen people.

The seabirds were loud and lively. They were all around, crying out in a deafening din. Hans Jonathan would never have heard

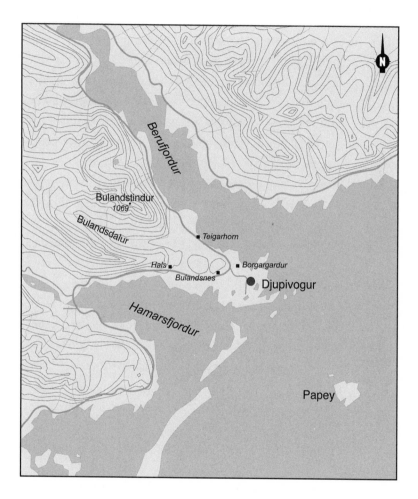

FIG. 10.2. Djupivogur and neighborhood.

anything like it—not in Denmark and not even on St. Croix. The cliffs of Papey Island were crowded with birds of many species, as was the sea all around. Hans Jonathan would not have recognized many of them, but in due course he would learn their names. In Iceland he would see no flamingos, pelicans, parakeets, or hummingbirds; instead he would grow accustomed to razorbills and guillemots, puffins and kittiwakes, eiderducks and gannets. Some traversed the calm surface of the sea at high speed, while others flew high into the sky to fling themselves hurtling down into the sea as they hunted for prey. Gannets splashed into the water like feathered cannonballs. Did Hans Jonathan flinch, recalling the great sea battle off Copenhagen? Farther inland other birdsongs were heard: golden plover, oystercatcher, snipe, and arctic tern. Their whistles and trills resounded from the rocks. Was this a symphony of destiny for the young slave, breathing the air of freedom?

Once Hans Jonathan's ship was safely in the bay, it dropped anchor, and the crew, the passengers and their luggage, and the cargo were ferried ashore in small boats. Would Hans Jonathan be free here, with the ocean and the Danish Empire on one side, the mountains and cliffs on the other? Wearing his blue cloak, he stepped onto Icelandic soil near Langabud, the general store—a wooden building that is still standing today. Under his arm he carried a violin.

DJUPIVOGUR

The small port of Djupivogur stands near the mouth of the Berufjordur in southeastern Iceland. Hanseatic merchants from northern Germany traded at Djupivogur in the fifteenth century. It provided a good landing place for boats, and the fjord had abundant fish stocks—important as a food source but also as a commodity. In 1589 the Germans set up shop at Djupivogur. In 1602, however, the king of Denmark imposed a trade monopoly on Iceland, after which the Germans were excluded and Icelanders could trade only with Danish merchants. Even after the monopoly was abolished in name in 1787, the Iceland trade remained confined to subjects of the Danish realm until 1854, when free trade was granted.

New ideas were emerging about commerce in Denmark. The mercantilist principles by which the state and the colonies had been governed gave way to a new economic theory: physiocracy. Physiocracy, developed in France and influenced by the Englishman Adam Smith's libertarian ideas about the "invisible hand" of the free market, highlighted the productive value of land rather than gold, paving the way for modern economic theory.

When the Danish trade monopoly in Iceland was abolished (in name at least), it was followed by a period of "free commerce" during which the crown sold off licenses to trade in specific ports. The license holders were entitled to a range of benefits, including tax privileges and interest-free credit. Merchants and their managers were provided with buildings, ships, and goods on very favorable conditions. But of all the licensed merchants in Iceland, only three were Icelanders; the rest were Danes.[3] Many of those who had acquired trading licenses in Iceland went back to Copenhagen once they had their businesses up and running, leaving them in the hands of managers, known as "factors."

This system worked well for the Danish owners, such as the Copenhagen-based J. L. Busch merchant business, which owned the general store at Djupivogur; with its headquarters in Denmark it could also trade with other countries. The liberating "invisible hand" had no noticeable effect in Iceland, and the market remained tightly controlled by Denmark. Many Icelanders in the early 1800s—farmhands, tenants, and laborers—had little more freedom than the black and mulatto slaves in the fields of the West Indies, although, of course, it was one thing to be a servant and quite another to be somebody's property.[4] Sometimes after the abolition of slavery in the West Indies, "free" laborers, black and white, were subjected to brutal practices of bondage and domination that in many respects replicated those of slavery.

When Hans Jonathan arrived in Djupivogur, he was unaware of

FIG. 10.3. Djupivogur, late nineteenth century. (Photo: Nicoline Marie Elise Weywadt. National Museum of Iceland, Reykjavik.)

a traumatic chapter in local history which had undoubtedly colored the residents' attitude toward outsiders.[5] In the summer of 1627, Barbary pirates from Algeria raided the east coast of Iceland. Since Algeria then belonged to the vast Ottoman Empire, the pirates were known in Iceland as "Turks." A brief contemporary account of the events appears in *Skard Annals*: "Raid on the East Fjords by Turks. They seized a merchant ship at Djupivogur in Berufjordur, with all its goods. They also drove livestock and people down to their ships, killed people, and chopped them in pieces."[6]

The Algerian corsairs went from farm to farm, capturing dozens of people, tying them up, and taking them to their ships. When they reached the parsonage at Hals, the household was all up at the summer pastures tending their livestock, but the pirates tracked them down. After the attack on Berufjordur they sailed around to the Westman Islands off Iceland's south coast. The place where they landed

FIG. 10.4. Djupivogur harbor, late nineteenth century. (Photo: Nicoline Marie Elise Weywadt. National Museum of Iceland, Reykjavik.)

is still known as Raiders' Point. Once again they took captives, while killing and mutilating other islanders. Hundreds were transported to northern Africa that summer to be sold on the slave markets. Some were eventually ransomed, and at least twenty-seven lived to return home to tell of their extraordinary adventures in "Barbary."[7]

The story of 1627, when the "Turks" ravaged the peaceful countryside and took people away in shackles, remained vivid in local memory in 1802 when Hans Jonathan arrived; it is not forgotten even today. Did it affect Hans Jonathan's reception in any way? To the people of Djupivogur was he "the mulatto," as he was called in Copenhagen, just another Dane? Or did he seem exotic, like the "barbarians" who had run wild nearly two centuries before? Or did the local people sympathize with him, since they knew what it meant to be enslaved captives? We cannot say. But whatever their initial reaction, the locals soon accepted Hans Jonathan as himself.

The hamlet of Djupivogur lay within the parish of Hals, which, according to the census of 1801, had a total population of 115. It was rather Danish in character. Although the environment was spectacularly different from what he knew, some of what Hans Jonathan found there would have been familiar: the general store itself, Danish customs and manners, and Danish-influenced personal names. Many of Iceland's trading centers were more or less Danish communities where Danish was the first or second language.

In the late eighteenth century there were twenty-five of these in Iceland, seven of them on the north and east coasts. They were sometimes termed "meat ports" (literally slaughterhouse ports) to distinguish them from the fishing ports. Under the monopoly system, merchants were obliged to sail to Iceland each year with necessities, such as grain, timber, iron, and sugar, and to buy the Icelanders' commodities, such as wool cloth and dried fish, in return. The system provided the Icelanders—who had no wood with which to build oceangoing vessels of their own—with a basic level of security in trade, and many officials profited personally from it.[8] But it left average Icelanders at the mercy of the merchants, forced to accept whatever they offered for Icelandic goods and to pay whatever price they demanded for their imported commodities; from the middle of the eighteenth century this led to rising discontent.

Some of the merchants at the Djupivogur store were particularly unpopular. One such was Georg Andreas Kyhn (1749–1828). He held the post for ten years, from 1778 to 1788, having assisted the previous manager, Christian F. A. Wulff, and married his daughter. Kyhn's problems were largely of his own making. Before he became manager, he argued with the subassistant, Jens Ørum, as a result of which Ørum left for Reykjavik. There, in partnership with Jens Andreas Wulff, he founded the trading company Ørum & Wulff, which would play an important role in commerce in Iceland—and in Hans Jonathan's future.[9] Kyhn's marriage did not last; he lived the high life, was an arrogant man, got involved in extensive lawsuits, and spent the last twenty-two years of his life in prison in Copenhagen. Judge

Magnus Stephensen, president of the Icelandic High Court, referred to him in a letter in 1821 as "argumentative, malevolent, and impervious to reason."[10]

AMONG BOOKLOVERS

Probably Hans Jonathan's first action on arriving in Iceland was to call on the manager of the Djupivogur general store, the Icelander Jon Stefansson (often written Stephensen or Steffensen to give his name a more cosmopolitan air). Hans Jonathan seems to have been engaged as his apprentice that very day; the arrangements may have been made by Hans Jonathan's friends and wellwishers before he even arrived in Iceland. Like anyone else, though, Hans Jonathan would need to learn his trade. It is likely that the requirements for being a shop apprentice had been relaxed after the abolition of the trade monopoly, but apprentices were still obliged to undergo commercial training. Many people—whether in Iceland or in Denmark—who had opposed the abolition of the monopoly system warned against a too-rapid changeover, as "real free trade would be unthinkable in Iceland until a class of people had emerged, equipped with sufficient knowledge and resources to undertake commerce."[11]

The trading post at Djupivogur had developed into a small hamlet by this time and probably included the following buildings: a draper's store selling textiles; the merchant's home; the cooper's workshop, called Siberia for some unknown reason; the general store, later known as Langabud (literally, Long Booth); a slaughterhouse; and a warehouse.[12] According to a local census, in 1801 the manager's household included seven people: Jon (1767–1819) and his Danish wife, Ellen Katrin; their two-year-old daughter Bolletta Kathrina; two workmen and two housemaids. This was to be Hans Jonathan's new working environment.

Outside the hamlet, he would come across zeolites—beautiful, and valuable, crystalized stones that had long been prized by collectors. But the countryside was marshy and difficult to traverse. Life had taught Hans Jonathan that vessels and people could be lost at sea; now he was in a place where it was possible to sink without trace in a bog on dry land.

He might also have found Icelandic a strange language, with its difficult grammar and declensions. In his day-to-day work he dealt with many people who spoke Danish, as that was the language of the ruling class and the merchants were predominantly Danes. But while all Icelanders had business with the Danish traders from time to time, the majority spoke only their mother tongue. As a child Hans Jonathan had lived in the multilingual environment of St. Croix; he must have quickly gained command of Icelandic. Before long he would have adopted the local vocabulary for describing his surroundings: Nordurland (Northland) lay to the northwest of Djupivogur, Sudurland (Southland) to the south and west, and Utland (Outland) to the south and east.

The first autumn after Hans Jonathan's arrival in Iceland was heralded by blizzards and such heavy snow that it was hardly possible to get from one house to the next, let alone to travel into the countryside or to visit other ports. Such weather conditions were entirely new for Hans Jonathan, and the blue cloak he had brought from Copenhagen would not have sufficed to keep him warm through the winter. Climate is sometimes said to influence character and even personality. How did the Icelandic climate affect Hans Jonathan? Perhaps the challenge of the weather helped him to take his final steps toward freedom. Part of his life journey had consisted of changing himself, of standing up for himself and looking the world boldly in the face. It was one thing to run away, quite another to become his own master, at peace with himself.

His new employer, Jon Stefansson, from Breiddalur in eastern Iceland, showed him the way. Jon is said to have been "a great bookman."[13] He founded a reading association and established a lending library for the hamlet. He collected manuscripts that would go on to form the foundation of the Icelandic Literary Society's collection in Copenhagen; tragically, most of the medieval manuscripts were later destroyed by fire. Jon was a talented poet. He enjoyed singing, and long after his death his drinking songs remained perennial favorites in Iceland's East Fjords.[14]

The Scottish missionary Ebenezer Henderson spent two days at Djupivogur in 1815. Like many travelers, he called on the merchant and his wife. "Madame Stephensen, whose father is a Norwegian clergyman," he writes, "received and treated me in the kindest and most hospitable manner. I had a large room assigned to me for my lodging, in which I was surprised to find a pretty voluminous circulating library, . . . for the cultivation of different branches of science."[15]

Jon Stefansson became Hans Jonathan's mentor and benefactor. The two worked together for seventeen years, until Jon's death in 1819. Jon and his wife, Ellen Katrin, must have enjoyed the opportunity to converse about Denmark and the West Indies with the young man from Copenhagen. And surely he must have appreciated the couple's company—and their library. Once again he found himself in a cultured home that had something in common with the Schimmelmanns' grand mansion in Copenhagen. But here his status was quite different: he was not a slave, or even a servant, but a promising young commercial assistant who might rise to be manager in his own right.

A collection of essays translated by Jon Stefansson from Danish into Icelandic between 1808 and 1809 survives.[16] Reflecting on the subject of slavery in Christendom, the author writes: "There can scarcely be a vice in the world more shameful than the slave trade—to sell one's fellow men into slavery, like a horse or other beast." He goes on to criticize the prophet Moses in no uncertain terms: "For the Laws of Moses were not so made that slavery, or the buying and selling of slaves, should ever be abolished, but that a master should compensate a slave woman for his dealings with her. . . . But that recompense meant no more than that, when the master wearied of her, he should grant her her freedom, and allow her to go where she wanted. But when she was old and poor, who would then take her in?" The author objects to the biblical statement that it is blameless to

FIG. 10.5.
Manuscript written by *factor* John Stephensen (Jon Stefansson). (The National and University Library of Iceland.)

"sell one's fellow men and women into lifelong slavery." He goes on to comment that the Bible is indisputably responsible for the prevalence of this "shameful vice against Nature and Man" among nations that call themselves Christians.

The author is aware of the growing opposition to slavery in Europe. He writes of events in England in 1799, when "various noble-minded men tried to abolish in Parliament the human trade in slaves" but were defeated; when the matter came to a vote, "sixty-one favoured abolition, while sixty-eight wished this human infamy to continue." His essay concludes: "Now when human beings' wailing and their laments over their slavery in the West Indies reach to heaven, and the parents and kinsmen of those slaves in the Guinea Coast of Africa beg heaven for vengeance on these European human traffickers, clerics are to blame for having convinced the nations that these shameful laws are spoken by God himself."

It can be no coincidence that the store manager at Djupivogur undertook to translate into Icelandic a foreign essay about the slave trade on Africa's Gold Coast, slavery in the West Indies, and the woes of slaves on the sugar plantations there. The obvious conclusion is that Jon Stefansson and Hans Jonathan must have discussed the subject in depth.

Thanks to the medieval Icelandic Sagas, nineteenth-century Icelanders were aware of the practice of slavery in early Iceland and Scandinavia. The early settlers of Iceland, around AD 900, brought many slaves with them, mostly from the British Isles. These slaves had the right to marry, and their owners were sometimes anxious about supporting them as their numbers increased. Unwanted infants might even be left outside to die. Slavery in Iceland died out by stages without any formal declaration; by 1100 only a handful of Icelanders remained in slavery, although certain legal provisions for slavery were not repealed until much later. The reasons for the end of slavery continue to be debated, but given the rural economy and the small-scale farming of medieval Iceland, seasonal labor contracts came to seem more practical to landowners than permanent slavery.[17]

The African slave trade and the plantation economies in the West Indies were not well known to Jon Stefansson and his contemporaries, but they were not completely ignored. In 1788, for instance, during his stay in England, the Icelandic scholar Grimur Thorkelin published his *Essay on the Slave Trade*. Thorkelin, who is best known for his transcription and Latin translation of the Old English epic poem *Beowulf*, spent much of his career as chief archivist in Copenhagen. In his *Essay* he reflected on the practice of slavery in Europe, emphasizing—in contrast to Jon Stefansson—the beneficial role of Christianity in securing the rights of slaves and in abolishing the slave trade. For him, however, the enslavement of Africans, "who at present are sunk into ignorance," was a "necessary evil."[18] He wrote, "It is impossible for the inhabitants of the Gold Coast to live free from those evils which introduce Slavery. . . . It appears to me that the abolition of the Slave Trade is by no means advisable, with a view to Christian duty and benevolence, as it also appears impracticable in the light of political interest."[19]

AT BUSINESS

The heart of Djupivogur was the building now known as Langabud. In the early nineteenth century there were two separate structures:

a warehouse and a slaughterhouse. They were of equal width and stood end to end several yards apart. The buildings had been constructed on the foundations of older structures, the timbers largely reused with the addition of repurposed wood from other buildings. Some of the roof beams have decorative moldings, indicating that they came from high-quality buildings—perhaps dwellings or commercial premises. At the end of the nineteenth century the gap between the buildings was roofed over to combine them into a single long structure. The name Langabud probably dates from that time.[20] Business was carried out mostly on the ground floor of the building. Upstairs in the loft, under a steeply pitched roof, valuables were stored in a sturdy iron-bound chest. People also gathered in the loft for various reasons. Many have carved their names in the wooden boards, along with a date—as if signing a guest book or making note of some important event.

For many years Hans Jonathan's life was bound up with his work at Langabud. A number of commercial documents written by him survive: memoranda of transactions with customers, stock taking, and other aspects of his work. His ornate handwriting was a product of the Danish colonial bureaucracy—and his signature is as flamboyant as any seen on documents signed by the wealthy sugar barons on St. Croix when he was a boy. But not all sugar barons wrote so well: Baron von Prock, for instance, who had owned Hans Jonathan's mother, Emilia Regina, had a cramped and inelegant hand.

As in every community in Iceland, the local authorities in Djupivogur kept records of all the residents and their assets, noting their economic status and their duties toward the indigent. Residents in the district were classified as farmers, landless people, or "abiding there"—that is, indigent people, paupers, invalids, the senile, and the bedridden. According to these documents, Hans Jonathan became a mate on a sailboat around 1804. (Perhaps it belonged to the Djupivogur general store?) Classified as a landless workman, he is briefly mentioned in local records of 1808, when the "Assistant" made a donation for the poor.[21] In subsequent years he is registered as an

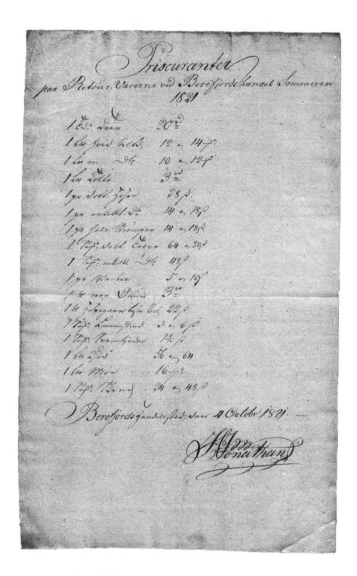

FIG. 10.6. Records of Hans Jonathan's transactions at the store in Djupivogur. (National Archives, Reykjavik.)

assistant and a workman, or as a "casual worker." His assets and his payments of the tithe to the church are recorded. At a regular meeting of the district council in 1810, to which both farmers and landless people were summoned, it was confirmed that Hans Jonathan owned a ewe, three yearling lambs, and a horse. The same assets are recorded the following year.

No documents survive for the next three years, but by 1815 Hans Jonathan owned four ewes, two yearling lambs, and one and a half boats. He may have co-owned one of the boats with his employer, Jon Stefansson, who is also recorded as owning one and a half. In 1817 Hans Jonathan owned two boats, probably the four-oared vessels named *Else* and *Delectation*, with one and two masts respectively: the shop assistant was spending his free time fishing.

Although he owned two boats, Hans Jonathan was not a wealthy man, and he was not subject to much tax, though he paid the required community tax and the dues for the poor. The records indicate that Hans Jonathan's position was unusual, as he was the only landless man who owned a boat. But he had established himself as a member of the community: he had his boats, kept a few animals, paid his taxes, and attended local meetings.

In 1819 Jon Stefansson fell ill and died, and his widow left Djupivogur and returned to Denmark. Hans Jonathan's position changed greatly. The merchant corporation Ørum & Wulff, which had a general store in Eskifjordur, another East Fjords port, purchased the Djupivogur store and promoted Hans Jonathan to manager. He appears to have proved his ability by taking over Jon's work during his final illness and to have earned a good reputation in his seventeen years in business.

WAS HE SAFE?

It is highly likely that Hans Jonathan came up with the bright idea of "stealing" himself—as his attorney put it during the court proceedings in Copenhagen—shortly before he took his fate into his own

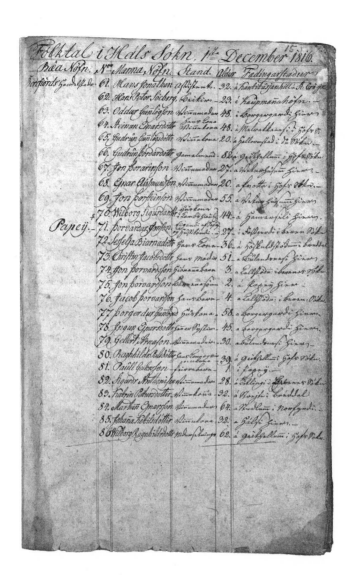

FIG. 10.7. Census of 1 December 1816. "Assistant Hans Jonathan, born on Kantitusjanhill, St. Cröjs." (National Archives, Reykjavik.)

hands and took ship for Iceland, where he would settle into a new environment, win respect, do good works, and make a name for himself in history. But was he not guilty of theft, or kidnapping—paradoxical as that may seem? Could one and the same person be both the object and the perpetrator of human trafficking? On his arrival in Iceland Hans Jonathan had two choices: he could conceal his true identity in order to evade discovery, or he could tell the truth without subterfuge. And he seems to have chosen the latter option, declaring himself a freed slave, formerly of "Kantitusjanhill, St. Croyx," as the local census would record.

He probably considered the risks minimal. After all, he had not been sentenced for anything, not even charged. Henrietta Schimmelmann had indeed been able to confirm, through her civil case, that he was her slave, but she would have had to take him back to the plantation world herself, or with the help of her servants, if she was still interested. In any case, the costs would probably have outweighed his value on the slave market in St. Croix. Also, things were changing in Copenhagen with respect to slavery, and time was on his side. Still, given the flaws of the courts in his case, under pressure from the sugar barons, he may have had nagging worries. In practice, on the other hand, he was a free man and an honorable one. Perhaps he passed, regarded as white or just as "one of us" by the locals of Djupivogur.

FIG. 11.1. Berufjord Pass, 2005. Jona Petra Magnusdottir, descendant of Hans Jonathan.
(Photo: Toggi [Thorgeir Eiriksson], 2005.)

MOUNTAIN GUIDE

HANS JONATHAN was not only valued by his employers. On two occasions he stood godfather to children baptized in the parish. He is
also said to have been outstandingly conscientious in dealing with
customers in the store. A story has been passed down that on one
occasion (and perhaps more than one) Hans Jonathan chased after a
customer who had left the shop, in order to rectify a mistake he had
made in giving change. In Djupivogur he was well known for always
correcting any error, even when he need not have done so and would,
in fact, have profited by keeping his mouth shut. He was quick on
his feet, well educated, and a good linguist, and he got to know new
people and places rapidly. All this made him an ideal travel guide for
visitors to Berufjordur like Gytha Thorlacius (1782–1861).

They first met in 1803, when Hans Jonathan had been in Iceland
for a year. Born in Denmark, Gytha was married to a young lawyer, Thordur Thorlacius, who was half-Icelandic. Thorlacius was
appointed district commissioner in South Mulasysla, in eastern Iceland. He was said to be "unpopular with the people and . . . one of
the harshest of all district commissioners."[1] After living for fourteen
years in Iceland, Gytha and her husband returned to Denmark in
1815. The year they left, Thorlacius was involved in an incident at the
trading station in Djupivogur. A local peasant was accused of, among

FIG. 11.2.
Gytha Thorlacius.

other things, acting disrespectfully toward the district commissioner and calling him "You dog!" Hans Jonathan was named as a witness.

About twenty-five years later Gytha started to write her memoirs, giving a perceptive and candid account of life in Iceland and Denmark. Her memoirs were published in Danish, considerably edited, by her son-in-law while she was still alive; they were republished in 1930, and in Icelandic translation in 1947.

Gytha Thorlacius had been not yet twenty years old when she moved to Iceland in 1801. The new country offered much that surprised her—and caused her problems. She was keen to encourage Icelanders to learn to grow vegetables and made many efforts in the East Fjords. Vegetables were not an important part of the Icelandic diet, partly because of the short growing season. Potato gardens, however, had become fashionable by the end of the eighteenth century. Some of Gytha's experiments were more successful than others, as the plants had to adapt to different soil, seasonal changes, and climatic conditions. On one occasion the crop failure was caused by man: while the Thorlaciuses were away, a farmer opened the gate to their vegetable garden and turned out his sheep to graze on their cabbage, rutabagas, chervil, and spinach. Many farmers regarded vegetable cultivation as a waste of land, believing that grassland for sheep (the pillar of the Icelandic agrarian economy) should always be given priority. Thorlacius took legal action against the farmer, who was ordered to pay a fine of two silver coins (*spesiur*) to the poor; this probably did not make the couple any more popular locally.[2] Despite such problems, Gytha's memoirs express affection for the people of Iceland.

Gytha's account of meeting Hans Jonathan in Iceland in 1803 must be regarded as one of the most reliable sources for his arrival in Iceland. Although she wrote her story many years later, her encounter with Hans Jonathan was connected in her mind to an unforgettable personal event—the birth of her son, who was to die at only two years old. Her husband was away when the boy was born on 13 May, but a few days later he returned home to Eskifjordur and celebrated the birth with his wife. According to Gytha he arrived by sea from Berufjordur, accompanied by a number of men in oilskins. Gytha recalls: "Several guests came with the district commissioner: merchant Jon Stefansson, merchant Busch, assistant Jonathan, and Ferslow, a cooper."[3] "Busch" was probably Eggert Christopher Busch (1782–1841), who was about the same age as Hans Jonathan, the representative of the Busch family who owned the store. Gytha points out that the event took place before the Danish merchant ships had arrived in Iceland that year. So Hans Jonathan must have arrived the previous summer, shortly after the conclusion of his court case.

In the autumn of 1808 Hans Jonathan and Gytha met again. Pregnant with her fifth child, Gytha set out on a journey from Eskifjordur to Djupivogur to meet her friend Ellen Katrin, the Danish wife of the store manager Jon Stefansson. Her husband, whose duties made it impossible for him to accompany her, hoped that she could bring back some necessary supplies for Christmas: "He wrote to merchant Jon Stefansson in Berufjordur and asked him to have his wife let us have a few pounds of grain, some rye biscuit, and a little coffee and sugar. He replied that his wife would let us have what we asked for, but asked us to come ourselves to fetch it, as they were so eager to see us and talk to us."[4]

The pregnant Gytha was nervous as she embarked on an arduous journey across the mountains with her attendant. "When we had gone a short distance from the house," she writes, "my attendant stopped, took off his hat, and held it before his face. As I looked back, I saw that the men in the farmyard were standing bareheaded, and the women with their hands before their faces, and they were praying for us—that our journey should have a happy outcome." This was not Gytha's first journey to Berufjordur: "As I crossed the Thordalsheidi heath," she writes, "I was always in a solemn mood, and on this occasion more than ever before." After staying the night in Skriddalur valley, she continued along the Oxi route to Berufjordur, where "I was very happy to be with my friends again."

Gytha enjoyed her friends' hospitality in Djupivogur for eight days before setting off for home. Ellen Katrin Stefansson and Hans Jonathan went with her part way:

> The merchant's wife and assistant Jonathan accompanied me for the first day's journey. They recommended taking a mountain route—but I soon regretted it. We had to ride along a high mountain. In one place there was a narrow path only wide enough for one person, eight or ten fathoms in length. The horses had to be driven across before us, during which sand and gravel tumbled down the mountainside. They all wanted me to cross first, and I too thought I could do it. But when I approached the place, and saw the abyss to my right and the rugged mountain close to my left, I seemed to take leave of my senses.[5]

Gytha took a little Communion wine to steady her nerves, but it did no good. Then Hans Jonathan took the initiative:

> Jonathan came up with the solution of walking backwards along the narrow path, holding me by the hands; and where the path was

narrowest he placed his foot crosswise, so as to make a wider place for me to tread. I placed my foot on his, keeping my eyes on the mountain to my left, so that I would not become dizzy by looking at the drop on the other side. God was kind to me, and I made the crossing safely. Although it is always regarded as a little risky to go by that narrow path, I think that the terror that overcame me was mostly due to my condition. That evening we reached Thorvaldsstadir in Breiddalur. We travelers slept that night in the barn, lying there in the hay—ladies in one corner, Jonathan and the escorts in another.[6]

To judge from Gytha's account, Hans Jonathan had a good head for heights. His chivalrous behavior under pressure is also striking. Gytha says no more of the man who kindly led her by the hands at this stressful point in their journey from one fjord to another while she fixed her eyes on the mountainside above.

When Gytha's memoirs were first published in Copenhagen in 1845, it seems that no one in Denmark made the connection between the "Jonathan" in her story and the runaway slave who had been the subject of a notorious court case roughly forty years before. Nor, apparently, did Gytha or anyone else in Iceland link the shop assistant at Djupivogur with the rebellious slave. And why should they? How could it occur to anyone that the Schimmelmanns' house slave, the mulatto from the West Indies, was the same person as the courteous, well-respected shop assistant in Iceland who guided travelers across the mountains in his spare time?

HANS FRISAK

Although merchant ships called at Berufjordur only during the spring and summer seasons, the area was far from being isolated. Merchant ships had visited since the Middle Ages, and many people made their way there for various purposes. Some were influenced by Enlightenment ideas, convinced that phenomena must be measured and documented and new truths proclaimed.[7] Among those who visited Iceland at this time were the Norwegian surveyor Hans Frisak, who trekked into the mountains and built cairns as landmarks, and the missionary Ebenezer Henderson, who traveled around laden with Bibles, preaching the Christian gospel of salvation. Each came across Hans Jonathan and wrote about the encounter. Hans Jonathan apparently relished the opportunity to be a guide. It brought in extra money, but it also brought him firsthand news of the outside world. Hans Jonathan was thus a pioneer of "cultural tourism" in the southeast of Iceland.

In 1800 the Danish Department of Finance decided to carry out an improved coastal survey of Iceland; the available maritime charts were inaccurate, and shipping was constantly at risk. A building was constructed in Reykjavik where the surveyors could store their equipment and make astronomical observations during the winter.[8] Intermittently from 1803 to 1818 the survey was carried out by Hans Frisak (1773–1834), his colleague Hans Jacob von Scheel, and a team of assistants. They built many cairns as triangulation points for the survey. Frisak stayed the night of 3 August 1812 with Jon Stefansson and his wife at Djupivogur. He was keen to go out to Papey Island and build a cairn there, but that had to be postponed.

In his unpublished journal Frisak writes that his guide was a shop assistant from the Langabud general store: "He is from the West Indies, and has no surname . . . but calls himself Hans Jonathan. He is very brown skinned, with coal- black woolly hair. His father is a European, but his mother is a negress. He was twelve years old when he came to Denmark from the West Indies with Governor Schimmelmann, and twenty-one when he came here [to Iceland] seven years ago."[9] Frisak is mistaken about the age at which Hans Jonathan arrived in Denmark from St. Croix; according to court documents he was younger than twelve. And the date of his arrival in Iceland (or his age at the time) also appears to be inaccurate, in view of Gytha Thorlacius's account.

Frisak and his surveyors had a hard time carrying out their work during the summer of 1812, due to the heavy fogs that are a typical feature of the East Fjords climate. The team would climb a promising hill and build a cairn, only to find that fog had descended and there was little or no visibility. On Mount Bulandstindur above Berufjordur it proved difficult even to build the cairn, as there was hardly a level patch anywhere on the mountain's steep rocky slopes. In addition, the fjord was full of drift ice—unusual for that time of year—so it was difficult to sail in or out of the harbor. Hans Jonathan guided the survey team through the uplands and mountains. On 6 August 1812 Frisak wrote in his journal: "The cairn on Papey Island was completed. In the afternoon I wrote some instructions for the stereometric calculations for Herr Steffensen, and then made a pencil drawing of a bird—a greeting to Hans Jonathan."[10] They had clearly forged a bond.

Two days later Frisak writes that "Mr Steffensen and Hans Jonathan . . . were so gallant as to accompany me along the way until 3 o'clock. How *extraordinarily* these people have behaved towards me." On 3 July the following year Frisak mentions his "gallant" new friends again: "Scheel, Stephensen, Hans Jonathan and I rode for 2 and a half hours to the deserted farm of Teigarhorn, which belongs to Stephensen, about a mile from the trading post. There are supposed to be magnificent stones sparkling in the fjord." Jon Stefansson helped Frisak pack some stones—perhaps zeolites—into boxes to be sent back to Copenhagen, and the following day he and Hans Jonathan accompanied Frisak to Hamarsfjordur: "For our farewell toast Stephensen contributed a bottle of wine from Tenerife, 3 glasses for each of us. Then we set off with these good men Stephensen and Hans Jonathan, and hurried across the fjord."[11]

Frisak was not equally impressed by all the Icelanders he met on his travels. In his work he had to rely on their assistance, but he complains that some were uncooperative and demanded too much money—although that may have been natural, as summer was a busy time on the farms. And he notes other vices than greed and indolence, recording his feelings about drunken clergy: "It is disgusting to see common people offering the vicar a drink from their liquor flasks in church, and to see the effect on the religious teacher when he is performing his priestly duties is scandalous in the highest degree, and all too common here in Iceland."

EBENEZER HENDERSON

The Scottish minister Ebenezer Henderson (1784–1858) met Hans Jonathan in 1814. Henderson spent much of his career with the British and Foreign Bible Society, traveling widely and distributing Bibles in many languages. He had intended to go to India as a missionary, but as the East India Company refused to transport missionaries he went to Copenhagen, hoping to sail from there. In 1812 he was appointed to handle the publication of a new Bible translation into Icelandic, which was well received although the translation was not perfect. Henderson made three journeys to Iceland, writing about them in *Iceland, or The Journal of a Residence in That Island*. He was an observant visitor who was keen to learn about the places he visited. A talented linguist, he learned Icelandic and wrote extensively about Icelandic society and nature, especially its geology. He traveled more widely than had any visitor to Iceland before that time.

Henderson reached an agreement with merchants to distribute his large stock of Bibles all over Iceland. "The natural formation of that island rendering it impossible to convey any quantity of Bibles from one place to another, it was requisite to forward a proportionate number to each harbour," he writes.[12] But when Henderson arrived in Iceland, intending to get to work, he found that local conditions forced him to compromise: summer transport by trains of packhorses had come to an end for the year. Undeterred, Henderson set off himself with his Bibles, riding from one community to another.

Arriving in Eskifjordur in the east, Henderson handed over to the district commissioner three cases of books: 430 copies of the New Testament and 110 complete Bibles. At the end of August 1814 Henderson arrived in Djupivogur, where he stayed for two days. The hamlet, he wrote, consisted of one mercantile house, a shop, and some warehouses, but because of its location "it possessed great local importance relative to the object of my mission."[13] Henderson had heard of Jon Stefansson as an Icelandic patriot with a keen interest in literature. Ellen Katrin showed Henderson the library of her husband's Reading Association.

Before leaving Djupivogur, Henderson went for a walk. He wrote, "I made a short excursion along the southern shore of Berufjord[ur], accompanied by Jonathan, Mr. Stephensen's assistant, who is native of the West Indies, and has spent several years at this place."[14] Like Frisak, Henderson has little to say about Hans Jonathan. Perhaps Hans was simply reticent about his origins and his history.

It is equally likely that Henderson may have been reluctant to get into a discussion of the controversial issues of the time, such as slavery and the sugar trade in the West Indies. At the beginning of his journey to Iceland, Henderson had declared that he was pleased to be making this expedition independently, not "on any predatory or murderous expedition"—only to come across a mulatto who had thrown off the shackles of slavery, a man from one of the worst slaveholding societies in the sugar trade, where a human being could be bought and sold like a lawyer's robe, or a dog. In Henderson's mind Hans Jonathan probably did not count as part of Icelandic society, nor belong among the rocks and mountains which he describes at length in his book. He may have seen him as being like a vagrant bird that had wandered far from its natural habitat. In his book, Henderson's brief reference to Hans Jonathan is followed by two pages describing natural phenomena that did catch his attention: columnar basalt, quartz, zeolites, and so on. Then he was on his way south, with his saddlebags crammed with Bibles, leaving the young shop assistant behind.

THE SECOND BATTLE OF COPENHAGEN

Visitors to Iceland often required the help of guides, but they did not necessarily make a note of their names in their journals. Yet Hans

Jonathan is mentioned by name several times by Gytha Thorlacius, Frisak, and Henderson. He enjoyed a certain status due to his position at the trading company, but he also made an impression with his good manners, his helpfulness, and his unusual background.

As he was guiding these visitors about the mountains of Berufjordur, Hans Jonathan must have considered the possibility that news of who—and where—he was might reach Copenhagen. Clearly some of the Danish merchants who traveled back and forth knew his name, and possibly his past. Would he find himself in trouble if someone were to write a letter to the right recipient? Several Icelanders, in fact, were in contact with Judge Ørsted, who had presided over *The General's Widow v. the Mulatto*. One such was Judge Magnus Stephensen, president of the Icelandic High Court, who lived in Reykjavik, on Iceland's west coast. The Icelandic judge wrote to his Danish colleague several times about material he wanted to publish in his law journal in Denmark. On 14 September 1824, for example, he wrote to a friend in Copenhagen: "Today I finally managed to write a line to Judge Ørsted offering him my Danish piece on fornication law, for his *Juridiska Tidskrift*."[15] Perhaps those in Denmark who were familiar with Hans Jonathan's case were simply not interested. And Danish slave owners and officials had their hands full with pressing matters closer to home.

The Napoleonic Wars, from 1807 to 1814, had a major impact on the Danish Empire. Developments in Denmark affected every part of the triangular trade in slaves and sugar. Once again Denmark was at war with England, following global disputes over merchant shipping and control of the oceans. At the very time the English feared an invasion by Napoleon's French troops, the Danes continued to provoke them. The English issued an ultimatum: Denmark could form an alliance with England, or it must hand over its entire fleet as a pledge of its neutrality. Otherwise the English were prepared to attack. Denmark rejected the ultimatum, and in September 1807 English warships with twenty-five thousand men aboard surrounded the city of Copenhagen. They bombarded it into submission, and the

Danish fleet was handed over. Following the second Battle of Copenhagen, the English occupied the islands of the Danish West Indies. The once-proud Danish Empire was humiliated and crippled. Without its sugar trade, the nation faced bankruptcy.

What did Hans Jonathan, far away in Iceland, know about events in Denmark? The clash with England disrupted shipping to Iceland: of forty-one ships that set off for Iceland in 1807, eighteen were captured and diverted to English harbors. But the postal vessel *Skarven*, which sailed in October 1807, made it to Iceland,[16] and by the beginning of 1808 the news had reached the East Fjords that the English were besieging Copenhagen and laying waste to whole districts of the city. A number of Icelandic students had enlisted in defense of the city.[17]

Hans Jonathan, singled out for heroism during the first Battle of Copenhagen, would surely have been concerned upon hearing about the second one. He must have worried that his mother and his friends there might not have survived the attack on the city and the fires that broke out as a result. He himself had witnessed the panic that erupted in 1795, when part of Copenhagen went up in flames.

But Denmark had refused him his freedom, Reykjavik was far away, and in Djupivogur Hans Jonathan was not only a free man but also a pillar of the community. It was time for him to get on with his life: to run the business, go out fishing on his boat, take care of his livestock, play his violin—and settle down and start a family.

FIG. 12.1. The ruins in Bulandsdalur. (Photo: Gisli Palsson.)

FACTOR, FARMER, FATHER

HANS JONATHAN had always been his name. A slave rarely had a family name, although he might take his father's name. But two names were useful for identification purposes. One method of demeaning slaves was to call out their first name, requiring them to answer with the second name or be punished.[1] Thus the slave was compelled to acknowledge his or her submission to authority: the first name led to the second, emphasizing that the owner was in charge. When slaves were freed, they often wanted to adopt a new name, in the presence of witnesses, to mark the end of their bondage, reclaim themselves, and establish their new place in society.

Hans Jonathan was a free man now, and he could use any name he liked. He might have been expected to take a new name when he reached Iceland. Icelandic tradition did not include family names but instead used patronymics drawn from the father's name. If Hans Jonathan's employer was called Jon Stefansson, that meant Jon's father's name was Stefan. Matronymics were not common in the 1800s, so Hans Jonathan would not likely have called himself Emiliuson (son of Emilia), as he might in Iceland today. But Icelanders were familiar with surnames, as the Danes who were so prominent in Icelandic society all had family names. Some Icelanders even sought to imitate them, altering Stefansson to Stephensen, for instance. Hans Jonathan arrived in Iceland like any other Dane, so his second name was automatically treated as a surname: "Assistant Jonathan," born at "Kantitusjanhill, St. Croyx," was recorded in the census of Hals Parish on 1 December 1816. He had put down roots in Icelandic soil.

Henrietta Cathrina Schimmelmann had died on 15 May 1816 at the age of seventy-five. Hans Jonathan may have heard of her death. What would his mother have done after Henrietta Cathrina's death, if she was still living? There is no record of where and when she died, or what happened to her after Hans Jonathan's court case at all. Little is known of the fates of enslaved persons in Copenhagen in general.[2]

The death of his mistress provided final confirmation that Hans Jonathan was a free man. He must have been quite sure that her children, and the rest of the Schimmelmann family, would leave him alone even if word reached them of his new life in Iceland. The widow Schimmelmann's obsession with "her mulatto" was not shared by her descendants. Hans Jonathan could begin to think of starting a family of his own.

His eye fell on Katrin Antoniusdottir of Hals. Hans Jonathan was fourteen years older than Katrin, and they had known of each other for some years before they started courting. The farm of Hals is close to Djupivogur, and the family would have frequented the general store. Katrin was regarded as a beautiful girl, and Hans Jonathan cannot have failed to notice her. A contemporary later wrote of her, "In most fields of activity [she] excelled over other women." She was "one of the most outstanding women in the east of Iceland, for many reasons."[3] Many years later, another author wrote that in his youth, "at a distance of four generations," Katrin was still renowned "for her beauty and character."[4]

Katrin could hardly have helped noticing Hans Jonathan either, with his exotic appearance and cosmopolitan manners. According to a late twentieth-century account, the new store manager was active in the community: "In a number of fields he was forward-looking: he taught carpentry and arithmetic and navigation, and spoke up against drunkenness in the hamlet."[5] Hans Jonathan was "the Danish factor," but of a kind never seen before in Berufjordur.

Katrin was the youngest child of Antonius Sigurdsson (1767–1852) and his first wife, Halldora Jonsdottir (1761–1801). Antonius was a respected farmer and the local *hreppstjori*, or leader of the district council. The couple had two other children: a boy, Sigurdur (b. 1791), and a girl, Steinunn (b. 1796). According to the 1801 census the household also included Antonius's parents, a twelve-year-old foster son, and a twenty-one-year-old maid. When Katrin was two years old her mother died. Her father's second wife was Thorunn Jonsdottir, a clergyman's stepdaughter. Antonius and Thorunn had five children.

Until the end of the nineteenth century there was no church at Djupivogur, and the local parish church was on the farm of Hals, which had been a church site for many centuries; it is listed in the register of churches of Bishop Pall Jonsson from around 1200.[6] Hals was originally an extensive estate, but over the years it was gradually subdivided into smaller farms.

In 1816 the household at Hals numbered nine people. The farm kept an average number of livestock for the region: two cows, about thirty ewes, and dozens of yearling sheep and lambs. Other assets included a boat and fishing gear. Antonius and his family were typical subsistence farmers, relying on the resources of land and sea to feed themselves and to provide a little extra, which could be exchanged for such goods as timber, grain, coffee, and sugar, all available from the Djupivogur general store.

A TRYST AT THE SHIELING

During the short Icelandic summer, sheep graze in upland pastures. In Hans Jonathan's time, whole households moved to the summer pastures and lived in small huts, or shielings, to watch over their livestock. The farmers of Hals had a shieling at the mouth of the Bulandsdalur valley. In June 1627, when the Barbary pirates raided east

Iceland, Hals had deserted when the corsairs arrived, as the family were all at their summer shieling, and the raiders had tracked them down there and taken them captive.

In the summer of 1819 young Katrin Antoniusdottir was at the shieling, keeping watch over the livestock with her friend Sigridur Jonsdottir, a twenty-year-old woman from a nearby farm. Katrin must have been expecting to see more of Hans Jonathan, who had shown an interest in her, but she surely did not think he would turn up at the summer pastures. Tradition says that when he came striding into the valley, his face ruddy after his brisk hike up from the village, Katrin was mortified to be seen in her work clothes, a rough wool skirt and—even worse—mismatched socks, one brown and one black. Not a promising start.

Hans Jonathan was not alone; he was accompanied by Herman S. Schou, his twenty-year-old assistant in the business. It seems that Herman was interested in meeting Sigridur. Local people later spoke knowingly of the two young men going for "a hike" into Bulandsdalur where they "met" the girls, as if by chance. So Hans Jonathan and his friend Herman set off on foot one sunny day from the seashore in Berufjordur, keeping to the north of the Bulandsa River and heading inland. They headed south initially around Mount Bulandstindur, after which their route lay almost straight northwest. They walked for about two hours, perhaps stopping here and there to consider the history written in the landscape. It was not an easy hike, over rocky scrubland and through birds' nesting colonies. But the young men were eager. Perhaps Hans Jonathan took his violin along to entertain the girls. Hans and Herman found them at the shieling and spent the rest of the day with them there; oral tradition says that by the time they went home that evening both men were engaged to be married.

Some people doubt this romantic story of the hike into the mountains and the young shepherd girl in her mismatched socks. It is dismissed as overly reminiscent of modern-day tales of young people finding love on camping trips, surrounded by wild nature. While emotions are common human attributes, embodied and experienced everywhere, their role and designation varies from one context to another and, moreover from one epoch to another.[7] The association of love and intimacy with marriage, for instance, is far from universal. Thus modern notions of romance may not be pertinent for the time and context of Katrin and Hans Jonathan; perhaps their union was largely a "practical" arrangement in modern Euro-American terms, at least in the beginning.

Shortly after this historic Icelandic-Danish "double date," the shieling appears to have been abandoned. A little over twenty years later it is mentioned in a description of the parish: "At Bulandsdalur there was once a shieling that belonged to Hals, which has not been used for a long time, for whatever reason that may be—for it is a beautiful location for a shieling, although it may provide [only] meager grazing for cows."[8]

MARRIED LIFE

Hans Jonathan and Katrin Antoniusdottir had made a life-changing decision. After the rendezvous at the shieling, Hans Jonathan would have approached Katrin's father to ask for her hand. The couple were married on 28 February 1820 in Hals Church. A note in the church register shows that the couple were to be "tenants in common," each owning half of their assets. There is no reference here to the common practice of a marriage settlement, paid by the groom to the bride, but when Hans Jonathan's estate was settled upon his death, the account recorded a widow's marriage settlement of "eight spesiur to be paid in cash in silver, sixteen rigsdalers." Hans Jonathan's best man was the manager of the Eskifjordur general store, who had undertaken a considerable journey to stand beside his colleague at his wedding. In midwinter the journey may have taken several days, depending upon the weather.

The couple probably hosted a wedding breakfast in the manager's house. Some years before, the surveyor Hans Frisak had found himself at a wedding feast there. In the dining room Frisak saw a huge

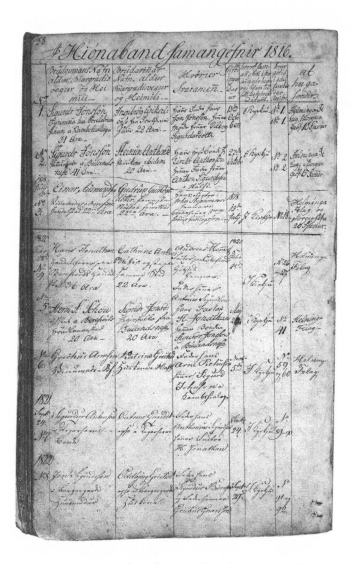

FIG. 12.2. Marriage certificate of Hans Jonathan and Katrin Antoniusdottir.
(National Archives, Reykjavik.)

coffeepot and "Fru Steffensen," the manager's wife, providing the refreshments. He and his team put up their tents outside the house and joined the party.[9]

The next entry in the church register after Hans Jonathan and Katrin were married is the wedding of their friends Sigridur Jonsdottir and Herman S. Schou, Hans Jonathan's assistant, about three months later. Schou's best man was recorded as "Factor Hans Jonathan." And when the Schous' daughter was baptized in January 1823, Hans Jonathan was her godfather. The two families were close.

Hans Jonathan and Katrin probably lived in the manager's house, where his predecessor Jon Stefansson and his family had made their home. It was a new lifestyle for "Fru Jonathan," as Katrin was known after her marriage: the solid bourgeois dining room where Frisak had watched the wedding guests dance as Fru Steffensen served coffee from a gigantic coffeepot; the reading association's "pretty voluminous circulating library" of books on science, which had so surprised Henderson; and other indicators of the high social status of the store manager. As for Hans Jonathan, he finally had a family again, after fifteen years—almost half his life—in his new country, far away from his own people. Their life was full of promise. And when Katrin became pregnant in the very first summer after their wedding, the newlyweds must have felt blessed.

On 26 May 1821 Katrin gave birth to a son, who was baptized Ludvik Stefan, with the surname Jonathan. Was he named in memory of Ludvig Schimmelmann, who had been Hans Jonathan's master and, possibly, his benefactor? Or was there some other reason for the name Ludvik—perhaps relating to the powerful Count Moltke, whose family may have helped Hans Jonathan to escape? This question will never be answered with any certainty, but we can be quite sure that the name was not chosen at random. A little over three years later, on 4 August 1824, a baby girl was born to the couple and baptized Hansina Regina. Obviously this little girl was named after her grandmother Emilia Regina. Was she named Hansina after her grandfather Hans Gram?

FRIEND OF THE POOR

Commerce and trade have a long history, and they have evolved naturally in many different ways over the centuries. What kind of men were the factors, the managers of general stores, in Iceland? It is sometimes said that there was a revolution in the world of commerce in the eighteenth and nineteenth centuries, probably related to developments in the sugar trade, among other things. Selfishness and self-interest, traditionally regarded as negative attributes—and quite probably a recipe for damnation—were now acknowledged as integral aspects of human nature, even creative forces for good.[10] *Homo economicus*, previously seen as a villainous type, was now regarded as entirely beneficial. Was it not in the nature of the shopkeeper to reach across the counter, to stand in the customer's shoes, and to establish a good rapport between two people—and sometimes two cultures as well? In 1769 Scottish historian William Robertson remarked that "commerce tends to wear off those prejudices which maintain distinctions and animosity between nations. It softens and polishes the manners of men."[11]

Whatever the truth of such ideas, merchants have always had a certain scope to act in their own way, and some have found it easier to reach across the counter than others, so to speak. Kyhn, the merchant at Djupivogur who ended his days in a Copenhagen jail after getting into disputes with his neighbors in Iceland, took moral standards to a new low under the monopoly trade of the eighteenth century. Sweet-natured Hans Jonathan, on the other hand, set the highest of ethical standards in the "free" commerce of the nineteenth century.

He was far from typical of the Danish factors in Iceland. Not only did he know for himself what it was like to be poor and disempowered, but he had also learned much from his reading about human rights. Hans Jonathan was well known in the region to have sympathy for the poor peasantry: in the words of a twentieth-century writer, "he was said to have asserted that the poverty in the trading area . . . was both harmful and shameful."[12] He was reluctant to send people out of the store without helping them, knowing that the goods he had for sale could make a crucial difference. On occasion he extended credit to customers in his own name, and in time he found himself in debt. According to the store's account books for 12 October 1818, around the time that Hans Jonathan was appointed manager, he owed 76 rigsdalers and 21 skildings—more than the average customer.

It is likely that his employer, the merchant company Ørum & Wulff, told Hans Jonathan that he must stop providing credit on his own account—that the store was not a charity and all debts must ultimately be settled. Near the end of his merchant career, on 12 July 1823, Hans Jonathan summoned "a number of debtors at the Berufjordur trading station to court, requesting that they settle their debts, giving them a certain time to respond before taking further action in accordance with the law and the courts."[13] There were twenty-seven names on the list. The average debt was roughly six rigsdaler. The document at the regional court specifies that the debtors, peasants in the community (including one widow), had shown up when requested, either expressing awareness of their debt or accepting it. There are no court records of how the cases were settled. Significantly, the store in the nearby community of Eskifjordur similarly summoned its debtors around the same time, a fact that indicates the decision was taken by the merchants' superiors. Did Hans Jonathan refuse to follow up on the claims? Was he fired, or did he resign? At any rate, a few weeks later, after five years as manager and over twenty years in the Djupivogur general store, Hans Jonathan left his job.

THE INDEPENDENT FARMER

When Hans Jonathan left the store, his own debts were documented. According to an entry in the legal records for the country of South Mulasysla on 28 October 1823, Hans Jonathan had declared all his assets two years before, in the context of his debt to the previous owner of the Djupivogur business, J. L. Busch.[14] Hans Jonathan appears to have used these assets as collateral for his debt. His assets at that time totaled 356 rigsdalers—nearly the same amount as the widow Schimmelmann had expected to sell him for on St. Croix. Hans Jonathan submitted a statement that he had declared all his assets except his own clothes and those of his wife and his son Ludvik Stefan. His father-in-law Antonius Sigurdsson pledged that none of the assets would be disposed of.

When Hans Jonathan left the Djupivogur store, he and Katrin became tenant farmers nearby, on a property called Borgargardur that belonged to the local authorities. Hans Jonathan was not the first store manager to settle at Borgargardur. Perhaps it was a tradition. As noted earlier, while employed in the business Hans Jonathan had owned a boat and a few farm animals, although he had no land of his own. He is unlikely to have had much time for his sheep, as he was a busy man, but he must have learned a good deal about animal husbandry during his years in Iceland, and ultimately he was able to become a farmer in his own right. Borgargardur commanded a range of peripheral resources, such as valuable eiderdown from an eider duck colony, as well as extensive grazing on islands and elsewhere. The house slave from the West Indies had remade himself as an Icelandic peasant farmer. Now he was his own master. He was also in the position of those to whom he had previously extended credit at the store, leading the precarious life of a subsistence farmer.

The value of property in Iceland is believed to have remained more or less stable from the Middle Ages until the nineteenth century.[15] But the value of individual lots and estates varied widely. Properties were valued in terms of *kugildi* (the value of a cow), *vætt* (a unit of weight), fish, ells of homespun woolen cloth (one ell equals about 24 inches) and *aurar* (silver coinage), but the most common unit of value was the *hundred* (equal to a hundred ells of woolen cloth). Major manors could be worth up to sixty hundreds, while an average-sized farm might be worth twenty. A description of the local parish in 1840 states that the farm of Hals was worth eight hundreds and Bor-

gargardur four hundreds.[16] The value of these properties was thus far
below the national average at the time. However, while properties in
the East Fjords were generally smaller than those in grassy lowland
areas of Iceland, they benefited from being close to the sea and its resources.[17] Still, Hans Jonathan's farm at Borgargardur was small even
by East Fjords standards—only half the value of Hals, where Katrin
had grown up. A year after the family moved to the farm, Hansina
Regina was born, putting further pressure on the household budget.
Hans Jonathan had to turn to increasing his livestock, cultivating the
land, and maintaining the farm buildings.

The inventory of Hans Jonathan's assets in the legal records of
1823 throws some light on the couple's years at Borgargardur. His
possessions included the two four-oared boats *Else* and *Delectation*
(with old sails), worn-out equipment for fishing and shark fishing, a
barn, a cattle shed, a small fishing shack, an old cow, two horses, four
ewes, two lambs, and a two-wheeled cart. Other items on the inventory give some insight into Hans Jonathan's lifestyle: a clock "which
does not work but should be useful if mended," a barometer, a ther-
mometer, a razor, and ice skates. Although there is no mention of
his violin, an organ is listed. So we know that Hans Jonathan played
music, made weather observations, and went skating when the fjord
froze over, perhaps with Katrin.

No less interesting is the list of the couple's reading material.
Given her parents' standing and common practice at the time, Katrin
must have been taught to read and write. In the couple's home was
"a bookcase with shelves" and a number of reference books on such
subjects as bookkeeping and English and Danish grammar. The latter was by a leading Danish literary scholar, grammarian, and educa-
tor, Jacob Baden (1735–1804). The library also included a collection
of poetry and prose published in 1798 by Judge Magnus Stephensen.

One of the books was listed as *Moralske Fortællinger* (Moral tales).
It was probably by the Danish author Charlotta Dorothea Biehl
(1731–88), who wrote four volumes of tales of human behavior and

morals, sometimes indirectly commenting on her contemporaries. She was an influential writer and the translator, for example, of Cervantes's *Don Quixote* into Danish. Another book was the work of the German writer Adolph Franz Friedrich Ludwig Knigge (1752–96). Knigge studied law and was a member of the Illuminati movement, which sprang from Enlightenment ideas and upheld principles of human rights and gender equality. He was strongly influenced by the French philosopher Jean-Jacques Rousseau and translated his *Confessions* into German. Knigge is best known for his work *Über den Umgang mit Menschen* (On human relations), which addresses issues of human interaction and provides guidance on etiquette and manners. Clearly Hans Jonathan had an interest in ethical questions, manners, and human rights, and kept up with the discourse on such issues in Europe.

He and Katrin largely raised Ludvik Stefan and Hansina Regina in keeping with the customs of Denmark and Iceland. But in view of the fact that they were familiar with Rousseau, their educational principles may also have been influenced by revolutionary ideas about human rights, although they reinforced traditional gender roles. In his *Émile, ou De l'éducation* (*Émile, or On Education*), Rousseau addressed the issue of the education of boys and girls, illustrated with examples. Émile, Rousseau implied, was to be educated to become an independent moral citizen, separated from his parents at an early age to be trained by an enlightened mentor, learning mostly through encounters with the natural world. While books were trivial for this task, Rousseau reasoned, Daniel Defoe's *Robinson Crusoe*, with its depiction of a shipwrecked man landing on a desert island, was crucial. Sophie, Émile's wife-to-be, in contrast, was to be taught in the context of the household, expected to be a good housewife, lover, and mother. Arguably, some of Rousseau's later writings indicate that he had serious doubts about such a division of gender roles. His key characters, both men and women, were often miserable and unhappy. The imbalance in gender roles which he had postulated, of course, did not resonate with his ideas of human rights.[18]

Bjorn Halldorsson (1724–94) of Saudlauksdalur, a pioneer of the Enlightenment in Iceland, kept up with the latest developments in Copenhagen, where he had spent time for medical treatment. His ideas about pedagogy and education, similar to those of Rousseau, were widely read.

FIG. 13.1. Musician Petur Bjornsson tuning the fiddle of his ancestor Hans Jonathan.
(Photo: Gisli Palsson.)

FAREWELL

IN THE SUMMER OF 1819, Katrin Antoniusdottir from Hals left the shieling in the hills and walked home, an engaged woman in spite of her mismatched socks. Were she and her fiancé a "mismatched pair" too? Questions inevitably arise about how the country people around Djupivogur received Hans Jonathan when he appeared in their midst. Few of them would ever have seen a "black" or "mulatto" before, although these terms were widely used within the Danish colonial empire. According to an early nineteenth-century book on Icelandic sayings and words of wisdom, "A black man does not make a good groomsman."[1] Is that what Katrin's friends and neighbors thought?

In Copenhagen around 1800, people were routinely categorized by their skin color, as if within a formal taxonomy. This racial hierarchy was the same as had evolved in the eighteenth-century sugar plantations in the West Indies, from which the concept of "negro" spread with slavery to the home country and into the Danish language.[2] In both the West Indies and Copenhagen, Hans Jonathan had been neatly categorized as a mulatto. But what vocabulary did his Icelandic neighbors have with which to describe him? So far as we know, no black or mixed-race person had ever been seen in or around Berufjordur.

Scholars have long debated this question of how we perceive the alien or "the other": Is it largely a matter of external appearance? Is "otherness" defined in terms of shades of skin color, while other physical attributes may also contribute? Do children see such differences before they have been conditioned to do so by their parents and society?[3] The answers to such questions are of great importance in the establishment of social groups. In some cases they give rise to racially based oppression, separatism, and even genocide.

Did the Icelanders simply see Hans Jonathan as having a deep tan?

The received version of Icelandic history tells us that the settlement of the island commenced in AD 874. The pioneers were mainly Norse people from Scandinavia, although some came from the British Isles, where Norse settlements had existed for some time. Ethnic mixing dates back to early Icelandic history, as many Norse settlers were accompanied by enslaved Celtic persons (and Celtic wives) from Ireland and Scotland, and people of other nationalities also found their way to Iceland. In modern times it has often been maintained that the island's Viking Age settlers represented a "racially pure" and homogenous population—overlooking or ignoring the fact that Iceland was, like many other pioneer communities, a melting pot.

The Icelandic sagas often refer to skin color. People are said to be "dark" or "black," others "white" or "light-skinned." But those definitions are a little more complex when viewed in context: "On their travels Vikings had encountered Negroes whom they designated, not as *svartir menn* [black men], but as *blamenn* (blue men). In other words, although *svartur* does not refer to race in the generally accepted modern sense, it nonetheless demonstrates an awareness of physical differences based on color."[4] Rather than applying it to black Africans, the sagas use the word *svartur*, meaning dark or black, to describe Celts: these are enslaved persons, or former slaves who have been freed. Many of them have been given Norse names such as Svartur (Black) or Kolur (Coal). And persons of such dark coloring are sometimes objects of hostility: *Vatnsdæla Saga* tells of a man named Svartur, "of Hebridean descent, a big strong man, not much blessed with friends and generally unpopular."[5] There is little evidence, however, of foreigners being harassed in medieval Iceland.[6] Foreigners were not necessarily perceived as "other," and a dark complexion was not invariably seen as a flaw.

There is no sign that Hans Jonathan's neighbors took any particular interest in his skin color or "race" or regarded him as "other." He was a member of the largely Danish commercial class and accepted as such. On several occasions he was called as a witness, along with other respected members of the local community, including his father-in-law and his superior at the trading station in Djupivogur. Like any Dane, he was obviously outside of the long-established network of genealogies that has always been so important in Iceland, but there is no indication that his unusual origins made any difference to the way he was treated by Icelanders. After his time "humorous" stories were sometimes told about the "black" man who had "colored" whole generations on the East Fjords, but such stories appear to have arisen much later, based on entirely different ideas about "race."

If Icelanders embraced Hans Jonathan, how did he react to them? Was he shocked by the first encounter at Djupivogur? It is difficult to tell, but it is tempting to refer to the experience of Tété-Michel Kpomassie, who as a young man in Togo in West Africa, not far from the land of Hans Jonathan's African ancestors, dreamed of traveling to the Arctic. In the 1960s he realized that dream as he visited Upernavik in Greenland. Later, having studied anthropology in France, he vividly described his stay among Greenlandic Inuit in his book *An African in Greenland*. Kpomassie, who had romanticized traveling on sledges and sleeping in igloos, was initially horrified by local food (especially whale blubber) and the "strange" manners of the Inuit, not least their excessive drinking and frequent spouse swapping.[7] In due course, however, he began to appreciate both the land and its people. Hans Jonathan was probably equally astonished at the beginning by the habits of the locals at Djupivogur, but he too clearly adapted. Such a move must have been easier for him than for Kpomassie. After all, Hans Jonathan had partly grown up in Copenhagen, a Danish subject like Icelanders.

A DARK DAY IN DECEMBER

On their small tenant farm at Borgargardur, it was difficult for the growing Jonathan family to make ends meet. They may never have escaped Hans Jonathan's debt from 1823, intensifying their dependency and the tensions between the family and the trading station—a familiar pattern in colonial economies. On 3 September 1827, District Commissioner M. H. Tvede summoned Hans Jonathan to answer charges made by the new store manager, Christian Thaae. Along with five others—local peasants and laborers—Hans Jonathan was requested "to explain the alleged disappearance of grain stored in the loft of the cooper's workshop since the time of the Ørums and landed by the ship *Normen* in 1824."[8] Again Hans Jonathan was fighting the injustice of the Danish colonial regime, though now at a different location and on radically different grounds. Was he bound to lose a second time?

A few weeks later, on 18 December 1827, Hans Jonathan was doing chores on his farm, where he was his own master. The winter was dim and dark, and when the sun peeked over the horizon it cast an eerie glow over the fjord. Down by the sea, the Ørum & Wulff trading post in Djupivogur was practicing "free" commerce—under which selfishness and self-interest were taken for granted. In the outside world, William Parry was attempting to reach the North Pole—without success. The previous summer in France, Joseph Nicéphore Niépce had succeeded in taking the first photograph, using a *camera obscura*, a technology that had hitherto been used as an aid for artists or for entertainment. The camera itself was still in the future; John Herschel would not coin the word *photography* until 1839.

Out in his field, Hans Jonathan suddenly collapsed. He had probably felt faint, had experienced numbness on one side of his body, and had lost control of his limbs and speech before he fell to the ground. He would have had no way of communicating at that point, but surely memories streamed through his mind: from Constitution Hill, Christiansted, Amaliegade, Langabud, the shieling in Bulandsdalur, and his croft at Borgargardur—mixed emotions about the sugar plantation, the Schimmelmanns, his long ocean journeys, the great sea battle, his unsettled debts—and his deep affection for his mother, his wife, and his children. He had only a moment to look back over his extraordinary life before it was over. There was no time to say goodbye. The man who had stolen himself had come to the end of his journey. Hans Jonathan, aged only forty-three, was gone. In Iceland, Denmark, or St. Croix during the first half of the nineteenth century, people did not expect to live longer than this, but still at Borgargardur the world was turned upside down. Katrin, suddenly widowed, was overwhelmed.

It is perhaps ironic that according to latter-day customs about wedding anniversaries, Katrin and Hans had just reached their "sugar anniversary." After only seven years of marriage Katrin had lost her lover, mentor, friend, and breadwinner. The loss of their father must also have been hard on six-year-old Ludvik Stefan and three-year-old Hansina Regina. December in Iceland is always dark and dim, but this year for them was worse than ever before.

Hans Jonathan was buried in the churchyard at Hals. His grave is unmarked, and its precise location is unknown. No obituary is known to have been written about him—which is curious in view of his popularity and his unusual history. But it is not surprising that no memorial marked Hans Jonathan's grave: few Icelanders of the time could afford such luxuries.

According to his death certificate Hans Jonathan died "of a stroke" (*af slagi*). This was not a precise diagnosis at the time but a general label covering a range of causes of death. An Icelandic medical textbook published in 1800 does not specifically mention "stroke." In 1884, more than half a century after Hans Jonathan's death, Jonas Jonassen (1840–1910), later surgeon general, published his *Medical Book for the Common People of Iceland*. It appears likely that those who were said to have died "of a stroke" in the first half of the nineteenth century had suffered what Dr. Jonassen defines as bleeding to the brain, that is, cerebral hemorrhage. "Bleeding to the brain may

FIG. 13.2.
Physician Hans Burch Gram.
(Kort- og Billedsamlingen, Royal
Library, Copenhagen.)

be caused by . . . a blockage in the blood vessels of the brain, or by blood congestion there due to diseases of the heart, lungs, or the blood vessels of the brain," he explains. "Either the hemorrhage may occur suddenly [*stroke*] with no warning signs, or it may come on more gradually . . . with symptoms of heavy-headedness, a buzzing in the ears, sleepiness and numbness, dizziness and blood congestion in the head, so that the face becomes flushed and swollen."[9]

It seems that Hans Jonathan's likely father and half-brother, both also named Hans, suffered a similar fate. Organist Hans Gram died suddenly in Boston in 1804 as he was setting off for Copenhagen to claim his inheritance, and later his legitimate son, Hans Burch Gram, a renowned physician and pioneer of homeopathy, died in much the same way at the age of fifty-two.[10] Hans Burch suffered "apoplexy" (a cerebral hemorrhage) and survived for some months, paralyzed on one side, before dying on 26 February 1840. He was buried in St. Mark's churchyard between Eleventh and Twelfth Streets in New York, with a fine marble stone to mark his grave.

LEGACY

On 12 May 1828, Hans Jonathan's estate was conscientiously settled in the fashion of the time.[11] District Commissioner Jon Eyjolfsson and Christian Thaae, then the manager of the Djupivogur general store, "undertook probate" of his assets, which had earlier been "listed and valued by the relevant leader of the district council," as the account notes:

> The year 1828, on the 4th of January, we the undersigned convened at Borgargardur in the district of Geithellnar, the same place as the estate of the deceased in question, to register and value the assets of the late farmer there, former Factor Hans Jonathan, who departed this life on the 18th of December 1827, and leaves the following heirs: The widow Katrin Antoniusdottir and their legitimate children, Ludvik Stefan, aged seven years, and Hansina Regina, aged four. The widow is represented by her father, Antonius Sigurdsson, and the conservator for the children is Sigurdur Antason of Teigarhorn.[12]

This statement is followed by a long list of the assets and debts of the deceased's estate. A total of eighty-one items are listed, in six categories: Livestock, Clothing and Bedding, Household Utensils, Miscellaneous, Books, and Tools. The category Livestock includes two cows, twenty ewes, ten lambs, one "worn-out horse," and one "colt, three winters old." Clothing and Bedding comprises two pairs of breeches (blue and gray), an old hat, three worn collars, two "used" overcoats (black and green), a "well-used" apron, two linen kerchiefs, a gold pin, and a worn quilt. Other garments are an old green coat, two waistcoats (one blue, the other light-colored), and two old jerkins (one gray and one blue). Could any of these blue items of clothing have been made from the blue cloak Hans Jonathan took with him when he disappeared from Copenhagen so many years earlier?

Under Household Utensils we find barrels, churns, baskets, pans, buckets, ladles, spades, rakes, a scythe, a teapot, a coffeepot, an old stove, spoons, and a vat. Miscellaneous includes such items as chests, a chest of drawers, a writing desk, a closet, a loom ("old and unserviceable"), a table, a lamp, chairs, a grinder, pictures, a spinning wheel, a mirror, combs, knitting needles, a barometer, a parlor clock, a pocket watch, and a violin. Books include hymnbooks in Icelandic and Danish, a number of books in Danish, and a year's worth of a monthly newspaper. The list of tools shows that Hans Jonathan was a handy man about the house: a lathe, five planes, two axes, tongs, two hammers, pliers, a chisel, a workbench ("little used"), a long saw, a "worn" hacksaw, knives, and a yardstick.

Comparing this list with the inventory compiled in 1821, when Hans Jonathan's debt to the trading company was documented, reveals that at his death he owned more livestock: two cows (one in 1821) and twenty ewes (previously four). But one of the boats was gone, as was the organ, while in exchange the family had acquired various equipment and furnishings for the home. Katrin and her father verified that "nothing belonging to the Estate has been omitted, and everything has been declared for the record." Hans Jonathan's estate was said to owe 42 rigsdalers and 56 skildings. This total included the funeral costs for the pastor and the church, six pallbearers, and the coffin maker, but the largest debt is to the trading company: 35 rigsdalers and eight skildings. Excluded from the account is "the widow's marriage settlement, 8 spesiur to be paid in cash in silver, 16 rdl [rigsdalers]."

Payments were settled in silver coin. The estate amounted to 140 rigsdalers and 76 skildings. Half went to Katrin, the other half to the children, Ludvik Stefan being entitled to twice as much as his sister. "The children's share of the inheritance," states the document, "is to remain in the keeping of their mother while they remain minors, against a pledge in her share of the estate and under the supervision of their conservator."

The inventory for Hans Jonathan's estate is probably typical for subsistence farmers of his day, who combined peasant agriculture with fishing, but there are unusual features that reflect the couple's origins, education, and interests. The violin, for instance, had been in Hans's possession since he arrived from Copenhagen, and the musical instrument itself has a history. Made in Germany around 1800, the violin passed to Hans Jonathan's son Ludvik and his descendants. It remained in the family at Djupivogur until about 1920, when it went to Reykjavik; from there it traveled to Vopnafjordur, back in the East Fjords. For two hundred years the instrument has been well cared for; it was recently examined and played by experts, including two violinists who are descendants of Hans Jonathan. It is not unlikely that Hans Jonathan had started to play the violin as a boy on St. Croix.

After the death of Hans Jonathan, his young widow did not have many options; she had to give priority to raising her two little children. Initially Katrin probably had help from her father and friends to remain on the croft at Borgargardur, but six years after Hans died she remarried. Her second husband was Bjorn Gislason (1806–82). An obituary written after Bjorn's death says that after he married Katrin "his preeminence over most farmers there in the east began to emerge," and indeed his wife was "the same inside the home as he was outside, that is thrifty, provident, early-rising, cleanly, and a good housewife."[13] She had, however, lived alone with her children for six years as a widow, and during that time she presumably did all the work of a subsistence farmer, indoors and out.

Hans Jonathan had traveled widely and had a varied experience of life. No doubt he had told his wife about his origins and his early life on St. Croix, followed by his youth in Copenhagen. Some parts of his story have been passed down in the family over nearly two centuries to the present day, while other aspects have been forgotten. Accounts of the descendants of Katrin and Hans Jonathan indicate that they had a loving marriage. One descendant, Kristin Vilhelmina Sigfinnsdottir in Djupivogur, remembers her grandfather telling her that Katrin once said, "All my honor I owe to Jonathan."

| IV |

DESCENDANTS

FIG. 14.1. Descendants of Hans Jonathan and Katrin Antoniusdottir. On the wall, Bjorn
Eiriksson (their daughter's son) and Susanna Weywadt. Below them, Emilia Bjornsdottir
(Bjorn and Susanna's daughter), her husband Magnus Magnusson, and their children
Emil Bjorn and Agusta. (Courtesy of Edda Emilsdottir.)

THE JONATHAN FAMILY

KATRIN ANTONIUSDOTTIR and her second husband, Bjorn Gislason, lived at Borgargardur for seven years, then moved to Bulandsnes, where they remained for the rest of their lives. Bjorn was from Rangarvellir in southern Iceland. Although the son of a clergyman, by the age of eighteen he "had neither learned to write, nor to reckon, in his father's house," according to his obituary.[1] The pastor is said to have fathered an illegitimate child but "dared not acknowledge the child, because of his position as a clergyman, and he claimed that his son Bjorn was the father, but Bjorn was displeased, and unwilling to cooperate in the deceit." As a result Bjorn left home and went to work for Chamberlain Tvede, the district commissioner at Bulandsnes in Djupivogur. Bjorn later went to Denmark to train as a mariner, then settled in Iceland, where he operated fishing boats and held various positions of responsibility: he was *hreppstjori* (leader of the district council) for thirty years, a caretaker in the local church, and chair of the county council for a time.

In the autumn of 1860, a ship called the *Fox* called in Iceland to explore the viability of laying a submarine telegraph cable across the Atlantic; Bjorn, then in his fifties, was commissioned to arrange horses for transport. The account of the ship's Danish representative, Theodor Zeilau, is not flattering: "Finally, on the evening of

August 14," Zeilau writes, "Bjorn arrived with horses, but it was impossible to arrange anything with him, as he arrived drunk as a lord and the horse trading had to be set aside for the time being until our friend Bjorn had slept off his intoxication; however, speaking of his excuse, which was that he had had a very strenuous ride all night through pouring rain, this of course probably made it difficult to calculate the balance between exterior and interior moisture."[2] Nevertheless, Bjorn Gislason was a good father to Hans Jonathan's children.

Ludvik Stefan was confirmed in 1835; he was said to be quite well versed in the catechism after two years of instruction by clergy. Later in life he built a fishing boat. One year, he and the crew, who numbered four or five men, decided to try fishing south along the coast. They found fish there, but then a sudden storm struck and swept the vessel ever farther south. On the fourth day they sighted the Westman Islands. Thirsty and tired, they were able to signal for help. The islanders welcomed them ashore and took care of them. They waited for an opportunity to get back to Djupivogur, but the weather was changeable and dangerous for their type of craft.

Finally Ludvik got an islander to ferry him across to Iceland's mainland, while his shipmates agreed to wait out the bad weather. Once he was ashore, Ludvik bought a horse and rode eastward. No news had been heard of the boat and its crew—they were believed lost at sea—and he was met with jubilation when he reappeared: "Around Midsummer Day, Farmer Jon was out checking on his ewes with their lambs. . . . Jon was heading home, and when he arrived he said to his wife that if his friend Ludvik were alive, he would believe he had seen him riding. And shortly afterward the news was heard of Ludvik's return, and the perils he and his companions had experienced—and they were regarded as having been snatched from the jaws of death."[3]

Ludvik Stefan married Anna Maria Johannsdottir Malmqvist (1822–68), from Stekkir in Djupivogur, and they had seven children, four of whom survived: Hans Kristjan (b. 1844), Katrin (b. 1845), Johann (b. 1848), and Ludvik (b. 1854). Hans Kristjan had eleven children, Katrin three, and Ludvik five. Johann moved to Copenhagen in 1863. Ludvik Stefan, like his father Hans Jonathan, died an untimely death, on 14 March 1855, aged only thirty-three.

When Hans Jonathan's daughter Hansina Regina was confirmed in 1839, she was said to be well versed in the catechism, intelligent, and well behaved. In 1846 she married Eirikur Eiriksson (1812–49), a farmhand at Borgargardur. They moved in with her mother and stepfather at Bulandsnes, where their elder son, Bjorn—named for Bjorn Gislason—was born in 1847. In 1849 Hansina gave birth to another son, Georg. Just a few days later, while beaching a boat, her husband Eirikur became caught between the hull and the roller beneath it. Although he managed to get home unaided after the accident, he collapsed shortly afterward and died from internal injuries.[4] Within six days Hansina Regina too was dead, of complications following Georg's birth. The two little boys were taken in by their grandmother and stepgrandfather, Katrin and Bjorn, who brought them up at Bulandsnes.

Despite being orphaned in infancy, Bjorn and Georg enjoyed a good childhood. Their grandmother and her husband were more prosperous than many others in the district, and their grandsons enjoyed the benefit. They grew up to be handsome, strapping young men and were said to have the look of their grandfather Hans Jonathan, with black curly hair, full lips, and dark eyes. In 1869 they were sent to Copenhagen for their education. Bjorn trained as a builder and furniture maker and returned to Iceland after six years. He settled in Eskifjordur in the east of Iceland, and had ten children. Georg remained in Denmark and married a Danish wife.

Little has been written about Hans Jonathan and Katrin's six grandchildren. Their grandson Ludvik, the son of Ludvik Stefan, however, was said to be a handsome man with a good reputation. A volume of genealogies from the East Fjords describes him as follows: "Ludvik was of average height, and dark in color, and very swarthy in the face—for his descent can be traced directly from a black person. He was a most gentle man, even-tempered and calm, a good

FIG. 14.2.
Ludvik Ludviksson, Hans Jonathan's
grandson. (Courtesy of Helga
Tomasdottir.)

man. He did not interfere with others and what they did. He was not
interested in money but wanted to earn a good living."[5]

From what we can tell, Hans Jonathan and Katrin's other grandchildren had a similar reputation. Many were described as polite and
considerate in their manner. Sometimes reference is made to a stately,
dignified air, like that of an aristocrat, yet without any sense of self-
importance or condescension. Some of them are said to have often
spoken formally—even to their parents, as a sign of respect. Yet they
were quick to put such formality aside when they made new friends.
There were musicians in the family: Bjorn Eiriksson, son of Hansina
Regina, played the organ like his grandfather Hans Jonathan; and
song and dance were part of the life of his household. Ever since,
Bjorn's descendants have been in the habit of singing together at social gatherings. Hans Jonathan's great-grandson Ludvik Hansson
(1873–1954), a harbor pilot, would play the violin at dances—it was
said that the real fun began when Ludvik began to play.

Katrin Antoniusdottir had the misfortune to lose both her children in the prime of life. Her six fine, healthy grandchildren must,

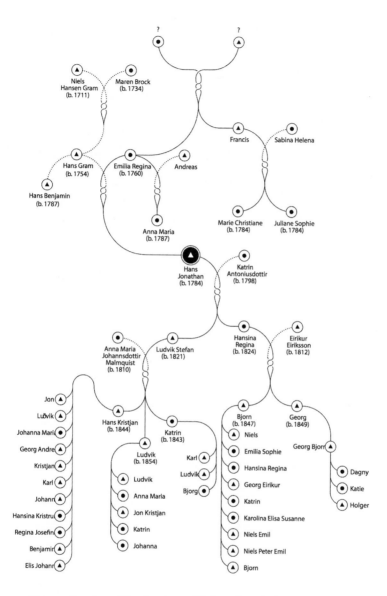

FIG. 14.3. Genealogy of Hans Jonathan and his descendants. (Sighvatur Halldorsson.)

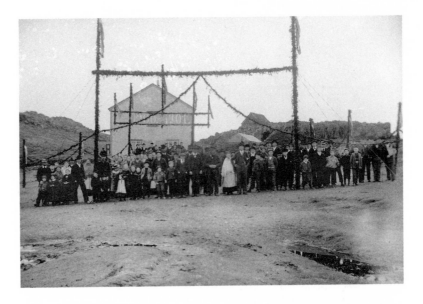

FIG. 14.4. Djupivogur celebrates a new century, 1901. (Photo: Nicoline Marie Elise Weywadt. National Museum of Iceland, Reykjavik.)

however, have provided some consolation for her losses. In due course there would be thirty great-grandchildren, but Katrin could not know that. She lived to be seventy-one, dying in August 1869.

On a summer day in 1901, the advent of the twentieth century was celebrated in Djupivogur. Below the rocky crags the people of the village and the surrounding countryside built a ceremonial arch—perhaps by walking through it one could enter the new age. It was a cold day, but the village was decorated with banners and heather, in the hope that the future would bring good times. The people gathered beside the general store, on Hans Jonathan's old territory and posed for a photograph to mark this important day. The photo shows most of them dressed up for the occasion: the men wear caps and neckties, the women elegant hats and ornate shawls. Some of their faces are blurred; photographs required long exposure times back then, and some people moved while the picture was being taken.

The photographer was Nicoline Marie Elise Weywadt (1848–

FIG. 14.5.
Hansina Regina Bjornsdottir. (Photo:
Nicoline Marie Elise Weywadt. National
Museum of Iceland, Reykjavik.)

1921). A daughter of the store manager in Djupivogur, she trained as a photographer in Copenhagen between 1871 and 1872—the first Icelandic woman to study in the field. Iceland's early photographers include a remarkable number of women; photography was one of few fields in which women could earn an independent living. Nicoline Wedwadt was said to be a woman of determined character who hated injustice of any kind. On occasion, if she took offense, she would stand up majestically, dust off her skirt and apron, and stalk out of the room. Nicoline's sister, Susanna Sophie, married Bjorn Eiriksson, Hans Jonathan's grandson. Susanna and Bjorn's daughter Hansina Regina (1884–1973) went to live with her aunt Nicoline at the age of four. She was trained as a photographer by her aunt and pursued further study in Copenhagen. Both women left photographic archives that provide important documentation of life in and around Djupivogur around the turn of the twentieth century.[6]

RACE AND THE COLONIAL EXHIBITION OF 1905

In the early nineteenth century, social upheavals were taking place which would inevitably have an impact on the descendants of Hans Jonathan. Debate was widespread over such issues as equality, skin color, race, and human dignity. The Danes were considering the possibility of an exchange with the English, trading Iceland for the sugar-growing Crab Island, one of the Virgin Islands.[7] At the same time, Icelanders were striving to convince themselves and the outside world that they deserved self-determination and a special place in the community of nations.

In the early years of the twentieth century, Iceland's campaign for self-determination rose to new heights. Having gained a parliament and a constitution in the nineteenth century, Iceland went on to win home rule in 1904 and sovereign status (though still under the Danish crown) in 1918. The independence movement fed on a growing pride in Icelandic history and culture—one that led inexorably to a focus on skin color or racial "purity." The descendants of the "mulatto" from St. Croix were inevitably affected by these ideas.

While racial ideas that occupied the colonial centers, one after another, in the wake of the slave trade arrived late to outposts such as Iceland, they were beginning to take hold in scattered isolated contexts. One example is the encyclopedia written by a self-taught naturalist, Jon Bjarnason of Vatnsdalur in northern Iceland, between 1845 and 1852.[8] He was in sporadic contact with foreign scholars, perhaps mixing prevailing religious themes and anthropological theories of evolution and the stages of "barbarism" and "civilization." While he was critical of "those who every year buy and sell many thousands of blacks for the lifelong burden of slavery and godless treatment, just like slaughtered sheep or inanimate objects," his system of "categories" of humans is clearly racist.[9] He placed humans in five categories; native Icelanders belonged to the superior class, while the blacks of the "Southern Territories" represented the lowest: "These have a black or rather dark color on their skin, and such human blackness shadows all the inhabitants of the Southern Territories. . . . Although some of them may be considered handsome by comparison with the most hideous, much like differences among us, between countries, counties, and among men, the main race is the same. Then, for example: the blacks of Guinea are strangely grotesque and carry with them an intolerable stench."[10] One of Bjarnason's volumes contained a series of drawings of "classes of human races and human variation," including a drawing captioned "The races of men; from Southern Territories, dark people [*Blamenn*], also called Negroes." Informed by Danish and European developments in commerce, politics, and science, such ideas would slowly catch on in Iceland, setting the stage for racial thinking.

In 1905, for example, a Danish Colonial Exhibition was held in Copenhagen. Iceland was to be included along with other Danish dominions, such as Greenland and the Caribbean islands. But Iceland's fervent nationalists were deeply offended at the idea of appearing alongside "primitive savages" from tropical islands. The Icelanders, after all, were the descendants of literary giants like Snorri Sturluson, whose *Prose Edda* the German scholar Jacob Schimmelmann had declared to be the oldest book in the world after the Bible! The Icelanders were mercilessly ridiculed in the Danish press for their sensitivity and rage—which incensed them even more. "Wherever our fellow countrymen met," wrote journalist Vilhjalmur Finsen about the Icelandic students in Copenhagen, "the talk was of this extraordinary scandal, as it seemed to us that the intention was to 'exhibit' us and our land among blacks and Eskimos, as a 'colony' of Denmark."[11] Vilhjalmur himself spoke plainly in an article published before the exhibition opened: "Can Iceland be known for taking part in such an exhibition, in which Icelandic women in their national costume are exhibited alongside Eskimos and negresses? I say no! This is a shameful smear on our nation and a disparagement of our culture."[12] For a time it seemed that Iceland would refuse to participate. In the end the exhibition was renamed "the Danish Colonial Exhibition, 'together with' an Exhibition from Iceland and the

FIG. 14.6.
Colonial Exhibition poster,
Copenhagen, 1905.

Faroes," distinguishing between two different kinds of colony or dominion.

The Icelanders had no objection to a colonial exhibition per se. They saw nothing wrong with the idea of exhibiting people like animals in a zoo; they were simply opposed to the idea of *Icelanders* being exhibited that way. Some Icelanders were unwilling to concede that Iceland should be called a colony at all, maintaining that Iceland and Denmark had a special relationship of quite a different nature.

Among the "exhibits" were two children from St. Croix, presumed to be of purely African descent. A little over a century after Hans Jonathan and his cousin Juliane Sophie left the fields of sugarcane behind them, a six-year-old boy, Victor Waldemar Cornelins, and a four-year-old girl, Alberta Roberts, had been sent to the Danish capital to be put on show.[13] The organizers of the colonial exhibition had dispatched a telegram to St. Croix: "Send two negro children!" In his autobiography Victor recounts the negotiations with his mother. Under pressure from the local authorities, his mother tearfully agreed to send her son to Denmark to take part in the exhibition. His time there was difficult, and far from what he had expected: "Staring was not enough; they let out cries of astonishment, and some disbelieving ones even fingered our faces to wipe off the black colour or touched our hair to make sure it was real. The crowd grew bigger, and soon it was almost impossible . . . to get us through."[14]

On the exhibition stand in Copenhagen's Tivoli Gardens, Victor was presented as a "wild boy" from the West Indies. Expected to pull grotesque faces at the public, he found his life as an exhibit tedious, and from time to time he crossed over and became a "visitor," viewing the Inuit and other colonial exhibits. He was particularly interested in the children in the Greenland exhibit, and sometimes he abandoned the role of both exhibit and visitor and simply played happily with the Inuit children among their dogsleds, hunting and fishing gear, and stuffed Arctic animals. But the exhibition stewards intervened to end the fun and locked him in a cage.

Little Alberta died young, and Victor would never return to St. Croix. Though much had changed, the colonial system was still in force.[15] After the exhibition closed there was no attempt to return Victor to his mother: he was placed in an orphanage, then fostered by a kind couple. He later married a Swedish woman, Vera, and they had three children. He went on to become a well-known academic and to write his autobiography.

The Colonial Exhibition of 1905 not only transformed the life of Victor Cornelins. It also underlined the tensions and paradoxes in Danish colonial rule and in the Icelandic campaign for self-determination, providing useful insights into attitudes to nationality, colonialism, and race in the Danish realm at the dawn of the twentieth century.[16] The phenomenon of the exhibition also throws light on the conditions and new attitudes faced by the descendants of Hans Jonathan in their everyday lives.

THE HEARTS OF MEN

The rising tide of Icelandic nationalism, with its emphasis on "noble" and "renowned" Icelandic families, had a considerable impact on individuals who were seen as "black" or "colored." The Jonathan family had no long or glorious history; they were part of the Antonius lineage—that is, Katrin's family—but Katrin's descendants were just one small branch of that family tree. At the peak of the nationalistic campaign for self-determination, even Icelanders with Danish blood in their veins were regarded as suspect, let alone those with African blood.

During the twentieth century, people of color became a more common sight on Reykjavik streets. The story is told that once during the 1930s the poet Tomas Gudmundsson witnessed a black person being refused admission to a Reykjavik restaurant. That incident is said to have led him to write his *Poem about a Young Woman from Sudan*. Gudmundsson, together with two companions, urged the waiter to submit his decision to a vote of his customers. The waiter protested that he was only following accepted international practice but agreed to allow a vote. Gudmundsson and his friends won, and the black customer was permitted to enter.[17] The first and last verses of Gudmundsson's poem are as follows:

> *In her veins is African darkness*
> *that flows with a restless beat.*
> *And a magical fire in her eyes,*
> *which either smolders or burns.*
> *For an ancient jungle from south in Sudan*
> *sleeps in her bosom,*
> *and the price of sixty black slaves*
> *glitters on a dark arm.*
>
> . . . .
>
> *And while the evening light loaded*
> *crystal and silk with an eerie glow*
> *and naked arms and raw music*
> *transmuted into a shining haẓe,*
> *I was captivated by her dark beauty.*
> *Yet I admired even more*

how much the hearts of men have in common
in Sudan and south Iceland.[18]

Tomas Gudmundsson's poem reflects common themes of the time—
the allegedly passionate black woman and the primitiveness of Africa.[19] But his concluding words about the "hearts of men" in Africa
and Iceland caught on and are often quoted in Iceland even today.

After World War II, when a US naval air base was established in
Iceland, African American military personnel were stationed there.
They encountered racial prejudice, and the Icelandic government
made a secret agreement with the Americans to prevent more blacks
from being sent there, partly to avoid racial mixing.[20] Yet at the same
time, another kind of brown skin began to enjoy a growing popularity: a deep suntan came to stand for a cosmopolitan, wealthy lifestyle,
in keeping with new fashion trends and the cult of youth. In 1958
suntan lotion was promoted in a newspaper advertisement aimed primarily at women: "Turns your skin a deep brown in no time, and
prevents peeling. Try Lytia Suntan Lotion and you'll be as brown as
a mulatto after just one day in the sun. Sold in all leading cosmetic
stores around the country."[21] Now it was possible to choose a skin
color—although it was not the same to be born a bona fide mixed-race person as to simply play the part for a while.

In recent years ideas relating to globalization and cultural diversity have played a growing role in debates in Icelandic society.[22]
Attitudes toward "colored people," legislation and rules on asylum
seekers and residence permits, and the rights of immigrants have undergone considerable change. Hans Jonathan has not been forgotten
in Iceland, although his story is not necessarily well known. Author
Stefan Jonsson, for instance, wrote about Hans Jonathan in 1987. He
writes that in East Iceland it was regarded as an honor to be able
to trace one's descent from Hans Jonathan; people mentioned it, he
says, "with disarming pride."[23] Various modern-day Icelanders have
been said, rightly or wrongly, to be descended from Hans, partly due
to Jonsson's engaging account.

A GOOD NAME

Hans Jonathan's descendants dispersed to many different places in the East Fjords, to the Westman Islands off Iceland's south coast, and to the capital city of Reykjavik. Some went abroad, to Denmark, Norway, the United States, and Mexico. They trained, studied, and worked in many different fields. Today they number about six hundred. They make up a diverse group, and most of them are curious about their roots in the Caribbean and West Africa. They also have their own stories to tell.

In view of the growing nationalistic feeling in Iceland in the first half of the twentieth century, it is hardly surprising that Hans Jonathan's African roots were sometimes a sensitive subject. It is said that some of his descendants were reluctant to admit any connection with "the black man." One member of the family reports a conversation with an elderly aunt in the middle of the twentieth century: "She was absolutely livid when I innocently asked her, as a child, whether it was true that there was a black person in our family. I swear, she stiffened up and banged her fists together, and declared it was all nonsense. Yes, she always maintained that people's reputation was being smeared and blackened, by alleging a connection with blacks— saying they were of black descent."[24]

Another member of the family recalled prevalent attitudes around 1970: "I remember it as a child, of course, and maybe as a teenager— being descended from a black—Good heavens above! It was absolutely taboo, of course."[25]

Some descendants of Hans Jonathan have suggested that old family photograph albums—probably some of the oldest such albums in Iceland—had been thrown away or burned in order to hide the dark faces. But such attitudes have changed, and the vast majority of Hans Jonathan's living relatives are proud of their origins, although some of their memories may have uncomfortable overtones. Says one, "My uncle always used to call me 'Svarta' [Blackie] or 'My little Blackie.' I was a little bit hurt if he forgot to call me Blackie, and insisted on my nickname. And his friends always called me Blackie too. It was an allusion to my origins. I really quite like it. There are a few of us who always call each other 'negro cousins,' or say 'my cousin in the negro family,' and so on."[26]

A member of the family who played soccer professionally alongside black players in England says: "I tanned well in the sun, and I have brown eyes, and it was always said that it was because I was 'related to' or 'descended from' Hans Jonathan. As a kid I was rather proud that there had been—how should I put it—a black person in my family—and I even mention it now, if I'm living abroad. And it's often been said, jokingly, that I'm partly—you know—of the same race as them."[27]

For some members of the family, their West African origins have led them to ask existential questions. One claims to sense "the black in me." She says, "I've always been a bit proud of being of African descent. I didn't know until last winter that it was an insult to say *negro*."[28] The family members were, as a rule, taught as children to respect people of other colors: "We'd have been spanked and locked up in the cellar or something, if we'd said anything bad about black people."[29]

Many make the point that Hans Jonathan's good name was paramount: "There was a certain—I suppose I have to call it 'mystique' about it. It was certainly seen as exotic. And I think the most important thing in the story was that he had such an excellent reputation. He was said to be a man of noble character, with many good qualities; and I felt it was that which determined what people thought of him. Not the color of his skin, or where he was from. But his own qualities—that was the attitude I was brought up with."[30] As the Old Icelandic poem *Havamal* (Words of the High One) says: "A good name shall never die."

Around 2000, one of Hans Jonathan's descendants, who lived in Hafnarfjordur in the southwest, hoped to do business with some people in Eskifjordur in the east of Iceland. He mentioned, as Icelanders often do, that his family was from the east, and was asked who they were. He replied that he was a descendant of Hans Jonathan. "Well then, it will be safe to do business with you," was the response.[31] And there are more such accounts. Many members of the family report friendly reactions when they explain whom they are descended from: "The old East Fjords people would often say: 'Oh, yes, you're descended from the black man.' Yes, I've had that a lot—elderly East Fjords people, maybe born before the turn of the last century. Which tells us that the story was kept alive in the region. 'Oh, yes! So you're descended from him.' They could instantly place you."[32]

RECOGNITION

On 2 April 2001 the Danish government symbolically honored Hans Jonathan and his descendants. To mark the bicentennial of the Battle of Copenhagen in 1801, Queen Margrethe of Denmark attended a memorial service and laid a wreath at the burial ground in central Copenhagen where the memory of the fallen is honored and the courageous defenders of the city are lauded. Along with royalty, the ceremony was attended by court officials, naval leaders, and representatives of some of those who took part in the battle two hundred years prior. These guests included a relative of Admiral Nelson—the English leader of the siege of Copenhagen—and a representative of the "mulatto" slave who ran away to enlist in the Danish navy, regardless of the wishes of his "owner" at Amaliegade 23. Helgi Mar Reynisson was invited to participate in the ceremony as a representative of Hans Jonathan's descendants, in honor of their ancestor's heroism, and in formal recognition on Danish soil of Hans Jonathan's struggle for freedom and the existence of a numerous family of his descendants in Iceland.[33] Despite his doughty performance in defense of Copenhagen and the Danish realm, Hans Jonathan was never formally a "free man" in Denmark. Now his case was recognized in the presence of royalty.

The following year on 15–16 June 2002—a few weeks past the bicentennial of the verdict in *The General's Widow v. the Mulatto*—

the descendants of Hans Jonathan and Katrin Antoniusdottir came together for their first family gathering. About 150 people attended, all of them Hans Jonathan's descendants or their partners. The event offered a rare opportunity to strengthen family bonds, recall old memories and stories, and exchange views. A website was launched, which includes old photographs and accounts contributed by family members as well as a family tree. The descendants now also have a Facebook page where they can keep in touch.[34]

The commemorative ceremony in Copenhagen and the Icelandic family gathering received some coverage in the Danish media, and a Danish film crew was present in Iceland. Alex Frank Larsen's documentary series *Descendants of Slaves* was later televised in Denmark and Iceland, drawing widespread attention to the story of Hans Jonathan and his descendants and to the history of Danish colonial slavery. In a sense these events gave rise to the birth, or rebirth, of Hans Jonathan's Icelandic lineage. His descendants were now keen to learn more about their roots. In due course, descendants of West Indian slaves in Denmark celebrated their discovery of a "new" Icelandic branch that shares their heritage.

The story of Hans Jonathan's descendants in Iceland has taken several turns. Originally their unusual background was simply taken for granted in a culture that showed little interest in race and skin color. Later on, in the wake of the nationalist movement with its emphasis on the notions of "purity" and Nordic ancestry, the Jonathan family sometimes experienced silence, gossip, and denigration. Still later many of them would celebrate their international connections and their African-Caribbean roots. These turns reflect the changing context of Icelandic society and its relations to the outer world. In recent decades Iceland has become a colorful melting pot, thanks to, among other things, interracial marriages, international travel in and out, transnational adoptions, and an influx of migratory workers, refugees, and asylum seekers from all parts of the world. At the same time, cultural distance has been redefined, partly by social and visual media; the exotic has become playful, softened and domesticated.

Given this context, the descendants of Hans Jonathan are impossible to distinguish from the rest of the community: spread throughout the country, occupying social positions of all kinds—and looking the same as everybody else.

While differences among Icelanders are often celebrated nowadays, the multicultural landscape remains unstable and sometimes contested. One important issue is the level of unemployment. Immediately after the financial meltdown of 2008, for instance, immigrants who had been welcomed during the boom years were increasingly seen as a threat, competing for jobs, housing, and social services—especially people of "different color."

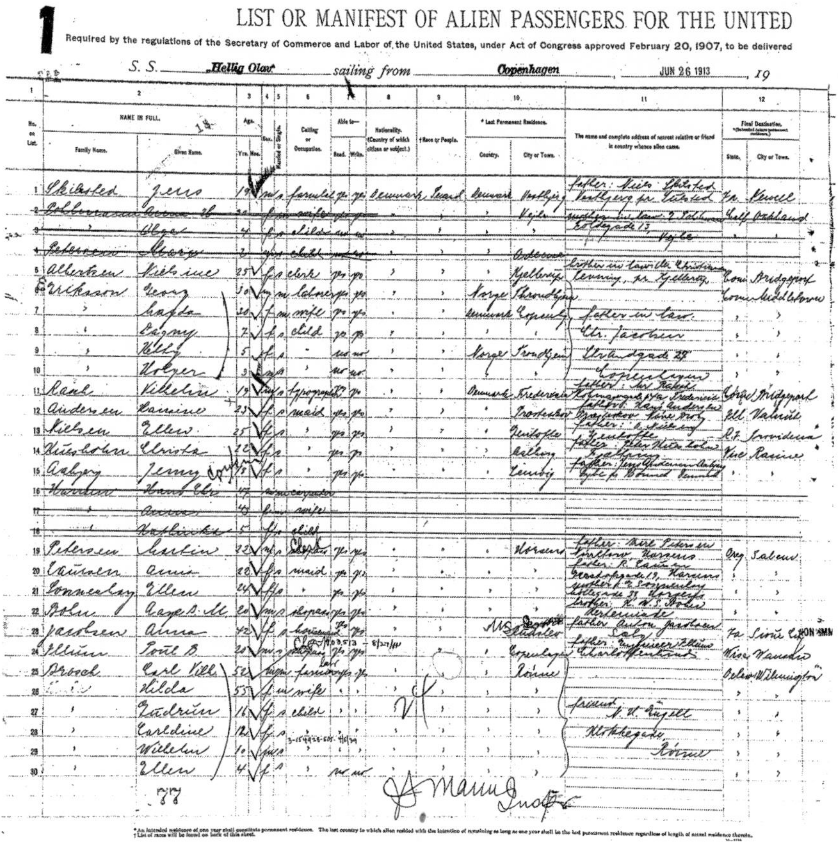

1

LIST OR MANIFEST OF ALIEN PASSENGERS FOR THE UNITED

Required by the regulations of the Secretary of Commerce and Labor of the United States, under Act of Congress approved February 20, 1907, to be delivered

S. S. Hellig Olav sailing from Copenhagen JUN 26 1913 19

FIG. 15.1. "Alien passengers." George Bjorn, Thora Martha, and children arrive in New York, 1913. (Ellis Island Foundation.)

THE EIRIKSSONS OF NEW ENGLAND

BJORN AND GEORG EIRIKSSON, grandsons of Hans Jonathan, went to study in Copenhagen in 1869. While Bjorn returned to Djupivogur, Georg stayed on and married a Danish woman, Birgitte Sindahl, who worked in the dairy industry. Georg joined the Danish navy, as his grandfather had done decades earlier when he tried to gain his freedom. But he served only a few years, and died at sea before his only child was born, in 1879. Birgitte named the boy Georg Bjorn Eiriksson, changing his father's traditional Icelandic patronymic ("son of Eirikur") into a Danish surname. Although his life was so short, Georg became the founder of a lineage of Eirikssons in a context radically different from that of his native Iceland: New England. But with Georg's premature death, their connection with his Icelandic family and its narratives about Hans Jonathan was severed. Struggling to maintain herself and her young son, Birgitte had other things on her mind than Icelandic family history. Perhaps she had never even heard of Hans Jonathan. The Eiriksson name, however, remained a reminder of an elusive Icelandic past.

Georg Bjorn Eiriksson was educated in a school for orphans in Copenhagen, possibly through high school. At the age of twenty-three he married Thora Martha Jacobsen. The couple lived near Copenhagen for a while, and their first child, Dagny, was born there.

FIG. 15.2.
Bjorn Eiriksson (left) and Georg
Eiriksson (right). Photo by Theodor
Hansen, Copenhagen. (Courtesy of
Roberta Dollase.)

Then they moved to Trondheim, Norway, where Georg Bjorn became manager in a factory and they had two more children, Katie (b.
1907) and Holger (b. 1909). Soon after that they decided to emigrate
to the United States, urged by Thora Martha's sister, who was already
settled in Middletown, Connecticut.

They returned to Copenhagen and in June 1913 boarded the
steamer *Hellig Olav* (Saint Olaf). The ship passed north of Scotland,
then turned west, too far from Iceland even to catch a glimpse of
it. *Hellig Olav* was a huge vessel, with accommodations for at least
a thousand passengers in first, second, and third class. Even if the
Eirikssons traveled third class, they had their own cabin. But while
they must have been excited about their journey, they would have
worried as well. In April the year before, the *Titanic* had struck an
iceberg and sunk on its maiden voyage on a similar route. More than
fifteen hundred passengers and crew drowned.

V. Jensen & Co.   Kjøbmagergade 11, Kjøbenhavn K.

FIG. 15.3.
George Bjorn Eiriksson.
(Courtesy of Roberta Dollase.)

The Eirikssons' trip, however, was without incident. After thirteen days at sea, the family disembarked at Ellis Island, New York, where papers had to be checked by port officials and health inspectors, and the adults cross-examined. The crowd was overwhelming and the atmosphere tense. While 1907 was the record year for immigration through Ellis Island, with no fewer than 1.25 million passengers processed, the flood of people from Europe continued until the United States entered World War I in 1917. Most were allowed to enter the country within a day, but any outward sign of illness might mean deportation. It was hard to miss the agony of families that were being split up, not knowing if and when they would be reunited. Not surprisingly, Ellis Island, the island of hope, gate to the adventures and opportunities of the New World, was also dubbed the "Island of Tears."

Once they were permitted to enter the country, the Eirikssons

FIG. 15.4.
George Bjorn and his children Katie, Holger, and Dagny. (Courtesy of Roberta Dollase.)

traveled to Middletown, where their relatives lived on a small farm. After a brief time there, they moved to Groton, where Georg Bjorn, a skilled craftsman, found work with the Bacon Banjo Company. Later he worked for the Electric Boat Company (now General Dynamics Corporation), which built submarines.[1]

Children in their neighborhood found the name of Holger, the youngest Eiriksson child, foreign and hard to pronounce. They gave him the nickname Buck, which remained with him for the rest of his life. He soon learned English and got along well with other children. Yet during World War I a nearby family would call him "a dirty little Hun" and refuse to allow him in their yard. Apparently, being Danish was too close to being German.

In June 1921 the Eiriksson family became United States citizens. George Bjorn signed the papers, while his wife and children were granted citizenship as his dependents. After eight years in the New World, the Eirikssons had found a home. In the 1940s the extended family built houses at Rogers Lake in Old Lyme, Connecticut, living close to each other while the grandchildren were growing up. Not long after moving to the lake, George Bjorn was diagnosed with stomach cancer. He died in the summer of 1947.

THE ELUSIVE ICELANDIC PAST

When Holger's children, Roberta and Karl, were in elementary school, their father told them that they were related to the discoverer of America, Leif Eiriksson. The family always used the Icelandic spelling of the name, Eiriksson (though without the accent mark an Icelander would use), not the Danish Erikson or the Americanized Erickson. Roberta's third-grade teacher told her it was not Leif Eiriksson but Christopher Columbus who discovered America—but she knew the teacher was wrong. When they were older, their father explained that in Iceland Eiriksson was not a family name but a patronymic; they were not directly related to Leif, after all, but their heritage was Icelandic.

For much of her life Roberta—a history major, then a high school teacher and administrator—has lived on the outskirts of Boston with her husband, Richard Dollase, and their children Chris, who grew up to become a lawyer, and Nancy, who became a doctor and professor of pediatrics. Roberta studied and taught American history throughout a more than thirty-year career. Her husband also taught American history and, with a professor whose scholarship focuses on historical and cultural issues, developed a high school curriculum for teaching about the experience of African Americans through their three hundred years in the nation's history. Their son Chris also studied American history. Early in his career he worked for a member of Congress who served on the Subcommittee on Civil Rights of the House of Representatives' Judiciary Committee.

Roberta's father knew that the Eirikssons came from Djupivogur in eastern Iceland, and he felt that he must visit at some point. In July

1985 he and his daughter finally did. Despite some translation problems, Roberta and Holger met people they thought they were related to. They sat down and tried to sketch out the family tree, starting with Katrin, Hans Jonathan's wife. One of their relatives told them that "the mulatto who had lived in the village" was their ancestor, adding that his name was Jonathan Moltke. At Hals they found Katrin's gravestone, which they found most exciting.

Roberta and Holger learned that the church records had been sent to the National Archives in Reykjavik. They visited the archives and found to their surprise that their ancestor was listed as Hans Jonathan. Were Hans Jonathan and Jonathan Moltke the same man? Where did he come from, and what did his "mulatto" status imply? The Icelanders seemed unable to answer such questions.

In early 2015, long after her father had died, Roberta returned to the issue. To her astonishment her brother Karl, who lives in Virginia, disclosed that their father had told him that their ancestor Hans Jonathan "was born a slave in St. Croix." Their father had said Karl would probably learn about it sooner or later, and he wanted to be the first to tell him. He specifically asked Karl not to talk with anyone about it. Out of respect for his father's wishes, Karl kept what he had learned to himself until Christmas 2014, when he told his youngest son, Jared.

Karl couldn't remember when the conversation with their father had taken place, but Roberta reasoned that it must have been after their 1985 visit to Iceland. Indeed, nine years after returning to the United States, Holger wrote to his contacts in Iceland requesting further genealogical details and documents. Eventually his inquiries were passed on to Edda Emilsdottir, a relative in Reykjavik who spoke English. They exchanged a number of letters, and early in 1995 Edda sent him a detailed account of their Icelandic family and of the general conditions in nineteenth-century Iceland. A retired biochemical technician, Edda has skillfully assembled genealogical records and family letters over the years, creating her own "archive," as she puts it. Her historic letter to Holger included the following comments on Hans Jonathan, reflecting what she and many of her relatives thought at the time:

Hans Jonathan was born . . . on St. Croix (a Caribbean island), a Danish colony at the time. His mother was a black slave named Regina. The father was presumed to be Heinrich Ludwig Ernst von Schimmelman (1743–1793), but that has not been confirmed. He was in charge of the family's sugar plantations and, later, governor of St. Croix. Regina worked in his home. Hans Jonathan was sent to Copenhagen for schooling. . . . He didn't stay on in Denmark. His position there was probably difficult as he was illegitimate (he didn't use a family name) and because he was black, which may explain why he left for Iceland. . . . Hans Jonathan was short-lived. He died of stroke at his home in Borgargardur in December 1827. He had a distinct presence thanks to his exotic looks and his upbringing. He was popular here, renowned for his honesty and kindness, and his death was a great tragedy to his family and the parish community.[2]

Holger thanked Edda for the information. He was living with Roberta and her family at the time, but he did not mention the letter. Nor did he pursue the issue with Edda, although he remained in contact with her, his last letter to Iceland being dated January 1998. With his death, the Eirikssons' link with their Icelandic kin and its sagas was once again severed.

A DELICATE ISSUE

Another Eiriksson in New England, Kirsten Pflomm, the granddaughter of Katie Eiriksson, suggests that Hans Jonathan was a delicate subject in her family as well. Her early life was in the same neighborhood as most of the Eirikssons in New England but was never particularly close to them; her parents divorced, and she grew up with her maternal grandparents, who were of Swedish descent.

Kirsten's interest in her ancestry was sparked by pure chance about ten years ago. One day, as she searched for her name on the internet, she was surprised to find a Kirsten Pflomm listed on an Icelandic website. She wrote to the site's Icelandic contact person, who explained the extensive genealogy on the website: unmistakably, Kirsten belonged to a family that descended from a Caribbean slave, Hans Jonathan, who had settled in Iceland about two centuries ago. Kirsten was puzzled to discover that she was related to "someone who was not blond-haired and blue-eyed."[3] She was reminded, however, of her last encounter with her father's brother Wilbur, who, shortly before he died in 1994, implored her: "Look into your family history! You'll find something interesting!"

"That's the big family secret!" she now concludes. "I think someone knew. With the discovery of Hans Jonathan everything kind of falls into place."

At the time that the Icelandic descendants of Hans Jonathan were finally gaining recognition at the turn of the last century, through the symbolic state event in Denmark and the documentary film shown on both Icelandic and Danish TV, their relatives in the United States remained hardly aware of their African ancestry. The real meaning of the Hans Jonathan connection is only now being discovered, as the families begin to explore their roots and history in the light of new evidence. Kirsten Pflomm and Roberta Dollase and their families and relatives are keen to learn more about their Icelandic-Caribbean roots and to connect with their distant relatives, embracing the genealogical details that had been lost or ignored since their relatives arrived in the New World. For the current generations of Eirikssons, much like most of their Icelandic relatives, discovery of the past is not a Pandora's box of troubles but an exciting new window into family history.

The tracing of one's roots to slave owners can be just as dramatic as discovering enslaved persons in the family tree. Often, however, the response is primarily denial and embarrassment. In 2015 a celebrity genealogy show listed the names of twenty-four enslaved people who in 1858 were owned by Benjamin L. Cole, the great-great-great-grandfather of Hollywood actor Ben Affleck. Affleck asked the show's producers to conceal his family's links to slavery, but later on, following disclosure by WikiLeaks, he publicly admitted: "I didn't want any television show about my family to include a guy who owned slaves. I was embarrassed."[4] While Euro-American relations to enslaved persons are increasingly documented, explored, and celebrated, relations with slave traders and slave owners have usually been carefully hidden from public view, despite the detailed head tax lists stored in many archives.[5]

Although Europe and the United States share a cultural and historical background, the two contexts exhibit one sharp difference. While the American cotton plantations were established at home, on the soil of the American South, European slavery took place far away, largely in the Caribbean. The inhabitants of Copenhagen, London, Hamburg, Amsterdam, and Lisbon, as a result, could carry on with their lives as if they had no relationships with slave owners or their estates, profits, and crimes. A growing body of literature on European slave ownership, however, has been emerging in most European contexts.[6] The records of British slave owners, now publicly available and scrutinized, show that slave ownership was far more common than previously assumed. Here, as in the United States, the euphemistic language of "planters" and "merchants" often concealed famous names associated with slave ownership.

In the United States, redefining race and color became the key issue for the civil rights movement of the twentieth century.[7] African Americans were continually subjected to practices and regulations that maintained segregation, poverty, and discrimination along the color line. "Jim Crow" laws barred the disenfranchised from public places, events, and opportunities freely enjoyed by whites. From 1877 to 1950 there were extensive lynchings of blacks, resulting in the deaths of four thousand people in twelve states.[8] Often these theatrical public executions were punishments for imagined crimes or trivial social transgressions, such as "talking back" to whites. These catastrophic events mainly took place in the South, but they set the stage for nationwide developments—racial segregation, forced migrations of blacks, and police violence in black neighborhoods, events that still recur in both northern and southern states. Civil rights activists, including Martin Luther King Jr., Rosa Parks, and Malcolm X, used civil disobedience to bring about change. The pressing question of "color" remains both extremely complex and unsettling.

Perhaps because of the logistics of North American slavery, the sheer proximity of the plantations, issues stemming from slavery repeatedly resurface in the United States, and along with them the racism on which slavery rested. One striking recent development has been the rise of the Black Lives Matter movement.[9] Growing out of raging discussions in social media in 2013 onward of the biases of all-white or near-all-white juries in connection with the shootings of unarmed black people and related public protests in several North American cities, it quickly became a political force of its own, sometimes referred to as the twenty-first century's first civil rights movement.

Written as a letter to the author's teenaged son, Ta-Nehisi Coates's best seller *Between the World and Me* captures the African American experience at this moment, reflecting on the deep history of color and racial violence and the gulf that continues to separate blacks and whites. Drawing upon his experience of growing up in the streets of Baltimore, Coates seems to provide the modern equivalent, and combined impact, of Frantz Fanon's *Black Skin, White Masks* (1952), James Baldwin's *The Fire Next Time* (1963), and Toni Morrison's *Beloved* (1982), outlining the manner in which racism dehumanizes blacks and the personal and political measures they must take to meaningfully respond and survive. Coates's text merges effective poetic language and powerful observations of black lives to capture the visceral experience of direct and insidious racial abuse, in a manner that few other recent books seem to do, appealing to many modern readers, not least young blacks.

It has sometimes been said that while the slave trade divided the world in two—into masters and slaves—it also forged connections between parts of the world that had previously been isolated. Such links are not just a feature of Hans Jonathan's story; it would be more accurate to say that he, along with the many others who shared similar experiences, paved the way for the global village we know today.

FIG. 16.1. Hans Jonathan's signature. (Records of the Langabud store, Djupivogur, Iceland; National Archives, Reykjavik, Iceland.)

WHO STOLE WHOM?

BETWEEN 1803 AND 1807 ten thousand slaves were transported from
West Africa to the West Indies. Danish ships took part in that trade,
sometimes sailing under foreign flags.[1] Despite the fact that the slave
trade was by then banned under Danish law, these forced transports
continued for a time. Yet in most places support for slavery was dwin-
dling as the nineteenth century progressed.[2] When Peter von Scholten was appointed governor of the Danish West Indies in 1833, he was
expected to pave the way for the emancipation of those who were enslaved. Scholten promoted a range of progressive measures: schools
were established for slave children, and laws were amended to allow freed persons to take certain jobs, mainly as skilled craftsmen.
In 1847, rules were introduced that all children born on the islands
should be deemed free—but the measure only heightened the sense
of injustice. Enslaved adults saw it as demeaning and unfair that they
should remain in slavery while their infants were born free. On the
nearby British Virgin Islands, slavery had been entirely abolished in
1834, and those enslaved on the Danish island of St. John could go
ashore as free persons on the British island of Tortola—if they could
cross the fifteen miles of sea to get there.[3] Meanwhile, the Danish
West Indies were still dominated by the white elite, and the bulk of
the black population of St. Croix and the other islands remained en-

slaved in the sugar fields, which was how the sugar barons wanted it. In the end it was an insurrection that set enslaved people free: they "stole" themselves—each and every one.

This revolt, when it came, was relatively peaceful, and soon over. Black islanders gathered en masse and marched on the Danish fort in Frederiksted on St. Croix, where enslaved Africans had tradition-ally been held on their arrival after the Middle Passage. The protest-ers demanded their freedom. A powerful threat they used was that they would set fire to the sugar fields. The sugar crop would go up in smoke—and sugar was, in the end, what mattered. The protesters did not confine their demands to freedom under the law; they also wanted to reap the profits of their labor. It would be only fair that those who worked the land should own it, and the white outsiders could go back where they came from. This was an epoch-making conflict over social rights, and the abolition of the bondage that en-slaved Africans and their descendants had endured since the planta-tions were founded.

Governor Scholten had done something to improve the position of enslaved people—and he himself lived with a woman of color, so perhaps he sympathized. He acceded to their demands and on 3 July 1848 issued a proclamation emancipating all slaves in the Danish West Indies. Prosecuted thereafter for stirring up the slave uprising, Scholten lost his position as governor. The governor had moved too fast, in the judgment of the authorities in Copenhagen, and had ul-timately been defeated by the slaves themselves. On appeal his con-viction was overturned and he was reappointed, but he died a broken man in 1854.[4]

White overseers and agents who ran the plantations for the sugar barons and profited handsomely themselves were expelled one by one. As the oldest photographs from St. Croix show, the blacks' ani-mosity was directed largely at the whites' personal possessions.[5] It would not do the enslaved people any good to burn the sugar crop. Instead they took out their anger on objects that signified white privi-lege: porcelain, fine bedding, and hardwood furniture. In the plant-

FIG. 16.2. Watchtower on one of the plantations on St. Croix, erected 1791. (Photo: Gisli Palsson.)

ers' former homes, blacks sawed the legs off grand pianos and destroyed beautiful mahogany tables that they had obediently polished to a fine shine for many years. They scratched the smooth wood and hacked at the tables with knives and machetes.

Yet while their freedom had been won and slavery was now a thing of the past, the newly freed agricultural laborers still faced a hard battle. The masters were still present, and the position of the laborers was precarious. Occasionally more trouble broke out. In protests on St. Croix three decades after the revolt, a large and sonorous bell on the Schimmelmanns' La Grange plantation, inscribed with their name, was taken down and broken up.[6] Cast in Copenhagen a century earlier, the bell had marked out the hours of the enslaved workers' long days laboring in the fields. Now it would ring no more.

In 1917 Denmark sold St. Croix and the rest of the Danish West Indies to the United States for twenty-five million dollars in gold. The First World War had redefined Danish and United States geopolitical interests. Also, with the end of slavery and the sugar plantations the colonies in the West Indies were increasingly considered a burden to the Danish state, plagued by social deprivation.

The Danish fort in Frederiksted on St. Croix is now a museum, popular with tourists, where various objects from the era of the slave trade are preserved. The contrast is shocking between the facilities of the guards on the upper floor and the conditions in which the enslaved people were kept below: European luxury above, beneath it bare walls and shackles. The cell where slaves were locked up for offenses or disobedience is claustrophobic, and those who summon up the courage to enter are met with a foul stench: over the centuries, generation after generation of slaves had to urinate where they lay, shackled and unable to move.

THE BANALITY OF EVIL

The slave trade is an atrocity on a scale larger than most crimes against humanity. How can we grasp the nature of this brutal practice? An obvious comparison is with the atrocities committed by the Nazis. German philosopher Hannah Arendt was present at the trial in Israel in 1961 of Adolf Eichmann, one of the architects of the Holocaust. She coined the phrase "the banality of evil" to convey her ideas about Eichmann's crimes and those of the Nazi regime.[7]

Arendt sought to depict the almost surreal "routine" attitude of the executioners, who unquestioningly followed orders, showing no sign of consideration or remorse. Eichmann himself stood proudly erect during his trial in Jerusalem, with no sign of shame or self-knowledge—as if he were in court for some minor traffic offense, or even saw what he had done as a good deed. Nazis came to take indescribable barbarism for granted, suffering no pangs of conscience or lack of sleep. They had a job to do. Most of them did their work conscientiously, almost without thinking, and that was what captured Arendt's attention. Her description has long been controversial: some critics felt that she was, in a sense, defending the Nazis—as if they were not personally responsible for their actions and felt nothing about them. A more recent study, *Eichmann before Jeru-salem*, convincingly argues, on the other hand, that Arendt failed to see through Eichmann's performance, disguising his evil agenda by conveying the image of the naive technocrat; actually Eichmann's papers show that he remained committed to his agenda and his crimes right to the end.[8]

Some have concluded that Arendt had pinpointed, and described with devastating accuracy, an entirely new phenomenon in human history. And perhaps that was also her view. She draws a clear distinc-tion between the slavery of past times and the concentration camps of the twentieth century, remarking that "throughout history slav-ery has been an institution within a social order; slaves were not, like concentration-camp inmates, withdrawn from the sight and hence the protection of their fellow men; as instruments of labor they had a definitive price and as property a definite value. The concentration-camp inmate has no price, because he can always be replaced; nobody knows to whom he belongs, because he is never seen."[9]

Arendt's concept of "the banality of evil" is, however, entirely applicable to the slave trade. Huge numbers of people got on with their jobs as if nothing could be more natural than human bondage: slave traders, planters, police officers, clergy, cooks and politicians, lawyers and executioners, coachmen and blacksmiths, physicians and gravediggers, sea captains and sailors. Many of them regarded the institution of slavery as a necessity—or even as a progressive step for the benefit of all. Weren't the slaves better off in the West Indies than they had been in Africa? Yet the everyday work of the slavers and slave owners brought misery and suffering to millions of human beings, many of them kept under restraint only to be exterminated in slow stages, out of the public eye, like the victims of the concen-tration camps—in the holds of slavers' vessels and on plantations in the colonies.[10]

Twelve and a half million Africans were transported across the Atlantic into slavery between 1527 and 1866. Individual tales from the terrible trade are heartbreaking. In the fall of 1781 the vessel *Zong*, owned by a Liverpool merchant, sailed from Africa to the Caribbean laden with enslaved captives. The ship drifted off course, water supplies ran out, and both crew and captives began to fall ill. Captain Luke Collingwood summoned the crew and informed them that if the Africans died a natural death, the costs would fall on the ship owner. But if, on some pretext regarding the safety of the crew, "they were thrown alive into the sea, it would be the loss of the underwriters."[11] The first mate is said to have objected, unsuccessfully. Over a hundred people were flung overboard to drown. The case led to a major scandal, and the underwriters refused to pay up.

Danish slave traders are believed to account for about 1 percent of the total slave transports across the Atlantic in the eighteenth and nineteenth centuries. The Danish role had long been quietly ignored—or hushed up[12]—before the author Thorkild Hansen lifted the veil of silence on this shameful stain on Scandinavian history.

In 1965 Hansen had been one of a group of Danish writers who went to Poland and visited the Auschwitz concentration camp. In his autobiography, *Søforhør* (Maritime court), Hansen recounts his experience of Auschwitz and how it led him to explore the subject of slavery:

> I had for many years nurtured a strong desire to go out to the former Danish colonies, especially the West Indies, where I knew that one would find a milieu from the Danish Golden Age, which had survived in its own niche. I was supported in this idea by my good friend Ib Andersen, whose watercolors from there I admired. It was the bright side of the subject, the aesthetic, but there was also, of course, another much darker side. This influenced me powerfully after I had been one of the delegates on a trip in April with Danish writers, not to the tropics, but just to Poland. And there . . . I don't know how to express it. It's kind of impossible to talk about.[13]

As the writers headed back to Krakow from the concentration camp, there was silence on the bus. Some of them were in tears. A friend of Hansen's suggested that he should work through his feelings by writing about the topic. The story of the Nazi camps had a personal meaning for Hansen: he was of Roma descent, an ethnic minority who were (and are) persecuted all over Europe. In Nazi Germany many Roma were given "a free trip to Auschwitz," as Hansen put it. The trains to the camps had a significance similar to that of the Danish ships on the Gold Coast of Africa: there was no way back. And Hansen's conclusion was similar to Arendt's: on the sugar plantations, as in the concentration camps, children were snatched from their parents, only to die, "but the people who had done this weren't members of the SS, Nazis, German, they were mostly quite ordinary Danes just like me."[14]

Nazi ideologies have a deep lineage that intersects with Icelandic ideas about race. In the early twentieth century, certain Icelandic intellectuals volubly espoused the idea of Iceland as a united nation with a strong sense of identity; some of these men and women had studied in Germany and had adopted ideas about racial anthropology and eugenics encountered there—which would be applied with horrifying consequences under the Third Reich. Gudmundur Hannesson (1866–1946), for example, was at one time Iceland's surgeon general. He was interested in improving and purifying the Icelandic "race." To his mind this effort was a form of preventive medicine: he was safeguarding public health.

Another of these intellectuals was Eidur S. Kvaran (1909–39), the first Icelander to qualify formally in physical anthropology. As a student in Germany, Kvaran was impressed by ideas of racial anthropology, such as those of the German geneticist Eugene Fischer, who praised the Nazis for being first to point out the importance of eugenics for the Germanic nations, and especially for the Nordic peoples.[15] Eidur graduated in 1936 with a doctorate from Greifswald, where he also taught Icelandic studies. He combined his anthropological ideas with an analysis of the Old Icelandic sagas. He read the sagas as literally true—as was common at the time; today they are more commonly viewed as literature than as history. He concluded that in early Iceland close attention had been paid to physical attributes; he maintained that the sagas are evidence that the Icelanders "realized, earlier and better than most other peoples, that individuals' qualities and instincts—whether good or bad—are heritable. That they are a legacy passed down to them by their ancestors. But the corollary of the legacy was a duty to ensure that it was not degraded by mixing blood with inferior lineages."[16]

Eidur made a study of the sagas' vocabulary for physical attributes, with the objective of deducing what "races" had settled Iceland. He found strong emphasis on physical build, facial features, and hair color. "Physical characteristics," he wrote, "are here described so clearly and in such detail, that an anthropologist can unhesitatingly draw conclusions from them about the race of the individuals. These descriptions are strongly reminiscent of modern anthropological studies, with the difference that all analysis of appearance . . . is described verbally, and not in statistical form, as we do today."[17] Hair color, he decided, was the best yardstick for the Old Icelanders' aesthetic sense. Black hair generally had some implication of evil, while fair hair was invariably mentioned in the context of beauty, splendor, and high status. There is no indication in Eidur's writings that he saw any problem with equating external features with character—or, indeed, "race."

Such ideologies persist today. In 2010 the Hans Jonathan website was mentioned on the neo-Nazi Stormfront website, under the heading "Black blood in Iceland?" The discussion was launched with the following comment:

> I always thought this was leftist propaganda and I was wondering if any Icelandic members could enlighten me on this subject. This site is dedicated to the descendants of Hans Jonathans, a negro slave who in the early 1800's fled Denmark and settled in Iceland where he started a family with an Icelandic woman. Apparently there are now hundreds of his descendants in Iceland, which seems a lot for a country of barely 300,000. I realise that this is only a single negro, but it would seem difficult for a country with such a small

population to maintain its genetic homogeneity with this infusion of black blood. Particularly with the genetic input of fairly recent non-white and non-Icelandic white (Eastern European) immigrants. What is truly upsetting is that these Icelandic descendants seem proud of having a negro ancestor.[18]

The next day more comments were made, addressing the significance in the short or long term of one black person in a small population, and whether, or how rapidly, "black blood" is "diluted." Among the comments are these two, reproduced verbatim:

> I would also say that those Icelanders who says to be proud of their black ancestor should be sent to Africa, there they will discover the beauty of the black race and how great is to live in their way . . . loosers!!!

> Hmm . . . I don't really believe it but . . . if they're proud of having negro blood, send them packing on top of an iceberg to Africa.

The World Wide Web is increasingly an active forum for white supremacists, their manifestos, and their plots. Operated out of Florida by a former leader of the Ku Klux Klan in Alabama, Stormfront, perhaps the most active website of its kind in the world, has tens of thousands of visitors a day. The killings of nine African American parishioners in a Charleston, South Carolina, church in June 2015 may have been partly instigated by discussions and blogs on Stormfront and similar sites.[19]

The Stormfront debate associated with Hans Jonathan included references to Heinrich Himmler and "the Jews"—and to the Schimmelmanns, who remain well known in Germany. The eighteenth-century patriarch Heinrich Carl Schimmelmann, who was hugely powerful in his time, is honored at the family's castle in Ahrensburg, and in Hamburg streets are named after him. In 2006 a bust of Heinrich Carl was erected in the Wandsbek district of the city, commemo-

rating "one of the leading slave traders of the eighteenth century."
Protests soon began, and artists arranged provocative street perfor-
mances reenacting the tight packing and forced transport of enslaved
Africans in past centuries. City officials hurriedly removed the bust
and placed it in storage.[20]

The Schimmelmann name may have had a specific resonance
for protesters in Hamburg and elsewhere because several Schimmelmanns in Germany and Denmark were enthusiastic Nazi col-
laborators during World War II.[21] One of these was Heinrich Carl
(1890–1971), a grandson of Ernst Carl Heinrich, Hans Jonathan's
contemporary, who grew up with him on St. Croix and in Copenhagen and enlisted in the Danish navy at the same time, before the Battle
of Copenhagen. Heinrich Carl Schimmelmann was the prominent
editor of the publication *Fædrelandet* (Fatherland) and supported the
Danish Nazi movement financially. In 1947 he was imprisoned for
treason, and some of his assets were seized.[22] The fate of Heinrich
Carl highlights with special clarity that the Holocaust of the twentieth century and the slave trade of the eighteenth were essentially the
same phenomenon.

SLAVERY TOURISM

In Africa, there is no clear milestone marking the "before" and the
"after" of slavery. The slave trade took place in many stages and periods. Well into the twentieth century, long after the European slave
trade had come to an end, slavery continued to exist in Africa. And
it persists today, though in altered form. The impact is still felt: vil-
lages and communities were formed under the influence of the slave
trade, and everyone had some connection with it—whether as a
victim, slave seller, dissident, accomplice of slave traders, or slave
owner. Many enslaved persons in Africa had family ties with their
African masters, and that painful and complex relationship is hard
to reconcile—not least in view of the prejudices and deprivation of
rights that enslave people have suffered. In some families, stories

have been passed down of raids by African slave catchers: of relatives vanishing from the fields, never to be heard of again, and others who managed to escape their captors and return home.

In recent years the history of slavery has been recounted and reenacted as part of a growing tourism industry.[23] Descendants of African slaves go on pilgrimages both to Africa and to St. Croix and the other Caribbean islands in order to learn about their history, seek out their roots, establish links with their relatives—or simply to find "people like us." In some places, like Benin and other West African countries that were major targets of the slave trade, there is not much to see: the slavers' camps consisted of simple huts that soon vanished and were forgotten. In Ghana and Nigeria, on the other hand, there is much to see and show: history lives on and is renewed by new generations, both at home and in the New World. This special niche in tourism is directed particularly at African Americans, the descendants of the slaves, who are keen to see where their ancestors came from, visit their ancestral lands, find their roots, and be reconciled with themselves and their origins.[24]

The pilgrimages of African Americans to Ghana reflect the slave trade of history. A popular Slave Route destination is the Pikworo Slave Camp near the northeast border of the country. Little remains at the site: rocks and cliffs surround grassy land, with an occasional tree. The lesson taught is that this is the starting point of the Ghanaian slave trade. Guides welcome the visitors and show them where the enslaved captives ate, where they were punished for disobedience, and where they were forced to perform to entertain their guards. A Ghanaian guide says: "At times when these black Americans come, when we take them round the history, some of them . . . weep . . . ; some of them will say, we and white people will never be together because they did bad to us."[25]

One of the pilgrimage projects is the "Slave Route," initiated by UNESCO in 1994. A striking aspect of this and similar projects is the silence regarding the African role in human trafficking.[26] The story of slavery is told, yet it is oversimplified and misinterpreted in various ways. Europeans alone are presented as slavers, while Africans appear exclusively as victims. This one-sided view, focusing on the slavers' ships, the sea passage, the ocean, the coastal forts, and the export of slaves, intensifies the dichotomy between the New World and the home country. This framing of the story ignores the fact that before they reached the coast, slaves had generally been seized and transported in "the jungle" by African slave traders, who had brutalized them long before they were offered for sale to European slavers. This silence about slavery of Africans by Africans arises partly from the fact that the descendants of slaves and of slave owners still live side by side, connected by familial ties. No one cares to examine too closely the old divisions or to experience the guilt and humiliation on both sides.[27]

Accounts of the hierarchies of the African slave trade are complicated by growing evidence of marriages between European slave traders and African women from the seventeenth century onward. The story of these marriages and the families involved is told in an important book by Pernille Ipsen, *Daughters of the Trade*. In the early days of globalization, Ipsen points out, Copenhageners and African business partners on the Gold Coast often established strong connections. While marriages between Danish men and African women were common and the themes of race and color were often subdued, at least early on before the real hype of sugar, in the interest of joint economic concerns, there is no evidence of women from the Gold Coast coming to Copenhagen with their husbands or partners.

Long suppressed due to the horrors of the African slave trade, the story of these families and their hybrid cultures deserves a place in the history of slavery, providing a more nuanced and complex picture of the Atlantic world than hitherto available. Some of this history is preserved in customs and embodied language: various words from the vocabulary of Danish slave traders remain in the language spoken in coastal Ghana. Many modern descendants of Danish Africans in Ghana feel the need to explore and celebrate their common

European roots, yet another aspect of the troubled remembrance of the Atlantic slave trade.

It is worth bearing in mind that slavery is deeply rooted in human history, over centuries and millennia. Leaders of Western philosophy as far back as Aristotle argued that slavery was a natural condition: not only were some people "natural slaves," but they were inherently "inferior" and hence *deserved* to be slaves. Immanuel Kant maintained that "the Negroes of Africa have received from nature no intelligence that rises above the foolish."[28] Kant was a seminal influence on Anders Sandøe Ørsted, the young judge who played such a crucial role in *The General's Widow v. the Mulatto*, and perhaps such racial prejudices colored the judge's views of Hans Jonathan.

Yet these assumptions were not unquestioningly accepted by all. Charles Darwin, for instance, condemned slavery; his opposition to racial stereotyping may have led him toward his theory of evolution.[29] The Scottish doctor James Grainger, who went to the West Indies and ultimately settled there, wrote a long poem, *The Sugar-Cane* (1765), in which he described the life of the sugar plantation in detail and urged the emancipation of the slaves.[30] Artists and photographers also played a role in the campaign for the abolition of slavery. Eighteenth-century drawings depict black people with severed limbs, or restrained in stocks, or hanged. Publications on the slave trade were illustrated with pictures of conditions aboard the slave ships, which were designed to make optimal use of space and keep the "livestock" under restraint during the sea passage. These became iconic images of slavery. Widely distributed, these graphic images of how enslaved people were "packed" opened many people's eyes to the appalling truth, and protests followed. Yet images of atrocities can also lead to what we now call compassion fatigue, and that was true in the slavery debate.[31]

Slavery still exists around the world.[32] In fact, more people are now enslaved than at any time in human history. The entire number of human beings transported across the Atlantic into slavery is estimated to have been only about half as many as are enslaved in the world today: twenty-five million. Today slavery is a secret phenomenon, carefully concealed. If any formal records are kept, they are certainly not intended for the public eye. And when information about slavery gets out, our reaction is horror and anger—unlike the apathy and indifference of the past. There are even open discussions today about our "slavery footprint," analogous to the "carbon footprint" which has gained currency in discussions of climate change. Our slavery footprint is meant to show "how many slaves work for" us—that is, how we as individuals contribute to modern-day slavery by buying goods whose production process includes slave labor.[33]

THE LESSONS OF HISTORY

RACE REMAINS A CONTESTED ISSUE. Debates over whether race is a social or a biological issue still rage in Iceland, Denmark, the United States, and many other countries. We should not underestimate the international movement that lies behind discourses about the purity of the "Nordic race." A follower of that ideology took action, for instance, on 22 July 2011 in Norway. The mass murders carried out in central Oslo and on Utøya Island have raised questions not only about the psyche of that one man and the Western society that shaped him but also about the roots of the Nordic and European world. Although the science of genomics has redefined the issues of race and ancestry—emphasizing that "color" is primarily a cultural construct, an idea in people's minds—the social divide is often intact, an everyday reality creating inequalities in opportunities, health, and well-being. Arguably, race is *both* social and biological, in the sense that social divisions and inequities become embodied biological realities.[1]

TO OWN ONESELF AND TO STEAL ONESELF

What does it mean to "steal oneself"? It is not simply a matter of throwing off the shackles of slavery, literally refusing to be classified as chattel. It also entails challenging received ideas about racial

222 · *Part IV, Descendants*

stereotyping, slavery, gender, class oppression, sexual orientation, and every form of systematic discrimination—and thus setting oneself and others free from the yoke of such ideologies. One aspect of "stealing oneself" in this broader sense is to change one's social status. Today people who are branded "black" in a "white" world tend to earn less and to have a less comfortable life. Such discrimination is often seen an integral part of an individual's personality—like a regional accent, taken for granted and very hard to shake off.

Beyer, Hans Jonathan's attorney in the lawsuit, poured scorn on the alleged "ownership" that was the premise of the case: if Hans Jonathan refused to obey the Widow Schimmelmann and left her home, against the orders of his "owner," Beyer said, then he must have "stolen himself." Beyer's argument serves to remind us that neither slavery nor freedom is necessarily permanent or durable: the individual is always a work in progress. The time had come for Hans Jonathan to "choose himself," as another Copenhagen resident, philosopher Søren Kierkegaard, called on his readers to do some years later. Probably the most important task of people in bondage consists in *choosing to be free*; in some cases there is scope for such a choice—but sometimes not. And a person can both gain freedom and lose it. Whatever happens, the principal task is oneself.

But is not freedom a prerequisite for the ability to make a choice? There is no evidence that Kierkegaard, who lived for a time on Bredgade, just around the corner from Hans Jonathan's former home at Ameliegade 23, made any effort to improve the lot of people of color. We know that he kept up with court cases and was well acquainted with Judge Anders Sandøe Ørsted, for whom he had great respect.[2] It is certainly ironic that the man who spoke so powerfully about the importance of choosing oneself should ignore the institution of slavery and commend a jurist who argued that some human beings had no right to choose. The paradoxes in Kierkegaard's views, and those of many others of his time, remind us how tenacious and insidious the opinion could be that people who are "other" are inferior or second-class. From that point the argument was easily made that slavery was normal—or even good.

I was on St. Croix at the time of the US presidential election when Barack Hussein Obama—another "mulatto," in the parlance of the sugar barons—was elected for a second term in the White House. Some of his opponents in the United States claimed that he was not US-born and thus ineligible to run for the presidency. They demanded that he produce documentary evidence of his birth and origins. Much has changed since Hans Jonathan's birth in 1784—but some things remain the same.

BIOGRAPHIES

I am not myself descended from Hans Jonathan. What was it that touched me, that urged me to write about slavery, that demanded I give Hans Jonathan a new life by writing his biography? There were many contributing factors. Ever since my years as a student of anthropology in Manchester, England, in the 1970s, I have been interested in the roots of racism. In England racism was almost an integral part of the landscape and architecture of the industrial revolution. As Karl Marx said, "Liverpool grew fat on the slave trade."[1] At the harbor there remain traces of the enslaved persons who were brought to England, then transported on barges to the industrial areas of Manchester and along the canals that crisscrossed the city, and the entire country, as slavery did in days gone by.[2] Textile production, industrialization, and slavery went hand in hand.[3] In retrospect, it is as if Hans Jonathan has been with me ever since I stood, a young student, fresh from Iceland and finding my way in a new language, on the banks of those canals in the English slave ports.

Or perhaps Hans Jonathan stood beside me still earlier, for some of his descendants lived in the place where I grew up, a fishing village in the Westman Islands, off the south coast of Iceland. In the village was a small general store run by Dagny Ingimundardottir, a descendant of Hans Jonathan, and her husband. In those days there was a deposit on soda bottles, and Dagny kept the returned empty bottles in a shed out back. We island lads would sometimes sneak in there, filch a few bottles, and take them into the shop to claim the deposit, which we used to buy candy. No doubt Dagny was aware of our small crimes but turned a blind eye—and nobody brought in the child protection authorities. Dagny could never have imagined that one of those thieves would set out to write the life story of her forefather. And I had no idea back then that this kindly shopkeeper was a descendant of people who had been enslaved. Ironically perhaps, one of the earliest written accounts of the islands where I was born and raised, from the Icelandic *Book of Settlements*, involves a narrative of enslaved persons who escaped to the islands in saga time only to get killed by the Norse settler who followed them. These were of Celtic background, "Westmen" in the language of the time—hence the "Westman Islands."

Writing Hans Jonathan's biography was for me a journey into the unknown—as is the writing of any biography, not only in the sense that all the facts of the story were not known to me before I began but also in that a single story may be told in many different ways, from a range of perspectives. Every biography is thus a work of fiction. The biographer brings out what the past *may* hold.

In recent years the genre has been the subject of lively debate.[4] Which individuals deserve to have their life stories written? How is that selection made? What is the author's attitude toward the subject? What motivates the author? And what methods do biographers use? Microhistory, with its focus on individuals and groups who have been marginalized in the historical grand narrative, has led to innovative ideas about appropriate subjects for biography. Figures who would once have been dismissed as unworthy are now brought out of the shadows in a different kind of biography, in which historians apply new approaches in narrative and style.[5]

In the past biographers (in European languages, at least) largely focused on free white individuals of some social standing. Documents and other sources tend to be silent regarding outsiders, such as people of color held in slavery; and this certainly makes the biographer's work more difficult. Not only is there little in the way of hard evidence, but it is hard to tell where the journey of discovery will lead the biographer—and the reader. For the life of an enslaved person, the documentary evidence is often meager. Slave owners did their best to leave a minimum of records, other than necessary letters and tax documents. The writing of any biography necessitates some use of the imagination, but the life story of an enslaved person requires more than most. Solid facts are so often lacking, because silence served the interests of the rich and powerful.

How are we to understand the *character* of a biography? The emphasis on a single consistent story, which has long typified the literary genre of biography, is a function of Western ideas about the individual as an autonomous being, to be viewed separately from his or her environment. We need to break out of that tradition. Although we concede that people "adapt" to circumstances and are "shaped" by the society in which they grow up, individuals still tend to be described as worlds of their own, and these worlds become the biographer's true subject—the unique and more or less immutable selves. Yet it is entirely possible to imagine a different kind of historical writing, one that focuses on relational beings firmly embedded in context.[6] The environment is in the person as much as the person is in the environment—both social and natural. This applies to every human being: no person is an island. That is the principle I have applied in writing this biography of Hans Jonathan. My focus is obviously on the man himself, but also on others who played a part in his life and in history, on the environment in which he grew up, on his descendants, and on many other phenomena that relate directly or indirectly to his life. Without his social network—without his friends, family, relatives, and neighbors—Hans Jonathan's efforts to gain his freedom could scarcely have been successful, and any freedom he won would have been a hollow victory.

The idea of biography—of recounting and commenting upon a real life—has its own life history. Such narratives and commentaries go back to the oldest writings and images—and beyond them into the mystery of ancient times. It is often said that the birth of humanity was marked by the tradition of bidding the dead farewell with some form of ritual, some funeral or burial customs. Burial rites, from ancient times to today, are intended to honor the memory of a person who is no longer alive, a life that has been lived. The word *biography* (from the Greek, meaning "account of a life"), on the other hand, has only a short history. It was coined around the time of Hans Jonathan's birth, a product of the combination of printing technology and the increased literacy of the eighteenth century.[7] This fact serves to remind us that biography, like the novel and other literary genres, is mutable, contingent upon the whims of writers and readers. No story can be told once and for all.

"Some day, perhaps, biography will be written almost in terms of structural chemistry," wrote the British chemist Henry Armstrong (1848–1937) in a brief comment in the journal *Nature* in 1931, "and the doctrine of descent stated in terms of the permutations and combinations effected between genes. . . . I merely wish to claim, in all modesty," he added, "that biography should be the recognised province of the structural chemist: he alone can appreciate the complete interdependence of character and structure." The discovery of the double helix, and the subsequent mapping and complete sequencing of the human genome, would have to wait for other generations, but Armstrong's comment was prescient. Currently, the genome of Hans Jonathan is being reconstructed. This reconstruction is the painstaking work of two anthropologists and their colleagues at deCODE genetics in Reykjavik, Iceland. Now Hans Jonathan's life is becoming the subject of another dramatic saga, far more futuristic than the chemist Henry Armstrong could possibly have imagined. The reconstruction of his genome is part of a larger study, based in Copenhagen, of transatlantic migrations in the wake of the slave trade.[8]

The principle of the "body of crime" (Latin *corpus delicti*) in Western jurisprudence stipulates that a crime must be proved to have occurred before a person can be convicted of having committed that crime. In the case of Hans Jonathan there is neither body nor crime, but how much can we learn about his body? While his own "chemistry" is not directly accessible for analysis (his grave site remains unknown), as in many criminal cases and detective stories there is some crucial circumstantial evidence—"beyond a reasonable doubt," in legal parlance. In a groundbreaking project, Agnar Helgason, Anuradha Jagadeesan, Kari Stefansson and their colleagues aim to reconstruct large fragments of Hans Jonathan's genome through the hereditary signatures of some of his living descendants in Iceland. This is possible thanks to several assets of the deCODE laboratory, including genotyping of thousands of living Icelanders (a substantial part of the national population), the comprehensive family histories stored in the computerized genealogical database known as the Book of Icelanders, and a series of bioinformatic innovations relating to the study of shared chromosome fragments.

Not only does this project reconstruct much of Hans Jonathan's genome, but it may throw new light on the West African background of his mother Emilia Regina and her parents, which until now has been shrouded in mystery. Having access to a series of recent studies of key reference populations in West Africa, and knowing that Hans Jonathan represents the only source of African admixture in the Icelandic population from the time in question, the researchers hope to be able to use his computed genome to make inferences about his ancestry. Further work on Hans Jonathan's genome might also establish the identity of his father, or rule out some of the candidates, assuming access to the relevant genomic data. Will the Danish relatives of Hans Gram prove to be related to Hans Jonathan?

In the fall of 2008 I went to Djupivogur to talk to schoolchildren there about Hans Jonathan. They were about the age I was when I was stealing bottles from Dagny—or that Hans Jonathan was when he sailed from St. Croix to Copenhagen. I told them briefly about his life—that his mother was from West Africa and his father probably from Denmark, that he had been born and spent his childhood in the

Virgin Islands, and that he had lived for a time in Copenhagen before coming to Iceland, where he lived for the rest of his life. I asked them to imagine what he may have looked like and to draw me a picture. I told them that we have no portrait of Hans Jonathan, no photograph, and so their ideas were as good as anyone else's. The children were responsive to the idea, and a few of them had heard of Hans Jonathan before. In the pictures they drew, Hans Jonathan was depicted in all sorts of settings and dressed in various ways, from a traditional Icelandic wool sweater to a suit and tie. I had taken care to make no reference to his skin color, and I had asked the pupils' teacher to do the same. One of the children humorously remarked that "if you mix black with yellow you ought to get green." "That's fine," I replied, "make him green, then!"

Hans Jonathan's story gives rise to many questions about the conditions that foster racism in our own time—about our ideas of who we are and what makes us different from each other. Where do our ideas about color, "purity," racial mixing, and diversity come from? Why do people become racists, and, perhaps more importantly, how can we interrupt that process? We must begin with schoolchildren like these. We must begin by changing the way we tell the story of the past. New times bring new writers, new perspectives, new technology, and a new history, for *Homo sapiens* is the eternal storyteller. Every story meets our need to understand the world and to set our imaginations free—while we strive to change the world, in the knowledge that everything could have been different.

| *Timeline* |

AROUND 1100 Slavery dies out in Iceland

1495 Columbus transports hundreds of enslaved Native Americans to Seville

1615 "Spanish Massacre" in Iceland—over thirty Basque whalers are brutally killed

1627 "Turkish Raid"—Barbary corsairs take hundreds of Icelanders captive in East Iceland and the Westman Islands

1658 Danish merchants establish themselves on Africa's Gold Coast

1712 Slave insurrection in New York City

1733 The Danish West India-Guinea Company purchases the island of St. Croix from France

1754 Hans Gram born in Copenhagen

1760 Emilia Regina, Hans Jonathan's mother, is born into slavery on St. Croix in the Danish Virgin Islands, probably on the La Reine plantation

1761 Arni from Geitastekkur, Iceland, sails by St. Croix

1770 Thomas William Schäffer purchases La Reine plantation from Baron Christian Lebrecht von Prock and acquires Emilia Regina together with other enslaved workers

1777 Schäffer's widow Henrietta Cathrina marries Ludvig Heinrich Ernst von Schimmelmann

1777 Vermont's constitution outlaws slavery

1782 Hans Gram is appointed secretary to Ludvig Heinrich
Schimmelmann

1784 12 April, Hans Jonathan is born on the island of St. Croix in the
Danish Virgin Islands; when he is christened, rumor claims that
his father is "the secretary"

1787 Monopoly on the Iceland trade (in force since 1602) abolished by
decree of King Christian VII of Denmark and Iceland

1788 Emilia Regina's second child, Hans Jonathan's half-sister Anna
Maria, is born and baptized on St. Croix

1788 Ludvig Heinrich Ernst von Schimmelmann and his wife
Henrietta Cathrina move to Copenhagen, taking with them
Emilia Regina and other enslaved persons but leaving Hans
Jonathan behind

1791–1804 Haitian Revolution: slaves and free people of color declare
independence from France

1792 Transport of slaves from Africa to the West Indies under the
Danish flag is banned under a decree that will take effect in 1803

1792 Hans Jonathan sails to Copenhagen, where he lives with his
mother and the Schimmelmann family at Amaliegade 23

1793 Ludvig Heinrich Ernst von Schimmelmann dies in Copenhagen

1798 Katrin Antoniusdottir is born at Hamarsel in southeast Iceland

1800 Hans Jonathan is confirmed in the Lutheran church in
Copenhagen

1801 Hans Jonathan runs away to join the Danish navy

1801 Hans Jonathan fights in the Battle of Copenhagen

1802 A verdict is handed down in the widow Schimmelmann's lawsuit
against Hans Jonathan

1802 Hans Jonathan arrives in Iceland and is employed as a commercial
assistant in the Djupivogur trading post

1803 Henrietta Cathrina Schimmelmann moves away from Amaliegade
23; Emilia Regina vanishes from history

1808 Britain and the United States outlaw participation in the African
slave trade

1816 Henrietta Cathrina Schimmelmann dies in Odense

1819 Hans Jonathan is appointed *factor* (manager) of the Djupivogur trading post

1820 Hans Jonathan marries Katrin Antoniusdottir

1821 Hans Jonathan and Katrin's son Ludvik Stefan is born

1821 Hans Jonathan gives an account of his assets and debts

1823 Hans Jonathan and Katrin become peasant farmers at Borgargardur in Berufjordur

1824 Hans Jonathan and Katrin's daughter Hansina Regina is born

1827 18 December, Hans Jonathan dies "of a stroke"

1833 Katrin Antoniusdottir marries Bjorn Gislason

1833 The American Anti-Slavery Society is founded

1843 Ludvik Stefan marries Anna Maria Johannsdottir Malmqvist

1846 Hansina Regina marries Eirikur Eiriksson

1848 Slaves on St. Croix are emancipated following an insurrection

1860 Abraham Lincoln is elected president of the United States

1862 President Lincoln issues Preliminary Emancipation Proclamation

1869 Katrin Antoniusdottir dies

1869 Bjorn and Georg Eiriksson, grandsons of Hans Jonathan, go to study in Copenhagen

1905 Colonial Exhibition in Copenhagen

1913 Georg Bjorn Eiriksson and his family emigrate from Denmark to the United States

1917 The United States purchase St. Croix from Denmark

1948 The United Nations Universal Declaration of Human Rights provides that "no one shall be held in slavery or servitude; slavery and the slave trade shall be prohibited in all their forms"

1957 The Gold Coast and former centers of the slave trade form part of a new nation, Ghana

1964 Knud Waaben, professor of criminal law at the University of Copenhagen, writes a paper about the verdict in Hans Jonathan's court case in 1802

1985 Holger Eiriksson and Roberta Eiriksson Dollase visit Djupivogur, Iceland

2001 Commemoration in Denmark of the First Battle of Copenhagen, 1801

2002 Descendants of Hans Jonathan and his wife Katrin gather in east Iceland

2008 Barack H. Obama is elected forty-fourth president of the United States

2013 The Black Lives Matter movement begins to take shape in the United States

2015 American and Icelandic descendants of Hans Jonathan visit St. Croix

| *Acknowledgments* |

The idea for this book came to me apparently out of nowhere in the summer of 2007. It had no connection with anything I had been working on during the preceding years, although I had been interested in issues of race and colonial history ever since my early days as a university student. I started out slowly, gathering information bit by bit. After that the process of writing, research, and travel to the sites of the story took up more and more time as the subject took hold of me, and as the opportunity arose. Before long this project became an overriding passion. The University of Iceland provided a number of grants for the research on which the book is based. The Icelandic Literature Center offerered a translation grant which made this publication possible. I twice had use of the scholar's apartment in the Icelandic Jon Sigurdsson House in Copenhagen, adjacent to some of the scenes of the events, as well as to helpful staff and vital archives.

Many people have also been of help. A decisive factor was my experience of interviewing a number of people connected to the saga of Hans Jonathan, who had gone to some effort to find out more about him and his life—not least Roberta Eiriksson Dollase, Edda Emilsdottir, Helgi Mar Reynisson, Kristin Vilhelmina Sigfinnsdottir, and Anna Maria Sveinsdottir, all of whom generously shared their time and passed on their detailed knowledge of the story of their forefather, corrected many errors, and repeatedly put me on the right path. They had begun their own quests for information in the early 1980s and knew more of the story than most others. All of these people, and many more, became the core of a dynamic research network that sometimes seemed to work independently of me, taking me by surprise, drawing my attention to new evidence and perspectives, and taking me to unfamiliar vistas and narratives.

Rannveig Larusdottir Reumert helped me search out information in archives and libraries in Copenhagen. She also independently and untiringly pursued various threads of the story in Denmark. Egill Thor Nielsson interviewed several descendants of Hans Jonathan and gathered historical sources in Iceland, and Sigurður Orn Gudbjornsson searched out important documents in libraries and online and drew my attention to importat sources. Kristin Erla Hardardottir provided crucial help over the years with administration, applications, and budgets.

Many colleagues and friends, mostly historians and anthropologists, have also assisted me in my research in different ways and advised me on particular aspects of the story recounted here: Anna Agnarsdottir, Lisa Birkner, Sveinn Ludvik Bjornsson, Ann Fabian, Erla Hulda Halldorsdottir, Gudni Th. Johannesson, Mar Jonsson, Alex Frank Larsen, Kristin Loftsdottir, Sigurdur Gylfi Magnusson, Sigurdur Hogni Sigurdsson, Olafur Arnar Sveinsson, and Anne Wolbom. Four experts in the fields of criminal law and legal history— Inger Dübeck, the late Vagn Greve, Pall Sigurdsson, and Henrik Stevnsborg—helped me to understand the court case that played such a decisive role in Hans Jonathan's life. George F. Tyson and Svend Holsoe helped me to search the St. Croix database and repeatedly offered important observations and advice. In addition to guiding me through the digital jungle, George Tyson also made introductions for me on St. Croix. Svend Holsoe and Lisa Birkner played an important role in tracking down the elusive Hans Gram. A sabbatical leave at the Center for Advanced Study in Oslo allowed me to make final changes to the manuscript. Thanks to Marianne Elisabeth Lien and her team for the invitation and the stimulating company.

The continued goodwill displayed by many people has encouraged me to persevere ever since I began this project. Among these people are Atli Asmundsson, Hrafn Baldursson, Helgi Bernodusson, Valdimar Leifsson, Rannveig Larusdottir Reumert, Andres Skulason, Anna Maria Sveinsdottir, and, last but not least, editor Gudrun Sigfusdottir, who skillfully handled the Icelandic production at Forlagið.

I am particularly grateful to Anna Yates, for her perceptive reading of my text, her excellent translation from the Icelandic, and her smooth collaboration on the final manuscript. Suzanne Looms offered her help with translating important texts from Danish. I am heavily indebted to my friend Nancy Marie Brown, who not only followed the project throughout but also significantly shaped its course through her editorial skills and her deep understanding of both Icelandic and American contexts. Timothy Mennel, editor at the University of Chicago Press, kindly expressed interest in the manuscript early on and consistently offered encouragement and advice on both practical procedures and narrative style. His skillful editorial work helped to set the right tone and to finalize the narrative and the text. Historian Terri L. Snyder and an anonymous reader for the Press offered extensive and highly valuable advice on language, historical context, and informative comparative works.

I thank Atli Asmundsson and Thrudur Helgadottir for their company on a memorable trip to St. Croix in November 2012. And I thank Hjordis Gudbjornsdottir and Kristjan Stefansson (in Florida) and Jon B. Stefansson and Gudrun Sveinsdottir (Breiddalur, Iceland) for their hospitality on my field trips. Finally, I wish to express my gratitude to my wife, Gudny S. Gudbjornsdottir, for lively discussions at all stages of the project and for accompanying me on my field trips in Iceland, Denmark, and St. Croix. And I must point out, as is customary, that while many people have contributed to this book, and while I have benefited from the invaluable assistance of all those named here and many others, any errors or faults are entirely my responsibility.

Reykjavik, April 2016

| *Photo Catalog* |

HALFTONES

The routes of the saga and the colonial world.

Karolina Elisa Susanna Bjornsdottir (b. 1889), great-granddaughter of Hans Jonathan. (Photo: Hansina Regina Bjornsdottir. National Museum of Iceland, Reykjavik.)

The fort at Frederiksted. (Photo: Gisli Palsson.)

Entrance to La Reine plantation. (Photo: Gisli Palsson.)

Behind 15 Queen's St. in Christiansted, where the house slaves of the Schimmelmann family may have lived, among them Emilia Regina. (Photo: Gisli Palsson.)

Mill tower at Constitution Hill with Schimmelmann's initials, 1778. (Photo: Mark Sellergren.)

Baptism of Hans Jonathan. Records of the Lutheran Church, St. Croix, 1780–94, 1/770-4. (National Archives of Denmark.)

The Lutheran church in Christiansted (rear entrance). (Photo: Gisli Palsson.)

Head tax list from Constitution Hill, 1785. (National Archives of Denmark.)

Letter of Ludvig Heinrich Schimmelmann from 10 March 1784,

witnessed by secretary H. Gram. (National Archives of
Denmark, Schimmelmann Private Archives, no 6285, box 31.)

Ludvig Heinrich Ernst von Schimmelmann. (Kort- og
Billedsamlingen, Royal Library, Copenhagen.)

St. Croix around 1766. The map was dedicated to Count Adam
Gotlob Moltke. (Kort- og Billedsamlingen, Royal Library,
Copenhagen.)

"The Death Song of an Indian Chief" by Hans Gram. (Special
Collections of the St. Louis Mercantile Library at the
University of Missouri–St. Louis.)

The mill at Constitution Hill. (Photo: Gisli Palsson.)

Title page of Jacob Schimmelmann's translation of the Prose
Edda, 1777.

The heart of Amalienborg, Copenhagen. (Photo: Gisli Palsson.)

Old Copenhagen. (Kort- og Billedsamlingen, Royal Library,
Copenhagen.)

Amaliegade 23 in Copenhagen, 1914. (Museum of Copenhagen.)

The Battle of Copenhagen, 2 April 1801. (Source: W. L. Clowes,
*The Royal Navy: A History from the Earliest Times to the
Present*, vol. 4 [London: Sampson Low, Marston, 1899].)

Letter of Crown Prince Frederik in support of Hans Jonathan,
dated 13 May 1801. (Privatarkiv Bille, Letters 1799–1816,
Case 1; National Archives of Denmark.)

Henrietta Cathrina von Schimmelmann. (Kort- og
Billedsamlingen, Royal Library, Copenhagen.)

One of the court documents regarding the case of Henrietta
Cathrina von Schimmelmann and "negro" Hans Jonathan.
(National Archives of Denmark.)

Grave of L. H. Schimmelmann at Garnison Church,
Copenhagen. (Photo: Gisli Palsson.)

The Schimmelmann mansion on Bredgade, Copenhagen.
(Photo: Gisli Palsson,)

Djupivogur around 1820. (From Poul de Lovenorn, *Beskrivelse
over den Iislandske Kyst og alle Havn* [Copenhagen, 1822].)

Djupivogur and neighborhood.

Djupivogur, late nineteenth century. (Photo: Nicoline Marie
Elise Weywadt. National Museum of Iceland, Reykjavik.)

Djupivogur harbor, late nineteenth century. (Photo: Nicoline
Marie Elise Weywadt. National Museum of Iceland,
Reykjavik.)

Manuscript written by *factor* John Stephensen (Jon Stefansson).
(The National and University Library of Iceland.)

Records of Hans Jonathan's transactions at the store in
Djupivogur. (National Archives, Reykjavik.)

Census of 1 December 1816. "Assistant Hans Jonathan,
born on Kantitusjanhill, St: Cröjs." (National Archives,
Reykjavik.)

Berufjord Pass, 2005. Jona Petra Magnusdottir, descendant of
Hans Jonathan. (Photo: Toggi [Thorgeir Eiriksson], 2005.)

Gytha Thorlacius.

The ruins in Bulandsdalur. (Photo: Gisli Palsson.)

Marriage certificate of Hans Jonathan and Katrin Antoniusdottir.
(National Archives, Reykjavik.)

Musician Petur Bjornsson tuning the fiddle of his ancestor Hans
Jonathan. (Photo: Gisli Palsson.)

Physician Hans Benjamin Gram. (Kort- og Billedsamlingen,
Royal Library, Copenhagen.)

Descendants of Hans Jonathan and Katrin Antoniusdottir: On
the wall, Bjorn Eiriksson (their daughter's son) and Susanna
Weywadt. Below them, Emilia Bjornsdottir (Bjorn and
Susanna's daughter), her husband Magnus Magnusson, and
their children Emil Bjorn and Agusta. (Courtesy of Edda
Emilsdottir.)

Ludvik Ludviksson, Hans Jonathan's grandson. (Courtesy of
Helga Tomasdottir.)

Genealogy of Hans Jonathan and his descendants. (Sighvatur
Halldorsson.)

Djupivogur celebrates a new century, 1901. (Photo: Nicoline

Marie Elise Weywadt. National Museum of Iceland, Reykjavik.)

Hansina Regina Bjornsdottir. (Photo: Nicoline Marie Elise Weywadt. National Museum of Iceland, Reykjavik.)

Colonial Exhibition poster, Copenhagen 1905.

"Alien passengers": George Bjorn, Thora Martha, and children arrive in New York, 1913. (Ellis Island Foundation.)

Bjorn Eiriksson (left) and Georg Eiriksson (right). Photo by Theodor Hansen, Copenhagen. (Courtesy of Roberta Dollase.)

George Bjorn Eiriksson. (Courtesy of Roberta Dollase.)

George Bjorn and his children Katie, Holger, and Dagny. (Courtesy of Roberta Dollase.)

Hans Jonathan's signature. (Records of the Langabud store, Djupivogur, Iceland; National Archives, Reykjavik, Iceland.)

Watchtower on one of the plantations on St. Croix, erected 1791. (Photo: Gisli Palsson.)

COLOR PLATES

The Constitution Hill plantation, 1833. (Frederik von Scholten, by permission of M/S Museet for Søfart, Helsingør, Denmark.)

The harbor at Christiansted, St. Croix. (H. G. Beenfeldt [1767–1829], by permission of M/S Museet for Søfart, Helsingør, Denmark.)

Heinrich Carl Schimmelmann and Caroline Tugendreich, around 1773–79. (Lorenz Lönberg; Museum of National History, Frederiksborg, Denmark). (Photo: Hans Petersen.)

The Battle of Copenhagen, 1801. (1901; C. Mølsted; Royal Danish Naval Museum, Copenhagen.)

The ruins at Borgargardur, Djupivogur, Iceland. (Photo: Gisli Palsson.)

"The races of men; from Southern Territories, dark people
(Blamenn), also called Negroes." (From a manuscript written
by Jon Bjarnason between 1845 and 1852; the National and
University Library of Iceland.)

Memorial service, Denmark, 2001. (Photo: Alex Frank Larsen.)

Meeting of Icelandic and American descendants of Hans
Jonathan in Djupivogur, Iceland, 1985. Left to right: Holger
Eiriksson, Kristjan Jonsson, Roberta Eiriksson Dollase,
Bjorn Jonsson, and Emil Bjornsson. (Courtesy of Roberta
Dollase.)

| *Notes* |

PROLOGUE

1. Raarup Andersen, interview, September 2013.

"A HOUSE NEGRO"

1. St. Clair, *The Door of No Return*.
2. Ipsen, *Daughters of the Trade*.
3. Hansen, *Slavernes skibe*.
4. Isert, *Letters on West Africa and the Slave Trade*.
5. Davis, *Problem of Slavery in the Age of Emancipation*, 93.
6. Oldendorp, *History of the Mission of the Evangelical Brethren on the Caribbean Islands of St. Thomas, St. Croix, and St. John*, 219.
7. Jensen, *For the Health of the Enslaved*, 132.
8. *Laws of Early Iceland: Gragas I*, 273.
9. Jensen, *For the Health of the Enslaved*, 60n158.
10. "Piracy," *Wikipedia*, https://en.wikipedia.org/wiki/Piracy. Accessed January 2012.
11. Oldendorp, *History of the Mission of the Evangelical Brethren*, 55.

12. Irving, *Life and Voyages of Christopher Columbus*.
13. West, *Hans West's Accounts of St. Croix in the West Indies*, 229–31.
14. Oldendorp, *History of the Mission of the Evangelical Brethren*.
15. Ibid., 225.
16. Ibid., 226–27.
17. Franklin and Schwedinger, *Runaway Slaves*.
18. Snyder, *Power to Die*.
19. Holsoe, "Coping with Enslavement."
20. See Hall and Highman, *Slave Society in the Danish West Indies*, 125–28.

"THE MULATTO HANS JONATHAN"

1. Garde, "Samboinden Charlotte Amalie Bernard og hendes efterkommere indtil 5. Led," 217.
2. Highfield, *Time Longa' Dan Twine*, 270.
3. Oldendorp *History of the Mission of the Evangelical Brethren*, 249.
4. Highfield, *Time Longa' Dan Twine*, 269.
5. Ibid., 270.
6. Schiebinger, *Plants and Empires*, 1.
7. Schmidt, *Various Remarks Collected on and about the Island of St. Croix in America*.
8. Ibid., 28.
9. Jensen, *For the Health of the Enslaved*, 72–74.
10. Schmidt, *Various Remarks*, 29.
11. Dunn, *Tale of Two Plantations*.
12. Oldendorp, *History of the Mission of the Evangelical Brethren*, 157.
13. *Generalmajorinde Henriette de Schimmelmann*; unpublished sources.
14. Oldendorp, *History of the Mission of the Evangelical Brethren*, 240.

15. Ibid., 239.

16. See Müller-Wille and Rheinberger, *Cultural History of Heredity*, 58.

17. Records of the Lutheran Church, Christiansted, 1780–194.

18. Records of the Lutherian Church, Christiansted, 1780–94.

19. Ibid.

20. Stoler, *Carnal Knowledge and Imperial Power*.

"SAID TO BE THE SECRETARY"

1. Svend Holsoe, anthropologist, e-mail 22 August 2013.

2. Hall and Highman, *Slave Society in the Danish West Indies*, 175; Highfield, *Time Longa' Dan Twine*, 292.

3. Degn, *Die Schimmelmanns im atlantischen Dreieckshandel*, 322.

4. Inger Dübeck, legal historian, interview, September 2013.

5. Jespersen et al., *Moltke*, 23.

6. Citation in ibid., 40.

7. Ibid., *Moltke*, 398.

8. Svend Holsoe, anthropologist, e-mail, 22 August 2013.

9. Gøbel, *Det danske slavehandelsforbud*.

10. Schimmelmann Private Archives, no 6285, box 31.

11. Pioneers of Homeopathy website.

12. *Dansk biografisk leksikon* website.

13. *Columbian Centinel*, 1795, 3.

14. *The Repertory*, 28 May 1806.

15. *New Hampshire Centinel*, 19 May 1804.

16. Gram, Holyoke, and Holden, *Massachusetts Compiler of Theoretical and Practical Elements of Sacred Vocal Music*.

17. Patterson, *Three American "Primitives,"* 43.

18. Sayre, "'Azakia,' *Quâbi*, and Sarah Wentworth Apthorp Morton."

19. See "Poetry," *Hallowell Gazette*, 4.

20. *Boston Centinel*.

21. "A Disgraceful Practice."

AMONG THE SUGAR BARONS

1. Oldendorp, *History of the Mission of the Evangelical Brethren*, 249.

2. Mintz, *Sweetness and Power*; see also Abbott, *Sugar*.

3. Knight, *Slave Societies of the Caribbean*, 2.

4. Highfield, editor's introduction to *Hans West's Accounts*

5. West, *Hans West's Accounts of St. Croix in the West Indies*, 12.

6. Ibid., 75–78.

7. Ibid., 23.

8. Ibid., 4, 24, and 84.

9. Degn, *Schimmelmanns im atlantischen Dreieckshandel*.

10. Brown, *Song of the Vikings*.

11. *Dansk biografisk leksikon* website, 129.

12. Sturluson, *Isländische Edda*.

13. Mintz, *Sweetness and Power*.

14. Rasmussen, *De Schimmelmannske skoler*, 4.

15. Ballegaard Petersen and Scott Sørensen, *Breve til Charlotte*.

16. *Dansk biografisk lexikon*, 15:139.

17. See Hall and Highman, *Slave Society in the Danish West Indies*, 37.

18. 4 August 1814 entry in "Hans Frisaks dagbøker 1810–1815," microfiche film 82 a II, Oslo University Library.

A CHILD NEAR THE ROYAL PALACE

1. Magnusson, *Ferðasaga Árna Magnússonar frá Geitastekk 1753–1797*, 102–3.

2. Rediker, *Slave Ship*, 251.

3. Quotation in Henningsen and Langen, *Hundemordet i Vimmelskaftet og andre fortællinger fra 1700-tallets København*, 122.

4. Henningsen and Langen, *Hundemordet i Vimmelskaftet og andre fortællinger fra 1700-tallets København*, 16–17.

5. Trouillot, *Silencing the Past*.

6. Davis, *Problem of Slavery in the Age of Emancipation*, 2013.

7. Ankestyrelsen website.

8. Rasmussen, *De Schimmelmannske skoler.*

9. Waaben, "A. S. Ørsted og negerslaverne i København."

10. Olsen, "Disse vilde karle."

11. Ipsen, *Daughters of the Trade*, chap. 3.

12. Bobé, *August Hennings dagbog under hans ophold i København 1802.*

13. Alexander Baumgerten, 1735, quoted in Gikandi, *Slavery and the Culture of Taste*, 222.

14. Tygesen, "Lighed," 146.

15. Andersen, *Mulatten, Originalt romantisk drama i fem akter,* 1840, 363.

16. Sigmundsson, ed., *Hafnarstúdentar skrifa heim*, 47.

17. Arason, *Gamla góða Kaupmannahöfn*, 38.

18. Stephensen, *Skémtileg Vina-Gledi In frodlegum Samrœdum og Liod-mœlum*, 103–7.

"HE WANTED TO GO TO WAR"

1. Scott, *Domination and the Arts of Resistance.*

2. National Archives, Copenhagen.

3. Copenhagen Census 1801.

4. "Generalmajorinde Henriette de Schimmelmann" (unpublished sources).

5. "Generalmajorinde Henriette de Schimmelmann."

6. Tamm, "Nogle tværsnit af Københavns byrets historie."

7. See, for example, "Forord," in Christensen, *Naturens tankelæser.*

8. Ballegaard Petersen and Scott Sørensen, *Breve til Charlotte*, 97.

9. Larsen, *Slavernes slægt*, 57; see also Feldbæk, *Slaget på Reden.*

10. Larsen, *Legenden om Denmark.*

11. Ibid., 58.

12. Bille's Private Archive, National Archives, Copenhagen.

13. "Generalmajorinde Henriette de Schimmelmann."

14. Ibid.
15. Dunn, *Tale of Two Plantations.*
16. Vagn Greve, professor of law, interview, September 2013.
17. "Generalmajorinde Henriette de Schimmelmann."
18. Ibid.

THE GENERAL'S WIDOW V. THE MULATTO

1. "Generalmajorinde Henriette de Schimmelmann."
2. "Generalmajorinde Henriette de Schimmelmann."
3. Ibid.
4. Ibid.
5. Göbel, *Det danske slavehandelsforbud,* 102–4.
6. "Generalmajorinde Henriette de Schimmelmann."
7. Ibid.
8. Ibid.

THE VERDICT

1. *Juridisk Maanedstidende,* 443–44.
2. See Waaben, "A. S. Ørsted og negerslaverne i København," 342.
3. Wiecek, "Somerset," 95.
4. See ibid., 86.
5. See ibid., 87.
6. Ørsted, *Haandbog over den danske og norske Lovkyndighed,* 2:47–48.
7. Algreen-Ussing, *Anmærkninger til personretten,* 78–83.
8. Dübeck, *De elendige,* 29.
9. Christoffersen, "De bortløbne slaver."
10. Thystrup website.
11. Helleberg, *Druknehuset,* 139.
12. Waaben, "A. S. Ørsted og negerslaverne i København," 343.
13. "Generalmajorinde Henriette de Schimmelmann."

A FREE MAN

1. Feldbæk, *Dansk søfartshistorie*, 28–29, 166.
2. Henderson, *Iceland*, 1:3.
3. Andresson, "Tveggja alda afmæli fríhöndlunar á Íslandi," 7.
4. For a comparative and historical perspective on different forms of bondage, see Newmann, *New World of Labor*.
5. Helgason, "Historical Narrative as Collective Therapy."
6. Jonsson, *Annalar þess froma og velvitra sáluga Bjørns Jónssonar á Skarðsá*.
7. Johannesdottir, *Reisubók Guðríðar Símonardóttur*.
8. Andresson, "Tveggja alda afmæli fríhöndlunar á Íslandi," 7.
9. Sigurdsson, *Eskja: Sögurit Eskfirðinga*, 5:7.
10. Stephensen, *Bréf til Finns Magnússonar*, 25.
11. Andresson, "Tveggja alda afmæli fríhöndlunar á Íslandi," 7.
12. *Langabúð*.
13. Sveinsson, *Djúpivogur*, 33.
14. Einarsson, "Bænarskrá bænda," 187.
15. Henderson, *Iceland*, 217.
16. Stephensen, "Aðskiljanlegt nýtt og gamalt sem er útlagt úr dönsku eftir ýmsum Autoribus."
17. Agnarsdottir and Arnason, "Þrælahald á þjóðveldisöld."
18. Thorkelin, *Essay on the Slave Trade*, 4.
19. Ibid., 29–30.
20. Hjorleifur Stefansson, architect, e-mail, May 2013.
21. Records of Geithellnahreppur 1797–1818.

MOUNTAIN GUIDE

1. See preface to Thorlacius, *Fru Gytha Thorlacius Erindringer fra Island i Aarene 1801–1815*.
2. E. O., "Íslendingar beittu búfé á kálplöntur frúarinnar," 11.
3. Thorlacius, *Fru Gytha Thorlacius Erindringer fra Island i Aarene 1801–1815*, 21.

4. Ibid., 48.
5. Ibid., 50.
6. Ibid., 50.
7. Thoroddsen, *Landfrædissaga Íslands III*.
8. Ibid., 191.
9. "Hans Frisaks dagbøker 1810–1815," 4 August 1812.
10. "Hans Frisaks dagbøker 1810–1815."
11. Ibid.
12. Henderson, *Iceland*, 1–2.
13. Ibid., 217.
14. Ibid., 218.
15. Stephensen, *Bréf til Finns Magnússonar*, 53.
16. Agnarsdottir, "Aldahvörf og umbrotatímar," 48.
17. Arason, *Gamla góða Kaupmannahöfn*, 272.

FACTOR, FARMER, FATHER

1. Benson, "Injurious Names."
2. Per Nielsen, historian, e-mail, September 2013.
3. "Minningargrein um Björn Gíslason," 41.
4. Jonsson, *Að breyta fjalli*, 30.
5. Ibid., 31.
6. Zoega, *Hálsþorp í Djúpavogshreppi*, 10.
7. Lutz and White, "Anthropology of Emotions."
8. Zoega, *Hálsþorp í Djúpavogshreppi*, 34.
9. "Hans Frisaks dagbøker 1810–1815," 2 July 1813.
10. Hirschman, *The Passions and the Interests*, 47.
11. William Robertson, quoted in ibid., 61.
12. Jonsson, *Að breyta fjalli*, 31.
13. Court records of Sudur-Mulasysla 1820–1827, 148–50.
14. ibid., 164–65.
15. Larusson, *Old Icelandic Land Registers*, 32–33.
16. Karlsson, Gislason, and Palsson, eds., *Sýslu- and sóknalýsingar Hins íslenska bókmenntafélags*, 556–57.

17. Jonsson and Magnusson, eds., *Hagskinna*, 925.

18. Gudbjornsdottir, "Uppeldishugmyndir Rousseaus í kynjafræðilegu ljósi."

FAREWELL

1. Jonsson, *Safn af íslenzkum orðskviðum*, 71.

2. Tygesen, "Lighed," 146.

3. Hirschfeld, "Children's Understanding of Racial Groups."

4. Jochens, "Race and Etnicity in the Old Norse World, " 81.

5. *Saga of the People of Vatnsdal*, 251; see also Birgisson, *Den svarte vikingen*, 31.

6. Jakobsson, "Útlendingar á Íslandi á miðöldum," 42.

7. Kpomassie, *African in Greenland*, 112.

8. Court records of Sudur-Mulasysla 1820–1827, 271–72.

9. Jonassen, *Lækningabók handa alþýðu á Íslandi*, 340.

10. Bradford, *Pioneers of Homeopathy*, 294–295.

11. Jonsson, *Sterbúsins fémunir framtöldust þessir*, 2015.

12. Constituency documents.

13. "Minningargrein um Björn Gíslason," 41.

THE JONATHAN FAMILY

1. "Minningargrein um Björn Gíslason," 41.

2. Zeilau, *Fox-Expeditionen i Aaret 1860 Over Faerøerne*, 56.

3. Sveinsson, *Djúpivogur: 400 ár við voginn*, 142–43.

4. Edda Emilsdottir, "Björn Eiriksson."

5. Hans Jonathan's Genealogy website.

6. Baldvinsdottir, *Ljósmyndarar á Íslandi*, 297.

7. Agnarsdottir, "Aldahvörf og umbrotatímar," 44–45; Agnarsdottir, "Danish Empire."

8. Bjarnason, *Bóndinn, spendýrin og fleiri undur alheimsins*, 43.

9. Ibid., 153.

10. Ibid., 151–52.

11. Finsen, "Hvað landinn sagði erlendis," 22.

12. Johannsson, "Af reiðum Íslendingum," 141.

13. See Freiesleben, *Boy of St. Croix.*

14. Cornelins, "From St. Croix to Nakskov," 155.

15. Bruun, *Illustreret Vejledning over dansk Koloniudstilling.*

16. Johannsson, "Af reiðum Íslendingum," 136.

17. Johannessen, *Svo kvað Tómas*, 120.

18. Gudmundsson, *Stjörnur vorsins.*

19. Loftsdottir, "Leifar nýlendutímans og kynþáttahyggju."

20. Whitehead, "Kynþáttastefna Íslands."

21. *Morgunblaðið*, 11.

22. Thorhallsdottir, "Fæddist í Indíum, dó á Djúpavogi."

23. Jonsson, *Að breyta fjalli*, 27.

24. Anna Maria Sveinsdottir (b. 1948).

25. Ludvik Matthiasson (b. 1954).

26. Anna Maria Sveinsdottir.

27. Ivar Ingimarsson (b. 1977).

28. Anna Maria Sveinsdottir.

29. Unnur Sveinsdottir (b. 1967).

30. Edda Emilsdottir (b. 1931).

31. Helgi Mar Reynisson (b. 1961).

32. Edda Emilsdottir.

33. Larsen, *Slavernes slægt*, 85–86.

34. Hans Jonathan's Genealogy website.

THE EIRIKSSONS OF NEW ENGLAND

1. Details of the family history of the Eirikssons were provided by Roberta Eiriksson Dollase, e-mail messages, March 2015.

2. Edda Emilsdottir, e-mail to the author, 5 March 2015.

3. Kirsten Pflomm, personal communication, February 2015.

4. Olusoga, "History of British Slave Ownership Has Been Buried."

5. Ipsen, *Daughters of the Trade.*

6. See, for instance, Hall et al., *Legacies of British Slave-Ownersip*; Gøbel, "Danish Shipping along the Triangular Route, 1671–1802"; and Tyson and Highfield, eds., *Danish West Indian Slave Trade.*

7. Brion Davis, *Inhuman Bondage.*

8. "Lynching as Racial Terrorism."

9. Ross, "How Black Lives Matter Moved from a Hashtag to a Real Political Force."

WHO STOLE WHOM?

1. Göbel, *Det danske slavehandelsforbud*, 131–32.

2. Nielsen, "Slaver og frie indbyggere 1784–1848"; Davis, *Problem of Slavery in the Age of Emancipation.*

3. Rostgaard and Schou, *Kulturmøder I dansk kolonihistorie*, 99–100.

4. Dübeck, *De elendige*, 32.

5. Rezende and Walbom, *St. Croix.*

6. Göbel, *Det danske slavehandelsforbud*, 140.

7. Arendt, *Eichmann in Jerusalem.*

8. Stangneth, *Eichmann before Jerusalem.*

9. Arendt, *Totalitarianism*, 142.

10. Trouillot, *Silencing the Past.*

11. Parker, *Sugar Barons*, 348.

12. Greve, *Træk af kolonistrafferetten i komparativ belysning*, 55.

13. Hansen, *Søforhør*, 145.

14. Ibid., 143.

15. Proctor, "From *Anthropologie* to *Rassenkunde* in the German Anthropological Tradition."

16. Kvaran, "Um mannfræðilegt gildi forníslenskra mannlýsinga," 84–85.

17. Ibid., 83.

18. White Pride World Wide website.

19. Wines and Saul, "White Supremacists Extend Their Reach through Websites."

20. Steinmetz, "A Monument under Lock and Key" (*German Review* website).
21. Browder, *Foundations of the Nazi Police State*, 80.
22. Schimmelmann website.
23. Hosley, *Routes of Remembrance*.
24. Fog Olwig, "'Successful' Return."
25. Schramm, "Slaves of Pikworo," 110–11.
26. Schramm, "Slave Route Projects," 71–98.
27. Hosley, *Routes of Remembrance*.
28. Kant quotation in Davis, *Inhuman Bondage*, 75.
29. Desmond and Moore, *Darwin's Sacred Cause*.
30. Grainger, *Sugar-Cane*, bk. 4, 241–43.
31. Sontag, *Regarding the Pain of Others*.
32. Bales, *Understanding Global Slavery*.
33. Slavery Footprint website.

THE LESSONS OF HISTORY

1. Palsson, "Ensembles of Biosocial Relations."
2. Tamm, "Søren Kierkegaard, assessor Wilhelm—og guldalderens retslive," 404.

EPILOGUE

1. Marx, *Capital*, 924.
2. Baucom, *Specters of the Atlantic*, 51.
3. Williams, *Capitalism and Slavery*.
4. See, for example, Hamilton, *Biography*.
5. Zemon Davis, "Decentering History"; Aslanian et al., "How Size Matters."
6. See Palsson, "Ensembles of Biosocial Relations"; Lock and Palsson, *Can Science Resolve the Nature/Nurture Debate?*
7. Hamilton, *Biography*, 2.
8. EUROTAST website.

| *Bibliography* |

PUBLISHED MATERIAL

Abbott, Elizabeth. *Sugar: A Bittersweet History*. London: Duckworth, 2011.

Agnarsdottir, Anna. "Aldahvörf og umbrotatímar." In *Saga Íslands*, 9:3–374. Reykjavik: Hið Íslenzka bókmenntafélag, 2008.

———. "The Danish Empire: The Special Case of Iceland." In *Europe and Its Empires*, edited by Mary N. Harris and Csaba Lévai. Pisa: Pisa University Press, 2008.

Agnarsdottir, Anna, and Ragnar Arnason. "Þrælahald á þjóðveldisöld." *Saga* 21 (1983): 5–26.

Algreen-Ussing, Tage. *Anmærkninger til personretten*. Copenhagen: Gyldendal, 1824.

Andersen, Hans Christian. *Mulatten, Originalt romantisk drama i fem akter, 1840*. In *Andersen: H. C. Andersens samlede værker; Skuespil II 1836–1842*, 275–372. Copenhagen: Det Danske Sprog- og Litteraturselskap, 2005.

Andresson, Sigfus Haukur. "Tveggja alda afmæli fríhöndlunar á Íslandi." *Lesbók Morgunblaðsins*, 9 April 1988, 6–7.

Arason, Gudlaugur. *Gamla góða Kaupmannahöfn.* Reykjavik: Salka, 2005.

Arendt, Hannah. *Eichmann in Jerusalem: A Report on the Banality of Evil.* Harmondsworth, UK: Penguin, 1984.

———. *Totalitarianism.* San Diego: Harcourt, 1968.

Aslanian, Sebouh David, Joyce E. Chaplin, Ann McGrath, and Kristin Mann. "How Size Matters: The Question of Scale in History." *American Historical Review,* December 2013, 1431–72.

Baldvinsdottir, Inga Lara. *Ljósmyndarar á Íslandi / Photographers of Iceland 1845–1945.* Translated by Anna Yates. Reykjavik: JPV and National Museum of Iceland, 2001.

Bales, Kevin. *Understanding Global Slavery.* Berkeley: University of California Press, 2005.

Ballegaard Petersen, Annelise, and Anne Scott Sørensen. *Breve til Charlotte: Fra Sølyst til Weimar.* Odense, Denmark: Syddansk Universitetsforlag, 2011.

Barnet, Miguel. *Biography of a Runaway Slave.* Willimantic, CT: Curbstone, 1994.

Baucom, Ian. *Specters of the Atlantic: Finance Capital, Slavery, and the Philosophy of History.* Durham, NC: Duke University Press, 2005.

Benson, Susan. "Injurious Names: Naming, Disavowal, and Recuperation in Contexts of Slavery and Emancipation." In *The Anthropology of Names and Naming,* edited by Gabriele vom Bruck and Barbara Bodenhorn. Cambridge: Cambridge University Press, 2006.

Bindman, David, and Henry Louis Gates Jr., eds.. *The Image of the Black in Western Art,.* vol. 1, *From the Pharaohs to the Fall of the Roman Empire.* New ed. Cambridge, MA: Harvard University Press, 2010.

Birgisson, Bergsveinn. *Den svarte vikingen.* Oslo: Spartacus, 2013.

Birkedal, Vilhelm. "Hans Benjamin Gram." In *En Livs-førelse.* Odense, Denmark: Forlaget af den Miloske Boghandel, 1863.

Bjarki. "Sala Vestindíaeyjanna." 21 November 1902, 1.

Bjarnason, Jon. *Bóndinn, spendýrin og fleiri undur alheimsins*. Edited by Arni H. Kristjansson and Sigurdur Gylfi Magnusson. Reykjavik: Háskólaútgáfan, 2014.

Bobé, Louis. *August Hennings dagbog under hans ophold i København 1802*. Copenhagen: Nordisk forlag, 1934.

Boston Centinel 33 (11 May 1804): 8558.

Bradford, Thomas Lindsley. *The Pioneers of Homeopathy*. Philadelphia: Boericke Tafel, 1897.

Browder, George C. *Foundations of the Nazi Police State: The Formation of Sipo and SD*. Lexington: University Press of Kentucky, 1990.

Brown, Nancy Marie. *Song of the Vikings*. New York: Palgrave, 2014.

Bruun, Andreas. *Illustreret Vejledning over dansk Koloniudstilling: Grønland og dansk Vestindien samt Udstilling fra Island og Færøerne*. Exhibition pamphlet. Copenhagen, 1905.

Christensen, Dan Ch. *Naturens tankelæser: En biografi om Hans Christian Ørsted*. 2 bindi. Copenhagen: Museum Tusculanums Forlag, 2009.

Christoffersen, Jonas. "De bortløbne slaver." *Weekendavisen*, 4 October 2013.

Coates, Ta-Nehisi. *Between the World and Me*. New York: Spiegel and Grau, 2015.

Columbian Centinel 17 (2 May (1792): 15.

———— 22 (18 February 1795): 47.

Cornelins, Victor Waldemar. "From St. Croix to Nakskov." In Birgit Freiesleben, *The Boy of St. Croix: A Historical Story about Two West Indian Children's Long Journey*. Ballerup, Denmark: ACER, 2002.

Dahl, Thorkel, and Kjell de Fine Licht. *Surveys in 1961 on St. Thomas and St. Croix*. Copenhagen: Royal Danish Academy of Fine Arts, 2004.

Engelstoft, Povl, with Svend Dahl, eds., *Dansk biografisk leksikon*. Copenhagen: J. K. Schultz Forlag, 1941.

"The Danish Steamer Hellig Olav." *Mercury*, 26 April 1912.

Dansk biografisk lexikon, vol. 15. Copenhagen: Gyldendal, 1901.

Davis, David Brion. "How They Stopped Slavery: A New Perspective." *New York Review of Books*, 6 June 2013, 59–61.

———. *Inhuman Bondage: The Rise and Fall of Slavery in the New World*. Oxford: Oxford University Press, 2006.

———. *The Problem of Slavery in the Age of Emancipation*. New York: Alfred A. Knopf, 2014.

Degn, Christian. *Die Schimmelmanns im atlantischen Dreieckshandel: Gewinn und Gewissen*. Neymünster, Germany: Wachholtz Verlag, 1974.

Desmond, Adrian, and James Moore. *Darwin's Sacred Cause: How a Hatred of Slavery Shaped Darwin's Views on Human Evolution*. Boston: Houghton Mifflin Harcourt, 2009.

"A Disgraceful Practice." *New-Hampshire Gazette* 92 (8 September 1846): 36.

Dübeck, Inger. *De elendige: Retshistoriske studier over samfundets marginaliserede*. Copenhagen: Jurist- og Økonomforbundets Forlag, 2013.

Dunn, Richard S. *A Tale of Two Plantations: Slave Life and Labor in Jamaica and Virginia*. Cambridge, MA: Harvard University Press, 2014.

E. O. "Íslendingar beittu búfé á kálplöntur frúarinnar." *Tíminn*, 11–12 November 1989, 11–12.

Einarsson, Stefan. "Bænarskrá bænda." In *Nordæla*, 178–87. Reykjavik: Helgafell, 1956.

Feldbæk, Ole. *Dansk søfartshistorie*, vol. 3, *1720–1814: Storhandelens tid*. Copenhagen: Gyldendal, 1997.

———. *Slaget på Reden*. Copenhagen: Politikens Forlag, 1985.

Finsen, Vilhjalmur. "Hvað landinn sagði erlendis." *Norðri*, 1958.

Fog Olwig, Karen. "The 'Successful' Return: Caribbean Narratives of Migration, Family, and Gender." *Journal of the Royal Anthropological Institute* 18 (2012): 828–45.

Franklin, John Hope, and Loren Schwedinger. *Runaway Slaves:*

Rebels on the Plantation. Chicago: University of Chicago Press, 2000.

Freiesleben, Birgit. *The Boy of St. Croix: A Historical Story about Two West Indian Children's Long Journey.* Ballerup, Denmark: ACER, 2002.

Garde, H. F. "Samboinden Charlotte Amalie Bernard og hendes efterkommere indtil 5. led, Et Bidrag til de dansk-vestindiske Øers Personalhistorie." *Personalhistorisk Tidsskrift* 15, no. 5 (1971): 212.

Gikandi, Simon. *Slavery and the Culture of Taste.* Princeton, NJ: Princeton University Press, 2011.

Gøbel, Erik. "Danish Shipping along the Triangular Route, 1671–1802." *Scandinavian Journal of History* 36, no. 2 (2011): 135–55.

———. *Det danske slavehandelsforbud: Studier og kilder til forhistorien, forordningen og følgerne.* Odense, Denmark: Syddansk Universitetsforlag, 2008.

Grainger, James. *The Sugar-Cane: A Poem.* London: R. and J. Dodsley, 1764.

Gram, Hans, Samuel Holyoke, and Oliver Holden. *The Massachusetts Compiler of Theoretical and Practical Elements of Sacred Vocal Music: Together with a Musical Dictionary and a Variety of Psalm Tunes, Chorusses, &c., Chiefly Selected or Adapted from Modern European Publications.* Boston: I. Thomas and E. T. Andrews, 1795.

Grandin, Greg. *The Empire of Necessity: The Untold History of a Slave Rebellion in the Age of Liberty.* New York: OneWorld, 2014.

Greve, Vagn. *Træk af kolonistrafferetten i komparativ belysning.* Copenhagen: Jurist- og Økonomforbundets Forlag, 2012.

Gudbjornsdottir, Gudny. "Uppeldishugmyndir Rousseaus í kynjafræðilegu ljósi: Afturhaldssemi, kvenfyrirlitning eða byltingarkennd framsækni?" *Tímarit um menntarannsóknir,* 2013, 78–95.

Gudmundsson, Tomas. *Stjörnur vorsins*. Reykjavik: Ragnar Jóns-son Víkingsprent h.f., 1940.

Hall, Catherine, Keith McClelland, Nick Draper, Kate Doning-ton, and Richard Lang. *Legacies of British Slave-Ownersip: Colonial Slavery and the Formation of Victorian Britain*. Cam-bridge: Cambridge University Press, 2014.

Hall, Neville A. T., and B. W. Highman, eds. *Slave Society in the Danish West Indies: St. Thomas, St. John and St. Croix*. Mona, Jamaica: University of the West Indies Press, 1992.

Hamilton, Nigel. *Biography: A Brief History*. Cambridge, MA: Harvard University Press, 2007.

Hansen, Thorkild. *Slavernes øer*. Copenhagen: Gyldendal, 1970.

———. *Slavernes skibe*. Copenhagen: Gyldendal, 1968.

———. *Søforhør: Nærbillede af Thorkild Hansen*. Copenhagen: Lindhardt og Ringhof, 1989.

Helgason, Thorsteinn. "Historical Narrative as Collective Ther-apy: The Case of the Turkish Raids in Iceland." *Scandinavian Journal of History* 22, no. 4 (2008): 275–89.

Helleberg, Maria. *Druknehuset*. Copenhagen: Samleren, 2008.

Henderson, Ebenezer. *Iceland, or The Journal of a Resdience in That Island, during the Years 1814 and 1815*. Edinburgh: Oli-phant, Waugh and Innes, 1818.

Henningsen, Peter, and Ulrik Langen. *Hundemordet i Vimmels-kaftet og andre fortællinger fra 1700-tallets København*. Copen-hagen: Jyllands-Postens Forlag, 2010.

Highfield, Arnold R. Editor's introduction to *Hans West's Ac-counts of St. Croix in the West Indies*, x–xxxiii. St. Thomas: Virgin Islands Humanities Council, 2004.

———. *Time Longa' Dan Twine: Notes on the Culture, His-tory, and People of the U.S. Virgin Islands*. St. Croix: Antilles Press, 2009.

Hirschfeld, Lawrence A. "Children's Understanding of Racial Groups." In *Children's Understanding of Society*, edited by

Martyn Barrett and Eithne Buchanan-Barrow. Hove, East Sussex, UK: Psychology, 2005.

Hirschman, Albert O. *The Passions and the Interests: Political Arguments for Capitalism before Its Triumph*. Princeton, NJ: Princeton University Press, 1977.

Holsoe, Svend. "Coping with Enslavement: A Women's Network in Christiansted." In *Negotiating Enslavement: Perspectives on Slavery in the Danish West Indies*, edited by A. R. Highfield and G. F. Tyson, 59–75. Christiansted, St. Croix: Antilles Press., 2009.

Hosley, Bayo. *Routes of Remembrance: Refashioning the Slave Trade of Ghana*. Chicago: University of Chicago Press, 2008.

Ipsen, Pernille. *Daughters of the Trade: Atlantic Slavers and Interracial Marriage on the Gold Coast*. Philadelphia: University of Pennsylvania Press, 2015.

Irving, Washington. *The Life and Voyages of Christopher Columbus*. Ware, Hertfordshire, UK: Wordsworth Classics, 2008.

Isert, Paul Erdman. *Letters on West Africa and the Slave Trade: Paul Erdmann Isert's Journey to Guinea and the Caribbean Islands in Columbia (1788)*. Edited by Selena Axelrod Winsnes. Legon-Accra, Ghana: Sub-Saharan, 2007.

Jakobsson, Sverrir. "Útlendingar á Íslandi á miðöldum." *Andvari* 43 (2001): 36–51.

Jensen, Niklas Thode. *For the Health of the Enslaved: Slaves, Medicine and Power in the Danish West Indies, 1803–1848*. Copenhagen: Museum Tusculanum Press, 2012.

Jespersen, Knud J. V., Carsten Porskrog Rasmussen, Hanne Raabyemagle, and Poul Holstein. *Moltke: Rigets mægtigste mand*. Copenhagen: Gad, 2010.

Jochens, Jenny. "Race and Ethnicity in the Old Norse World." *Viator* 30 (1999): 79–104.

Johannesdottir, Steinunn. *Reisubók Guðríðar Símonardóttur*. Reykjavik: Forlagið, 2001.

Johannessen, Matthias. *Svo kvað Tómas: Matthías Jóhannessen ræddi við skáldið*. Reykjavik: Almenna bókafélagið, 1960.

Johannsson, Jon Yngvi. "Af reiðum Íslendingum: Deilur um Nýlendusýninguna 1905." In *Þjóðerni í þúsund ár*, edited by Jon Yngvi Johannsson, Kolbeinn Ottarsson Proppe, and Sverrir Jakobsson. Reykjavik: Háskólaútgáfan, 2003.

Jonassen, Jonas. *Lækningabók handa alþýðu á Íslandi*. Reykjavik: Sigm. Guðmundsson, 1884.

Jonsson, Bjorn. *Annalar þess froma og velvitra sáluga Bjørns Jónssonar á Skarðsá*. Hrappsey, Iceland: Hið Konúnglega príviligeraða bókþrykkerie, 1774.

Jonsson, Gudmundur. *Safn af íslenzkum orðskviðum, fornmælum, heilræðum, snilliyrðum, sannmælum og málsgreinum*. Copenhagen: Hið íslenzka bókmennta-félag, 1830.

Jonsson, Gudmundur, and Magnus S. Magnusson, eds. *Hagskinna: Sögulegar hagtölur um Ísland*. Reykjavik: Hagstofa Íslands, 1997.

Jonsson, Mar. *Sterbúsins fémunir framtöldust þessir: Eftirlátnar eigur 96 Íslendinga sem létust á tímabilinu 1722–1820*. Reykjavik: Háskólaútgáfan, 2015.

Jonsson, Stefan. *Að breyta fjalli*. Reykjavik: Svart á hvítu, 1987.

Jørgensen, Troels G. *Anders Sandøe Ørsted: Juristen and Politikeren*. Copenhagen: Arne Frost-Hansens Forlag, 1957.

Juridist Maanedstidende, vol. 1. Copenhagen: Forlaget af Arnszen and Hartier, 1802.

Karlsson, Finnur N., Indridi Gislason, and Pall Palsson, eds. *Sýslu- og sóknalýsingar Hins íslenska bókmenntafélags 1839–1874*. Reykjavik: Hið íslenska bókmenntafélag, 2000.

Knight, Franklin W., ed. *The Slave Societies of the Caribbean*, vol. 3 of *General History of the Caribbean*. London: UNESCO Publishing, 1997.

Kpomassie, Tété-Michel. *An African in Greenland*. New York: New York Review Books, 2001.

Kvaran, Eidur S. "Um mannfræðilegt gildi forníslenskra mannlýsinga." *Skírnir* 108 (1934): 63–101.

Langabúð: Menningarmiðstöð Djúpavogshrepps. Djúpivogur, Iceland: Djúpavogshreppur, 1997.

Larsen, Alex Frank. *Legenden om Denmark: Den danske slave, der
ændrede USA's historie.* Copenhagen: Gyldendal, 2013.

———. *Slavernes slægt.* Copenhagen: Danmarks radio, 2008.

Larusson, Bjorn. *The Old Icelandic Land Registers.* Lundur, Iceland: Gleerup, 1967.

Laws of Early Iceland: Gragas I. Translated by Peter Foote and
Richard Perkins. Winnipeg: University of Manitoba Press,
2007.

Laxness, Halldor. *Independent People.* Translated by James An-
derson Thompson. New York: Alfred A. Knopf, 1934.

Lock, Margaret, and Gisli Palsson. *Can Science Resolve the
Nature/Nurture Debate?* Oxford: Polity, 2016.

Loftsdottir, Kristin. "Leifar nýlendutímans og kynþáttahyggju:
Ljóð Davíðs Stefánssonar, Tómasar Guðmundssonar og
deilur um skopmynd Sigmunds." *Skírnir* 184 (Spring 2010):
121–44.

Loftsdottir, Kristin, and Gisli Palsson. "Black on White: Danish
Colonialism, Iceland, and the Caribbean." In *Scandinavian
Colonialism and the Rise of Modernity: Small Time Agents in a
Global Arena*, edited by Magdalena Naum and Jonas M. Nor-
din. New York: Springer, 2013.

Lutz, C. A., and G. White. "The Anthropology of Emotions."
Annual Review of Anthropology 15 (1986): 405–436.

"Lynching as Racial Terrorism" [editorial]. *New York Times*,
February 11, 2015.

Magnusson, Arni. *Ferðasaga Árna Magnússonar frá Geitastekk
1753–1797.* Reykjavik: Ísafoldarprentsmiðja, 1945.

Marx, Karl. *Capital: A Critique of Political Economy*, vol, 1 [orig.
1867]. Translated by Ben Fowkes. Harmondsworth, UK:
Penguin Books, 1976.

McConville, Chris. "'Just Sugar'? Food and Landscape along Queensland's Sunshine Coast." In *Dining on Turtles: Food, Feasts and Dining in History*, edited by D. Kirkby and T. Luckins New York: Palgrave Macmillan, 2007.

McCusker, John J. *Money and Exchange in Europe and America, 1600–1775: A Handbook*. Chapel Hill: University of North Carolina Press, 1978.

Meier, Gudrun. "Preliminary Remarks on the Oldendorp Manuscripts and Their History." In *Slave Cultures and the Cultures of Slavery*, edited by Stefan Palmie. Knoxwille: University of Tennessee Press, 1996.

Melsted, Bogi Th. "Smágreinar." In *Ársrit hins íslenska fræðafélags í Kaupmannahöfn*, 158–64. Copenhagen: Hið íslenska fræðafélag í Kaupmannahöfn, 1919.

"Minningargrein um Björn Gíslason." *Norðanfari* 22 (1883): 19–20.

Mintz, Sidney. *Sweetness and Power: The Place of Sugar in Modern History*. New York: Penguin, 1986.

"Monument to Dr. Gram." *Salem Register*, 11 October 1869.

Moore, R. B. *The Name "Negro": Its Origin and Evil Use* [orig. 1960]. Baltimore: Black Classic Press, 1992.

Morgunblaðið. 2 August 1960. Reykjavik.

Müller-Wille, Staffan, and Hans-Jörg Rheinberger. *A Cultural History of Heredity*. Chicago: University of Chicago Press, 2012.

Naum, Magdalena, and Jonas M. Nordin. "Introduction: Situating Scandinavian Colonialism." In *Scandinavian Colonialism and the Rise of Modernity: Small Time Agents in a Global Arena*, edited by Naum and Nordin. New York: Springer, 2013.

New Hampshire Centinel 6, no. 270 (19 May 1804): 3.

Newman, Simon. *A New World of Labor: The Development of Plantation Slavery in the British Atlantic*. Philadelphia: University of Pennyslvania Press, 2013.

Nielsen, Per. "Slaver og frie indbyggere 1784–1848." In *Fra slaveri til frihed: Det dansk-vestindiske slavesamfund 1672–1848*. Copenhagen: Nationalmuseet, 2001.

Ogasapian, John. *Church Music in America 1620–2000*. Macon, GA: Mercer University Press, 2007.

Oldendorp, Christian Georg Andreas. *History of the Mission of the Evangelical Brethren on the Caribbean Islands of St. Thomas, St. Croix, and St. John* [orig. 1777]. Edited by Johann Jakob Bossard. Ann Arbor, MI: Karoma, 1987.

Olsen, Poul Erik. "Disse vilde karle: Negre i Danmark indtil 1848." In *Fremmede I Danmark: 400 års fremmedpolitik*, edited by Bent Blüdnikow. Odense, Denmark: Odense Universitetsforlag, 1987.

Olusoga, David. "The History of British Slave Ownership Has Been Buried: Now Its Scale Can Be Revealed." *Guardian*, 12 July 2015.

Ørsted, Anders Sandøe. *Haandbog over den danske og norske Lovkyndighed*, vol. 2. Copenhagen, 1825.

Palmadottir, Elin. "Þrælaeyjar." *Morgunblaðið*, 9 January 1994, B1–5.

Palsson, Arni. "Lok þrældóms á Íslandi." In *Á víð og dreif*, 342–57. Reykjavik: Helgafell, 1947.

Palsson, Gisli. "Ensembles of Biosocial Relations." In *Biosocial Becomings: Integrating Social and Biological Anthropology*, edited by Tim Ingold and Gisli Palsson. Cambridge: Cambridge University Press, 2013.

Parker, Matthew. *The Sugar Barons: Family, Corruption, Empire, and War in the West Indies*. New York: Walker, 2011.

Patterson, Relford. *Three American "Primitives": A Study of the Musical Style of Hans Gram, Oliver Holden, and Samuel Holyoke*. St. Louis, MO: Washington University, 1963.

"Poetry." *Hallowell Gazette* 2, no. 7 (1815).

Pollan, Michael. *The Botany of Desire: A Plant's-Eye View of the World*. New York: Random House, 2001.

Proctor, Robert. "From *Anthropologie* to *Rassenkunde* in the German Anthropological Tradition." In *Bones, Bodies, Behavior: Essays on Biological Anthropology*, edited by George W. Stocking Jr. Madison: University of Wisconsin Press, 1988.

Rasmussen, Alexander. *De Schimmelmannske skoler*. Aalborg, Denmark: Aalborg Stiftsbogtrykkeri, 1914

Rediker, Marcus. *The Slave Ship: A Human History*. New York: Viking, 2007.

The Repertory [Boston] 3. no. 95 (28 May 1806): 3.

Rezende, Elizabeth, and Anne Walbom. *St. Croix: Historic Photos*. Copenhagen: Danish West Indian Society, 2009.

Ross, Janell. "How *Black Lives Matter* Moved from a Hashtag to a Real Political Force." *Washington Post*, 19 August 2015.

Rostgaard, Marianne, and Lotte Schou. *Kulturmøder I dansk kolonihistorie*. Copenhagen: Gyldendal, 2010.

The Saga of the People of Vatnsdal. Translated by Andrew Wawn. In *The Sagas of the Icelanders*. New York: Penguin, 2001.

Samtíðin 10 (1955). 13.

Sayre, Gordon. "'Azakia,' *Quâbi*, and Sarah Wentworth Apthorp Morton: A Romance of the Early American Republic." *Princeton University Library Chronicle* 64, no. 2 (2003): 313–32.

Schiebinger, Londa. *Plants and Empires: Colonial Bioprospecting in the Atlantic World*. Cambridge, MA: Harvard University Press, 2004.

Schmidt, Johan Christian. *Various Remarks Collected on and about the Island of St. Croix in America* [orig. 1788]. Transllated by Svend Holsoe. St. Thomas: Virgin Islands Humanities Council, 1998.

Schramm, Katharina. "Slave Route Projects: Tracing the Heritage of Slavery in Ghana." In *Reclaiming Heritage: Alternative Imaginations in West Africa*, edited by Michael Rowlands and Ferdinand de Jong. Walnut Creek, CA: Left Coast, 2008.

————. "The Slaves of Pikworo: Local Histories, Transatlantic Perspectives." *History and Memory* 23, no. 1 (2011): 96–130.

Scott, James C. *Domination and the Arts of Resistance: Hidden Transcripts*. New Haven, CT: Yale University Press, 1990.

Scott, James C., John Tehranian, and Jeremy Mathias. "The Production of Legal Identities Proper to States: The Case of the Permanent Family Surname." *Comparative Studies in Society and History* 44, no. 1 (2002): 4–44.

Sigmundsson, Finnur, ed. *Hafnarstúdentar skrifa heim: Sendibréf 1825–1836 og 1878–1891*. Reykjavik: Bókfellsútgáfan, 1963.

Sigurdsson, Einar Bragi. *Eskja: Sögurit Eskfirðinga*, vol. 2. Eskifjördur: Byggðasögunefnd Eskifjarðar, 1977.

————. *Eskja: Sögurit Eskfirðinga*, vol. 5. Eskifjördur: Byggðasögunefnd Eskifjarðar, 1986.

Snyder, Terri L. *The Power to Die: Slavery and Suicide in British North America*. Chicago: University of Chicago Press, 2015.

Sontag, Susan. *Regarding the Pain of Others*. London: Penguin Books, 2003.

Stangneth, Bettina. *Eichmann before Jerusalem*. New York: Alfred A. Knopf, 2014.

St. Clair, William. *The Door of No Return: The History of Cape Coast Castle and the Atlantic Slave Trade*. New York: BlueBridge, 2007.

Stephensen, Magnus. *Bréf til Finns Magnússonar*. Copenhagen: Hið íslenska fræðafélag, 1924.

————. *Skémtileg Vina-Gledi In fródlegum Samrædum og Liódmælum / leidd í ljós af Magnúsi Stephensen, lögmanni yfir Nordur og Austur lögdæmi Íslands*. Leirargardar, Iceland: Björn Gottskálksson, 1797.

Stoler, Ann Laura. *Carnal Knowledge and Imperial Power: Race and the Intimate in Colonial Rule*. Berkeley: University of California Press, 2002.

Sturluson, Snorri. *Die isländische Edda, Das ist Die geheime*

Gottes-Lehre der ältesten Hyperboräer. Translated by Jacob Schimmelmann. Stettin [Szczecin, Poland]: Struck, 1777.

Svalesen, Leif. *The Slave Ship Fredensborg*. Kingston, Jamaica: Ian Randle, 2000.

Sveinsson, Ingimar. *Djúpivogur: 400 ár við voginn*. Djúpivogur, Iceland: Búlandshreppur, 1989.

———. *Djúpivogur: Siglt og róið um firði og eyjasund*. Djúpivogur, Iceland: Djúpavogshreppur, 2003.

Tamm, Ditlev. "Nogle tværsnit af Københavns byrets historie." In *Med lov skal land bygge*, edited by John Erichsen. Copenhagen: Gad jura, 2006.

———. "Søren Kierkegaard, assessor Wilhelm—og guldalderens retslive." *Juristen* 10 (2002): 397–404.

Thorhallsdottir, Rannveig. "Fæddist í Indíum, dó á Djúpavogi: Saga Hans Jónatans 1784–1827." *Austurland* 5 August 1998, 5.

Thorkelin, Grimur. *Essay on the Slave Trade*. London: G. Nicol, 1788.

Thorlacius, Gytha. *Fru Gytha Thorlacius Erindringer fra Island i Aarene 1801–1815*. Copenhagen: Munksgaard, 1930.

Thoroddsen, Þorvaldur. *Landfræðissaga Íslands III: Hugmyndir manna um Ísland náttúruskoðun og rannsóknir fyrr og síðar* [orig. 1900–1902]. Reykjavik: Ormstunga, 2005.

Trouillot, Michel-Rolph. *Silencing the Past: The Power and the Production of History*. 20th anniv. ed. Boston: Beacon, 2015.

Tygesen, Peter. "Lighed." In *1700 tallet: Parykker, profit og pøbel*, edited by Ulrik Langen. Copenhagen: Golden Days, 2010.

Tyson, George F., and Arnold R. Highfield, eds. *The Danish West Indian Slave Trade: Virgin Islands Perspectives*. St. Croix: Antilles Press, 1994.

Valsson, Pall. *Jónas Hallgrímsson: Ævisaga*. Reykjavik: Mál og menning, 1999.

Waaben, Knud. "A. S. Ørsted og negerslaverne i København." *Juristen*, 1964, 321–43.

Watkins, Priscilla G. *Government House St. Croix: Its History and*

Special Furnishings. Frederiksted, St. Croix: St. Croix Landmark Society, 1996.

West, Hans. *Hans West's Accounts of St. Croix in the West Indies*. Edited by Arnold R. Highfield. St. Thomas: Virgin Islands Humanities Council, 2004.

Whitehead, Thor. "Kynþáttastefna Íslands." *Lesbók Morgunblaðsins* 49, no. 2 (13 January 1974): 4–6, 14.

Wiecek, William M. "Somerset: Lord Mansfield and the Legitimacy of Slavery in the Anglo-American World." *University of Chicago Law Review* 42, no. 21 (1974): 86–146.

Williams, Eric. *Capitalism and Slavery*. Chapel Hill: University of North Carolina Press, 1944.

Wines, Michael, and Stephanie Saul. "White Supremacists Extend Their Reach through Websites." *New York Times*, July 5, 2015.

Winkle, Stefan. "Der dänische Sklavenhandel." *Hamburger Ärzteblatt* 12 (2003): 530–37.

Wolf, Eric. *Europe and the People without History*. Berkeley: University of California Press, 1982.

Zeilau, Th. *Fox-Expeditionen i Aaret 1860 Over Faerøerne, Island Og Grønland, Med Oplysninger Om Muligheden Af et Nordatlantisk Telegraf-Anloeg*. Ann Arbor: University of Michigan Library, 2009.

Zemon Davis, Natalie. "Decentering History: Local Stories and Cultural Crossings in a Global World." *History and Theory* 50 (May 2011): 188–202.

Zoega, Gudny. *Hálsþorp í Djúpavogshreppi: Fornleifaskráning*. Glaumbaer, Iceland: Byggðasafn Skagfirðinga, 2004.

UNPUBLISHED SOURCES

Bille's Private Archive, National Archives, Copenhagen.
Constituency Reports. National Archives, Reykjavik.
Copenhagen Census 1801. National Archives, Copenhagen.

Court records Sudur-Mulasysla V-1, 1820–1827. National Archives, Reykjavik.

Edda Emilsdottir. "Björn Eiríksson, Súsanna Weywadt og fjölskylda þeirra." Unpublished manuscript, 2011.

"Generalmajorinde Henriette de Schimmelmann contra mulatten Hans Jonathan 1802." Landsover, samt Hof- og Stadsretten Justidskontoret. Transskription af dokumenter fra pådømte sager [transcription of documents on concluded legal cases]. Nr. 356/1801. 1801 maj 24–juni 22 [24 May–22 June 1801]. National Archives, Copenhagen.

"Hans Frisaks dagbøker 1810–1815." Microfiche film 82 a II. Oslo University Library.

Holsoe, Svend 2011. "Virgin Islands Families: Schimmelmann."

Lutheran Church records, Christiansted 1780–1794. National Archives, Copenhagen.

Records of Geithellnahreppur, 1797–1818. National Archives, Reykjavik.

Schimmelmann private papers (no. 6285, box 31). National Archives, Copenhagen.

Stephensen, John. "Aðskiljanlegt nýtt og gamalt sem er útlagt úr dönsku eftir ýmsum Autoribus af Factor John Stephensen, Anno 1808–1809." Skrifað á Hofi In Álftafirði anno 1811 og 1812 af Sveini Péturssssyni. JS 243 4to. The National and University Library of Iceland, Reyjavik.

Store records, Djupivogur. National Archives, Reykjavik.

WEBSITES

Ankestyrelsen. Historien bag Ankestyrelsens bygninger i Amaliegade 23–25, midt i Frederikstaden; http://www.ast.dk /artikler/default.asp?page=557. Accessed 12 September 2013.

Dansk biografisk leksikon. http://www.denstoredanske.dk

/Dansk_Biografisk_Leksikon/Kunst_og_kultur/Musik /Organist/Hans_Gram. Accessed 25 July 2013.

EUROTAST. http://eurotast.eu/services/esr11-computational -reconstruction-of-hans-jonatans-genome/. Accessed 21 June 2015.

Hans Gram. http://en.wikipedia.org/wiki/Hans_Gram _(composer). Accessed 25 July 2013.

Hans Jonathan's Genealogy. http://www.simnet.is/hans jonatan/index.html. Accessed 24 October 2013.

NAXOS: The World's Leading Classical Music Group. http:// www.naxos.com/catalogue/item.asp?item_code= 9.80118–19. Accessed 29 July 2013.

Pioneers of Homeopathy. http://www.homeoint.org/seror /biograph/gram.htm. Accessed 25 July 2013.

Piracy. http://en.wikipedia.org/wiki/Piracy. Accessed 19 October 2011.

Schimmelmann, Heinrich Carl. http://da.wikipedia.org/wiki /Heinrich_Carl_Schimmelmann_(1890–1971). Accessed 28 December 2012.

Slavery Footprint. http://slaveryfootprint.org/#where_do _you_live. Accessed 27 December 2012.

St. Croix Database. http://stx.visharoots.org/db.html. Accessed 7 October 2013.

Steinmetz, Georg. "A Monument under Lock and Key: Seeking Germany's Colonial Lieux de Mémoire." *German Review*. http://www-personal.umich.edu/~geostein/docs/Stein metzGermanic.pdf. Accessed 20 February 2013.

Thystrup, Amalie G. *Dansk retshistorie*. Faculty of Law, University of Copenhagen (closed website). Accessed November 2006.

White Pride World Wide [chat room]. "Black Blood in Iceland?" http://www. Stormfront.org/forum/t717629/. Accessed 10 February 2011.

Index

Page numbers in italics refer to illustrations.

Antoniusdottir, 150, 152–53; death
in 1827 of stroke at age forty-three,
166–68; godfather to children baptized in parish, 137; legacy, 169–
71; marriage certificate of Hans
Jonathan and Katrin, *154*; as mate
on sailboat, 130; ownership of two
four-oared boats, 132; promoted to
general store manager after death
of Jon Stefansson, 132; record of
in census of 1816 listing birth-
place in St. Croix, *133*–34; records
of assets and payments of tithe to
church, 132; records of transactions at Langabud in Djupivogur,
130–*31*, *206*; second name treated
as surname, 150; tax payments for
community and dues for poor, 132;
teaching of carpentry, arithmetic,
and navigation, 64, 150–51; travel
guide for visitors to Berufjordur,
137–47
Hans Jonathan, paternity, theories
of: Count Moltke, 34–38; Hans
Gram, 38–41; Ludvig Heinrich von
Schimmelmann, 32–34; "said to be
the secretary," 31, 38
Hans Jonathan, reconstruction of genome of, 228–29
Hans Jonathan, on St. Croix: baptism
at Lutheran Church, Christiansted,
23–25; birth in 1784, xii, 22; education, 49; left in St. Croix when
Schimmelmanns moved back to

Copenhagen, 59; listed as "mu-
latto" on slave register of Constitution Hill in 1785, 26
Hans Jonathan saga: routes of saga, *x*;
timeline of saga, 231–34
Hans Jonathan website, discussion of
on neo-Nazi Stormfront website,
214–15
Hansson, Ludvik (great-grandson of
Hans Jonathan), 178
"happy slave hypothesis," 13
Havamal (Words of the High One),
189
Heegaard, Anna, 32
Helgason, Agnar, 229
Helleberg, Maria, *Druknehuset*,
111–12
Hellig Olav (steamer), 196
Henderson, Ebenezer, 117, 127, 142;
distribution of Bibles in Iceland,
144–45; *Iceland, or The Journal of a
Residence in That Island*, 144; meet-
ing with Hans Jonathan in 1814,
144–45, 146
Henning, August, 71
Herschel, John, 166
Holocaust, relationship to the slave
trade, 211–12, 214–16

Iceland: adoption of Christianity ca.
AD 1000, 118; coastal survey of
from 1803 to 1818, 142–44; control
of market by Denmark, 121, 124;
and Danish Colonial Exhibition of

"stealing oneself," 113, 208, 221–22

Stefansson, Ellen Katrin, 125, 127, 139–40, 145

Stefansson, Jon, 139–40, 142; death in 1819, 132; founder of reading association and lending library and collector of manuscripts, 126, 145; household of in 1801, 125; manager of Djupivogur general store, 125; manuscript written by, *128*; mentor and benefactor to Hans Jonathan, 127; translation of collection of essays about slave trade from Danish into Icelandic, 127–28

Stefansson, Kari, 229

Stephensen, Magnus: correspondence with Judge Ørsted in Copenhagen, 146; "An Entertaining Compendium for Friends with Enlightening Discourses and Poems," 73; reference to Kyhn, 124–25

Stewart, Charles, 109

Stormfront website: discussion of Hans Jonathan website, 214–15; most active white supremacist forum in world, 215

Sturluson, Snorri, *Prose Edda*, 183

sugarcane: availability to general public in sixteenth and seventeenth centuries, 52; first global economic bubble, 52; introduced in Caribbean islands by Spanish, 51; reached Copenhagen in 1374, 51

sugar plantations, workings of, 51, 52–54

Sveinsdottir, Anna Maria (descendant of Hans Jonathan), 31, 34

Tams, David, 89, 105–6, 112

Thaae, Christian, 166, 169

Thorkelin, Grimur, *Essay on the Slave Trade*, 129

Thorlacius, Gytha, 137–41; meeting with Hans Jonathan in 1803, 137, 139, 142; meeting with Hans Jonathan in 1808, 139–41; memoirs published in Copenhagen in 1845, 138, 141; portrait of, *138*

Thorlacius, Thordur, 137–38, 139–40

Titanic, 196

Tortola, 207

Tugendreich, Caroline, portrait of, ca. 1773–79, plate 3

Tvede, Chamberlain, 175

Tvede, M. H., 166

United States, race relations in, 203–5; Black Lives Matter movement, 204; persistence of issues related to slavery, 204

Vanderbourg, Charles Bouden, 33–34

Vatnsdœla Saga, 164

Vesey, Denmark, 83

vilde karle (wild men), 70

Virgin Islands, named by Christopher Columbus, 8–9

Waaben, Knud, 112

Walterstorff, Ernst Frederik von, 108